COURTLY SPLENDOR

Twelve Centuries of Treasures from Japan

王朝貴族の美術

Museum of Fine Arts, Boston

Exhibition dates:
Museum of Fine Arts, Boston
October 17 to November 25, 1990

"The entry explanations in the catalogue were written by the staff of the Art and Crafts Section, Agency for Cultural Affairs, Japan. For sculpture: Matsushima Ken, Nakamura Yasushi, and Nedachi Kensuke. For painting: Miyajima Shin'ichi, Hayashi On, and Kobayashi Tatsuroh. For craftworks: Suzuki Norio. And for sword mounting: Ogawa Morihiro, Museum of Fine Arts, Boston. They were translated by Kaneko Shigetaka, and edited by Margaret Miller Kanada, with the assistance of Maribeth Graybill (especially Cat. Nos. 22, 23, 30, 31). Margaret Miller Kanada and Jan Fontein, research curator, edited the introduction."

Cover design:
Carl Zahn (Director of Publications, MFA, Boston).

Catalogue design:
Ohishi Kazuyoshi

Printing:
Otsuka Kogeisha, Inc., Tokyo

Front Cover: Detail from BUGAKU DANCERS (Daigo-ji, Kyoto), by Tawaraya Sōtatsu.

The exhibition is organized to honor the enthronement of Emperor Akihito of Japan, and to celebrate the centennial of the Department of Asiatic Art, Museum of Fine Arts, Boston.

COURTLY SPLENDOR: TWELVE CENTURIES OF TREASURES FROM JAPAN

October 17-November 25, 1990

This exhibition was organized by the Agency for Cultural Affairs, Japan, and the Museum of Fine Arts, Boston.

The exhibition was made possible by the generosity of:

The Mitsui Group
Mitsubishi Group
The Sumitomo Group

Toyota Motor Corporation

The Dai-Ichi Mutual Life Insurance Co.
The Fuji Bank, Limited
Honda Motor Co., Ltd.
Nippon Life Insurance Company
Nissan Motor Co., Ltd.
The Nomura Securities Co., Ltd.
Nippon Steel Corporation
Tokyo Electric Power Company
The Yasuda Fire & Marine Insurance Co., Ltd.
The Yasuda Mutual Life Insurance Company
The Yasuda Trust & Banking Co., Ltd.
The Kansai Electric Power Company, Incorporated
American Family Life Assurance Company of Columbus
Japan Airlines Company, Ltd.

The assistance of The Japan Foundation and the Japan Art Renaissance Association has been essential to
the realization of the exhibition. An indemnity has been granted by the Federal Council on the Arts and Humanities.

「王朝貴族の美術」 12世紀に亘る日本宝物展

会期　1990年10月17日—1990年11月25日

本展覧会は日本国文化庁とボストン美術館との企画により開催されます。

この展覧会は次の企業の御援助により実現が可能となりました。

三井グループ	日産自動車株式会社
三菱グループ	野村證券株式会社
住友グループ	新日本製鐵株式會社
	東京電力株式会社
トヨタ自動車株式会社	安田火災海上保険株式会社
	安田生命保険相互会社
第一生命保険相互会社	安田信託銀行株式会社
株式会社富士銀行	関西電力株式会社
本田技研工業株式会社	アメリカンファミリー生命保険会社
日本生命保険相互会社	日本航空株式会社

国際交流基金とジャパン アート ルネサンス協会の御協力は、本展を開催する為に欠く事のできぬものでした。
又、アメリカ合衆国芸術・人文科学評議会より保険保障の御援助を戴き、ここに御礼申し上げます。

Honorary Committee for Japanese Support and Funding

Chairman: **Goro Koyama**
Honorary Chairman   The Mitsui Taiyo Kobe Bank, Ltd.

Member: **Gaishi Hiraiwa**
Chairman   Tokyo Electric Power Company

Takashi Ishihara
Chairman   Keizai Doyukai
(Japan Association of Corporate Executives, J.A.C.E.)

Rokuro Ishikawa
Chairman   The Japan Chamber
of Commerce & Industry

Ichiro Isoda
Chairman   The Sumitomo Bank, Ltd.

Josei Ito
President   Nippon Life Insurance Company

Shoichiro Kobayashi
Chairman   The Kansai Electric Power Company,
Incorporated

Yosoji Kobayashi
President   The Japan Newspaper Publishers and
Editors Association

Takuji Matsuzawa
Senior Advisor   The Fuji Bank, Limited

Yohei Mimura
Chairman   Mitsubishi Corporation

Akio Morita
Chairman of the Board   Sony Corporation

Yoshihiko Morozumi
Member of the Policy Board   The Bank of Japan

Yoshiki Paul Otake
Japan President   American Family Life Assurance Company
of Columbus

Eishiro Saito
Chairman   Keidanren
(Japan Federation of Economic Organizations)

Yoshio Sakurauchi
Speaker   House of Representatives

Yoshio Sasaki
President   The National Association
of Commercial Broadcasters in Japan

Keiji Shima
Chairman   NHK (Japan Broadcasting Corporation)

Eiji Suzuki
President   Japan Federation of Employers' Associations

Haruo Suzuki
Chairman   Association for Corporate Support of the Arts

Shoichiro Toyoda
President   Toyota Motor Corporation

Yoshihiko Tsuchiya
President   House of Councillors

Toshikuni Yahiro
Senior Advisor to the Board   Mitsui & Co., Ltd.

Manager-in-Charge: **Natsuaki Fusano**
Managing Director   Keidanren
(Japan Federation of Economic Organizations)

Executive Director: **Momoco Tsuchiya**
Chairman   Japan Art Renaissance Association

王朝美術展協賛委員会

（敬称略　ABC順）

委員長　小山五郎　株式会社太陽神戸三井銀行　相談役名誉会長

委員　平岩外四　東京電力株式会社　取締役会長

石原　俊　社団法人経済同友会　代表幹事

石川六郎　日本商工会議所　会頭

磯田一郎　株式会社住友銀行　会長

伊藤助成　日本生命保険相互会社　代表取締役社長

小林庄一郎　関西電力株式会社　代表取締役会長

小林與三次　社団法人日本新聞協会　会長

松澤卓二　株式会社富士銀行　相談役

三村庸平　三菱商事株式会社　取締役会長

盛田昭夫　ソニー株式会社　代表取締役会長

両角良彦　日本銀行政策委員会　委員

大竹美喜　アメリカンファミリー生命保険会社　社長

斎藤英四郎　社団法人経済団体連合会　会長

桜内義雄　衆議院　議長

佐々木芳雄　社団法人日本民間放送連盟　会長

島　桂次　日本放送協会　会長

鈴木永二　日本経営者団体連盟　会長

鈴木治雄　社団法人企業メセナ協議会　会長

豊田章一郎　トヨタ自動車株式会社　取締役社長

土屋義彦　参議院　議長

八尋俊邦　三井物産株式会社　相談役

代表監査役　房野夏明　社団法人経済団体連合会　常務理事

事務局長　土屋桃子　ジャパン アート ルネサンス協会　理事長

Lenders to the Exhibition

Agency for Cultural Affairs
Daigo-ji, Kyoto
Fuji Art Museum, Tokyo
Fujita Art Museum, Osaka
Fukui Prefectural Museum
Fukushima Prefectural Museum
Gotoh Museum, Tokyo
Hakutsuru Art Museum, Hyogo
Hōryū-ji, Nara
Idemitsu Museum of Art, Tokyo
Imperial Collection
Imperial Household Agency
Itsuō Museum of Art, Osaka
Iwaya-dera, Aichi
Izumi City Kubosō Memorial Museum, Osaka
Jinshō-ji, Shiga
Kōryū-ji, Kyoto
Kotohira Shrine, Kagawa
Kyoto National Museum
Mantoku-ji, Aichi
Matsudaira-Kōekikai, Kagawa
MOA Museum of Art (Sekai Kyūseikyō Foundation), Shizuoka
Nara National Museum
National Museum of History and Ethnology, Chiba
Seikadō Library
Shitennō-ji, Osaka
Shōjōkō-ji, Kanagawa
Suntory Museum of Art, Tokyo
Tō-ji (Kyōōgokoku-ji), Kyoto
Tōkei-ji, Kanagawa
Tokyo National Museum

Contents

Preface

The Museum of Fine Arts, Boston, is pleased and honored to present the extraordinary exhibition documented in this catalogue. It demonstrates to the American public for the first time the unique role played by the Japanese Court as patron of the fine arts through twelve centuries. It is also an exhibition composed of art treasures of an exceedingly high degree of refinement and subtlety, reflecting the aristocratic patronage which gave rise to the work. Most of these art objects have rarely, if ever before, left Japanese shores. Our Museum is thus deeply grateful to the lenders and to the Japanese government for allowing these rarities to travel to Boston. Organized in Japan by the Agency for Cultural Affairs (Bunka-cho) exclusively for viewing at the Museum of Fine Arts, the exhibition and catalogue commemorate the 1990 Centennial of our Museum's Department of Asiatic Art, while simultaneously celebrating the enthronement this year of Emperor Akihito, who has visited Boston twice and appreciated our rich and extensive holdings of Japanese art, unparalleled outside Japan.

The Museum of Fine Arts' cooperative and productive relationship with the Japanese art world has always been a source of great gratification. In the case of this exhibition we extend heartfelt gratitude to Kawamura Tsuneaki, Commissioner for Cultural Affairs in Tokyo, and to his predecessor, Ueki Hiroshi, for their keen interest in and support of this project, At the Bunka-cho we have had the pleasure of working with Yamamoto Nobuyoshi and Watanabe Akiyoshi. As Director of the Fine Arts Division of the Agency for Cultural Affairs, Mr. Watanabe was responsible for most of the complex arrangements for this show, the selection of loans, and the preparation of the catalogue. Many scholars of Japanese art were invited to contribute to the catalogue, and we are truly grateful for their participation. Ogawa Morihiro, our Museum's representative in Japan, contributed generously of his time, knowledge, and energy over the past several years, shuttling between Tokyo and Boston, and serving as an indispensable intermediary.

The curatorial team working on the exhibition in Boston consisted of Mr. Ogawa; Wu Tung, Curator of Asiatic Art; and Anne Nishimura Morse, Assistant Curator of Asiatic Art. At a critical moment, Jan Fontein, Matsutaro Shoriki Curator for Research, provided invaluable assistance. As usual, the logistical planning for the exhibition benefited enormously from the involvement of Linda Thomas, Registrar; Désirée Caldwell, Exhibition Program Manager; Carl Zahn, Director of Publications; Tom Wong, Exhibition Designer, and their superlative staffs. Mort Golden, Deputy Director, played a key role in the negotiations surrounding this project and was indispensable to its success.

From the outset Hogen Kensaku, the Japanese Consul-General in Boston, has been extremely interested and involved in this project and has provided the friendly and welcome support of his office.

Finally, I wish to express special thanks to Tsuchiya Momoko, Chairman of the Japan Art Renaissance Association in Tokyo. Mrs. Tsuchiya played a key role in finding the financial support needed to realize this ambitious exhibition. Elsewhere in this catalogue you will find a list of 18 corporations which have generously contributed to this undertaking, testimony to the widespread interest, support and good will this exhibition has engendered in Japan. The Museum is also grateful for the indeminification of this exhibition granted by the Federal Council on the Arts and Humanities.

It is my hope that American viewers will enjoy this rare opportunity to view and enjoy the most remarkable treasures of Japanese art ever gathered for a loan exhibition.

Alan Shestak
Director, Museum of Fine Arts, Boston

序　文

　ボストン美術館は、このカタログに所載された、卓越した展覧会を開催できる事を大変嬉しく、また光栄に存じます。

　この展覧会は12世紀にわたり、日本の宮廷が美術のパトロンとして、ユニークな役割を果していたことをアメリカの人々に知らしめる初めての機会となりましょう。本展は又、貴族が後援した事により、作品がより高尚になったことを如実に示す殊のほか優雅で繊細な美術品により構成されております。

　これらの美術品の多くは今だかつて日本を離れた事はありません。ボストン美術館はそれ故に貴重な作品をボストンまで御出品下さいましたご所蔵者と日本政府に対し心から感謝致しております。

　ボストン美術館での鑑賞だけの為に文化庁が日本に於てとりまとめたこの展覧会とカタログはボストン美術館東洋部が1990年に100周年を迎える記念であるとともに、今年の明仁天皇の即位をお祝いするものでもあります。明仁天皇はボストンを何度も訪問され、ボストン美術館が日本以外では他に類を見ない豊富で幅広い日本の美術品を収集している事を賞賛されました。

　ボストン美術館と日本美術界との協力的で建設的な関係は常に大変満足できるものでありました。

　今回の展覧会につきましては、東京の文化庁長官川村恒明氏と前任者の植木浩氏より、本計画への強い関心とご支援を賜り、厚く感謝を申し上げる次第です。文化庁では山本信吉氏及び渡辺明義氏と作業を共にする光栄に浴しました。

　文化庁美術工芸課長として渡辺氏は、今回の展覧会の複雑な手続の大半と、出品作の選択、そしてカタログの準備を担当されました。また、多くの日本美術研究家からこのカタログへご寄稿いただけた事を心から感謝しております。

　私共美術館の日本代表である小川盛弘氏はかけがえのない仲介者として、この数年間に亘ってボストンと東京間を頻繁に往復し、彼の貴重な時間、知識そして精力を惜しみなく費やされました。

　ボストンでの展覧会の学芸管理面での担当者は、小川盛弘氏、呉同東洋部長、そしてアン・ニシムラ・モース東洋部長補佐です。困難であった時期にヤン・フォンテーン正力松太郎記念研究部長が測り知れない程の援助を提供されました。

　リンダ・トーマス管理部長、デズリー・コードウェル展覧会計画マネージャー、カール・ザーン出版部長、トム・ウォン展示デザイン部長及び彼らの有能なスタッフ達が参加し得た事はいつもながら、展覧会の運営面での様々な計画に於て、大いに助けとなりました。モート・ゴールデン副館長はこの計画にまつわる各種の交渉で重要な役割を果たし、又、その成功には欠くべからざる存在でした。

　当初からボストン駐在日本総領事の法眼健作氏はこの計画に非常に興味を持たれ又、関わられて、総領事として友好的で心からなるご支援を下さいました。

　最後になりますが、東京のジャパンアートルネサンス協会の土屋桃子女史は、この野心的で大がかりな展覧会を実現させる為に必要だった財政的な支援者探しに大変重要な役割を果たされました。

　このカタログにこの事業に惜しみなくご寄付下さった18の日本企業のリストがございます。これはこの展覧会について多くの日本の人々が深い関心と支援と善意の心を示された証しであります。またアメリカ合衆国芸術・人文科学評議会より保険金保証のご援助を賜り、御礼申し上げます。

　私はアメリカの方々がいまだかつてないほど日本美術の名作が集められた本展を鑑賞される貴重な機会を楽しまれる事を希望いたします。

ボストン美術館　館長

アラン　シェスタック

Foreword

We at Japan's Agency for Cultural Affairs are exceedingly pleased to join with the Museum of Fine Arts, Boston, in presenting the exhibition "Courtly Splendor: Twelve Centuries of Treasures from Japan". Recently, the Agency for Cultural Affairs has worked almost every year with an art museum overseas to hold an exhibit to help introduce the cultural history and art of Japan. But it is a rare and indeed auspicious occasion to celebrate with this exhibition two historic events that involve both the United States and Japan.

The year 1990 marks the hundredth anniversary of the Asiatic department at the Museum of Fine Arts, Boston. The department was established under the direction of Ernest Fenollosa, who had in 1890 just returned from an extended stay in Japan. The second curator, his Japanese student, Okakura Tenshin, continued in the work of organizing the Japanese art and expanded the Chinese holdings to create a sizeable collection of works from throughout the Far East. Friends and colleagues in scholarship and love of Japanese traditions, both men played an important part in the rediscovery and preservation of Japanese art during the turbulent second half of the nineteenth century. At that time Japan, racing headlong into modernization, often lost sight of the value of its ancient culture. Because at the Agency for Cultural Affairs one of our primary responsibilities is the protection of Japanese art and artifacts, we can never forget either the example set by Fenollosa and Okakura, or the special connection they created between our agency and the Museum of Fine Arts, Boston.

This year, 1990, also marks the celebration of the enthronement of a new emperor in Japan. As Crown Prince, Emperor Akihito made two visits to Boston to view the esteemed collection. In turn the Museum has designated the exhibition to be in honor of his enthronement.

The term "Courtly Splendor" in the title refers to the imperial court of the Heian period (A.D. 794–1185). Political power during that time rested in the hands of the court and a few aristocratic families. The nobility, during several hundred years largely untouched by internal conflict or influence from the Asian continent, adapted and polished the legacy of the previous period of borrowing into a truly Japanized culture. The visual arts saw unique developments in elegance and refinement, based in a sense of luxurious ease and sensitivity to personal emotions that may be said to underlie Heian courtly taste. Although there are several ways to approach the cultural history of Japan, indispensible is an understanding of the Japanization of the arts during the Heian period, and of the continuing influence of that Japanized aesthetic.

The artworks on exhibit span a wide variety of genre to offer a representative sample of courtly art, from the Gotoh Museum's *Illustrated Handscroll of the Diary of Murasaki*

Shikibu, the Buddhist paintings of the Moon and Wind Gods (Kyoto National Museum), to the calligraphic masterpiece, the "Katsura Version" of the *Man'yō-shū,* on loan from the Imperial Collection, or a metalwork basket (Jinshō-ji). Aristocratic tastes and their stylistic expression were handed down during later periods to become a major current in the arts of Japan. One of the primary vehicles of that continuity was the inexhaustible inspiration offered by THE TALE OF GENJI. Therefore, this exhibition not only brings together art from the Heian period but attempts to present the courtly tradition in masterpieces from later times. A measure of the quality and central importance of works on exhibit is the fact that eleven pieces are designated as National Treasures. Their priceless value and attendant problems of care and preservation mean it is difficult to gather so many registered works for an exhibit in Japan. The event becomes momentous when so many treasures travel so far.

Finally this exhibition marks one more occasion of note. For the first time since the Edo period when handscrolls of *The Tale of the Heiji Era Rebellion* passed into the possession of different families, the three extant scrolls, through the cooperation of the Tokyo National Museum, the Seikadō Library, and of course the Museum of Fine Arts, will be on view in one exhibition.

Our appreciation goes to all those museums and collections that have generously made objects available for this exhibition. Tsuchida Naoshizu, director of the National Museum of History and Ethnography (Chiba), wrote the introductory historical essay for the catalogue. We also thank Alan Shestack, director; Mort Golden, deputy director; Wu Tung, curator, and the staff of the Museum of Fine Arts, Boston, especially Ogawa Morihiro, research fellow, who unstintingly served as representative and liason between the Museum and our agency. We cannot fail to mention our gratitude to the corporate sponsors, without whose support this exhibition would not have been possible. And finally our thanks to all the others, too numerous to mention, who have contributed to the success of the show.

In conclusion, it is my personal hope that this occasion will strengthen the ties of friendship and understanding between our two countries.

Kawamura Tsuneaki
Commissioner
Agency for Cultural Affairs
October 1990

　文化庁は、諸諸外国の美術館に協力して我が国の文化財による展覧会を毎年のように開催し、日本の美術や文化の歴史の紹介に努めてまいりましたが、このたびは、アメリカ合衆国の世界的美術館であるボストン美術館と共同で「王朝貴族の美術」展を開催することになったことを大変嬉しく思っております。この展覧会はボストン美術館の東洋部が1990年に開設百周年を迎えるにあたり、先ずこれを記念すべく計画されました。よく知られているように、ボストン美術館東洋部は1890年に、日本から帰国したアーネスト・フェノロサを初代部長として開設され、二代目部長には岡倉天心が就任し、蒐集作品の整理にあたりました。両者は、師友の間柄にあり、日本の歴史の変動期であった明治時代に、日本美術の価値の再発見と保護に努めた先覚者でありました。文化財の保護を重要な任務の一つとしている文化庁にとって、両者は忘れ得ぬ歴史上の人物であるわけであり、ボストン美術館と文化庁は特別な縁で結ばれているといえるでしょう。

　ところで、1990年は、日本国民にとって大変目出たい年に当っています。今上陛下の御即位の盛儀が挙行される年であるからです。そこで、ボストン美術館はこの展覧会を御即位を慶祝する展覧会としたい旨関係筋にお願いし、そのお許しを得「御即位記念」と銘うつことになりました。今上陛下は皇太子時代に二度、ボストン美術館を訪問しておられますが、ボストン美術館はこれを大変名誉に思い、わが皇室に対する敬愛の念を深くしているということであります。こうして、展覧会は二つの特別な意義を持って開催されることになったのですが、国際間の一つの展覧会が、これほど時誼を得るということも珍しいと思います。

　展覧会の題名にあたる「王朝」は歴史学的には平安時代を指しています。平安時代は政治の中心は宮廷にあり、貴族たちは安定した生活を背景に文化の創造者、指導者として活躍し、文化全般にわたって「国風」を成立させたからです。美術も同様であり、雅びで繊細な表現と様式が完成しました。「紫式部日記絵詞」（五島美術館）、「月天像」（京都国立博物館）、「桂本万葉集」（御物）、華篭（神照寺）など、分野は異なっ

ていますが、貴族の美意識を見事に表現した作品です。このような貴族的な美と様式
の世界は伝統として後代に継承され、日本美術の大きな流れを形成しておりますが、
展覧会はこのような平安時代の国風の美とその伝統の行方を主題としています。日本
の美術の歴史を理解するにはいくつもの視点が考えられますが、この展覧会の主題は、
最も有力な視点の一つであると云えます。国宝も11件という多数が出陳されますが、
一つの展覧会でこれだけの国宝を出陳するということは我が国においても容易にでき
ないことであります。

　さて、展覧会には、もう一つの見所が用意してあります。それは、ボストン美術館、
東京国立博物館、静嘉堂各々所蔵されている「平治物語絵巻」が同時に陳列されるこ
とです。これらの絵巻は江戸時代以前に散逸していますが、それ以来、三巻が一堂に
会するのは初めての出来事です。

　以上のように、この展覧会は話題多い内容となっていますが、このように立派な展
覧会が実現しましたのは、展覧会の意義の大きさとボストン美術館関係者の熱意であ
り、これに心よく応えて下さったご所蔵者の好意であります。ご所蔵者の方々、アラ
ン・シェスタック館長、モート・J・ゴールデン副館長、呉同東洋部長等ボストン美
術館の展覧会関係者の方々、ボストン美術館日本代表として絶えず文化庁との連絡調
整にあたった小川盛弘氏に心から敬意を表します。またこの展覧会には各方面から様々
なご支援がありました。国立歴史民俗博物館土田直鎮博士は展覧会図録のために總説
を執筆していただきました。これ等のご支援とご好意に対し心から御礼申しあげます。
最後にこの展覧会が日米親善に大きく寄与するであろうことを祈念して私の挨拶とい
たします。

　　1990年10月

文化庁長官
川村垣明

The Age of Aristocracy: Historical Background

Tsuchida Naoshizu
Director, National Museum of History and Ethnography

1) The Heian Period and Aristocratic Society

Following the example of the Tang dynasty (618–906) which ruled the great empire of China, Japan tried to establish a national government structure based on a penal regulation code (*ritsu*) and a civil or administrative code (*ryō*), a process that was successfully completed in the course of the eighth century. The core of this governmental structure was a centralized national bureaucracy organized by a small elite aristocracy, centered around the emperor or reigning empress. The nation from Tohoku in the northeast of the main island to Kyushu was divided into sixty provinces (*kuni*). It was an orderly, functioning government, in which local administrators were dispatched from the capital for tours of duty to outlying areas and in which communication and tax-collection from the provinces was maintained by a huge traffic of documents.

The national capital was the city of Nara and the period during which this city served as the center of the government is known as the Nara period (710–774). For the aristocracy of this metropolis, a culture in the Tang style set the tone. The aristocrats who occupied the key positions in the government were descendants of leading local clans. They had ruled the central part of Japan, the Kinki area around Nara, since the fifth century, and they had succeeded in bringing the entire country under their control with the emperor at the center.

Towards the end of the eighth century the capital was transferred to Heian, present-day Kyoto. The following period of four hundred years, called the Heian period (794–1185), lasted until the rise to power of warrior families from the provinces toward the end of the twelfth century.

During the Heian period the administrative system underwent some changes, but the basis of the national structure remained the same. Except at the inception and conclusion of the period, which were marked by warfare, the central government did not become involved in armed conflicts, and although political changes occurred, they took place without loss of life of the nobles involved. Exile from the capital was the favored solution.

The Japanese archipelago lies only a short distance from the Asian continent; although it experienced an influx of cultural elements from the continent it did not suffer any hostile invasions by foreign countries. In the course of the ninth century, the Tang dynasty in China and the Silla dynasty on the Korean peninsula saw their power decline as a result of protracted civil wars. Both perished during the tenth century. Subsequently, except for occasional visits by priests, merchants, and pirates, international communication between Japan and the Asian continent ceased, and outside influence was rare. It was under these circumstances that the Fujiwara clan achieved hegemony over the other aristocratic families. One branch of the Fujiwaras, known as the Northern family (Hokke), occupied a powerful position from the eleventh century onwards, and reached its apex under Fujiwara no Michinaga (966–1027). They gave their daughters in marriage to emperors, and when a son born from such a marriage was called to the throne, the Fujiwaras acted as regents (*sessho* or *kampaku*), keeping the emperor under their tutelage, and securing power for themselves by their close association with the imperial authority.

During the same period, it became customary to rank the aristocracy in accordance with the lineage of their families, shifting the basis of rank from achievements to heredity. One group of high officials was named *kugyō*. They were the chief executives of the chancellory which consisted of several ministers (*daijin*) who had under them councilors. Most of them came from families affiliated with the Northern branch of the Fujiwaras and some from the imperial clan. The class of officials just below the rank of *kugyō* consisted of about thiry or forty court nobles called *tenjobito* ("men having admission to the Imperial Palace"). They were permitted to enter the emperor's residence and took turns in serving the emperor in a variety of matters; their status was one of high prestige. All of them were administrators occupying leading positions in various government offices. Provincial governors (*kokushi*) were in charge of the administration on the local level. Although their rank was regarded as lower than that of *tenjobito* their positions were much in demand because of the financial benefits they provided. They built their own fortunes and vied for even more lucrative offices by making gifts to their superiors, for the highest ranking aristocrats had full control of personnel. The aristocracy which consisted for the most part of these officials and their families was thus a very small elite.

This aristocratic society remained firmly entrenched from the second half of the tenth to the first half of the twelfth century. During this period, the status of these families remained fixed in accordance with their lineage and gradually all privileges assumed an hereditary character. Great importance was attached to precedent and custom, while formalities and rules of conduct were strictly adhered to, not only in everyday life and during court ceremonies, but also in the execution of affairs of state. All of these matters were regulated down to the smallest detail, explained and codified in several books on protocol.

Under these circumstances neither innovation nor leadership was manifest in the affairs of state. Although important matters were brought up in meetings of the highest-ranking aristocrats, no rule existed for a decision by the majority. When no consensus could be reached, the matter was reported to the emperor and the *kampaku*. The emperor and *kampaku* handed down their decision by mutual agreement. As it was again the rule to search for precedents and to rely upon them in making decisions, there was little scope for despotism, and no exceptional promotions or degradations occurred.

The aristocracy resided in the eastern half of the Heian capital, in an area of about five kilometers square. There they attended to their duites in the Imperial Palace or the nearby government offices, discharging their various major and minor obligations, each according to his rank. Their duties included all aspects of religious and court life ranging from ceremonies at Shinto shrines and Buddhist rituals, to poetry composition, patronage of the fine arts, and attendance at banquets, almost three hundred different items. For each of these duties a customary rule existed, and to perform them faultlessly came to be considered a meritorious achievement for all aristocrats in official life. Their activities centered around the imperial court and took place in or near the capital; they rarely travelled to distant places. The concern of the provincial governors (*kokushi*), who were appointed as local administrators for four-year terms, was invariably focused upon the capital. In their provincial offices they performed their duties as they did in the capital, never failing to pay attention to developments there. Each time an occasion presented itself, they would return to the capital until finally they remained permanently, sending their deputies to conduct affairs in the provinces on their behalf.

The religion of the nobles and common people was characterized by beliefs in the native gods (*kami*) and their cycles of myths, a shamanistic tradition which recognized the existence of spiritual power in all natural phenomena. Many Shinto shrines, large and small, dedicated to the *kami,* were scattered throughout the country. During the eight and ninth century nearly two thousand of the principal Shinto shrines were placed under national protection. The priests who occupied hereditary offices were government officials in charge of Shinto affairs. During the Heian period there were about twenty shrines at which members of the aristocracy worshipped. The foremost of these was at Ise, dedicated to the ancestral deities of the imperial clan. The festivals performed at these shrines were considered national affairs. Among the shrines were various kinds: those dedicated to the ancestral deities of such leading noble families as the Fujiwaras; those dedicated to deities of myths concerning the creation of the country; those of the tutelary deities of the capital, and protectors of agriculture etc. Frequently, imperial and other emissaries were dispatched to make offerings at three shrines enjoying special status. These were the Kasuga Shrine, Nara, dedicated to the tutelary deities of the Fujiwara clan, the Kamo Shrine, dedicated to the tutelary deity of the Heian capital and the Iwashimizu Hachimangū, dedicated to Hachiman and which also had close Buddhist ties. The imperial messengers participated in colorful pageants that were part of the shrine festivals. Noblemen and commoners alike enjoyed watching the festivities.

In contrast to the traditional beliefs of Shinto, which had no historical founder or organized central doctrine, Buddhism consisted of the teachings of the Buddha Sákyamuni (Jp: Shaka). Originating in India around the fifth century B.C. it was imported into Japan during the sixth century A.D. by way of China and Korea. Buddhism brought with it Buddhist temple architecture, sculpture, painting, applied arts and sacred texts written in Chinese characters — visual expressions of the highest culture of that time. Moreover, Buddhism was not an exclusive monotheistic religion but recognized many different Buddhas, guardian spirits and demigods, the worship of whom could be reconciled with that of the native *kami* as all were beings who ward off evil and bring happiness. Especially during the eighth century Buddhism prospered and brought stability and peace to the country. The Tōdai-ji and other great Buddhist temples in the capital at Nara and provincial temples (*kokubun-ji*) at various provincial centers were built by the nation and they supported large cohorts of Buddhist priests and nuns.

Part of the reason for the transfer of the capital from Nara to Heian (Kyoto) in 794, however, was to check the influence exerted by the Buddhist church which was seen as interfering excessively in affairs of state. The noblemen who made up the national bureaucracy did not reject Buddhism, but supported government control of the clergy. Under strict government protection Buddhist temples became henceforth places of worship and houses of prayer directly enlisted to ensure the peace and prosperity of the nation.

At the beginning of the Heian period, esoteric Buddhism was introduced into Japan from China by Kūkai (774-835) and other priests. Rooted in deep religiosity, characterized by complex doctrines and elaborate rituals, esoteric Buddhism emphasized the supernatural power of the Buddhas. Its practitioners frequently used awe-inspiring rituals and incantations to ward off disaster and to seek benefits, practices that found wide acceptance among members of the nobility. From the ninth century, Buddhist temples of the esoteric Shingon and Tendai sects were built one after the other as houses of prayer for the nation and the aristocracy. Buddhist statuary and Buddhist paintings became icons for various types of rituals. Many of these temples were located in mountainous areas that were deemed suitable for sacred precincts.

By the eleventh century a compromise between Buddhist and Shinto divinities had developed. Buddhist divinities and native *kami* were interpreted as being identical, even though they manifested themselves in different forms. The concept sprang from the realization that spiritual power was omnipresent. Any means of providing happiness was welcomed by nobles and commoners alike. While on one hand, splendid temples were built in the capital, on the other hand, the ancient cults of mountain worship blended with the occultism of esoteric Buddhism and resulted in the flourishing of *shugendō*, the Japanese tradition of wandering mountain-climbing ascetics (*yamabushi*), and a belief in the existence of powerful Buddhist and Shinto deities in sacred precincts deep in the mountains.

From about the end of the tenth century, a new Buddhist approach gradually gained adherence in the complex world of religious beliefs. It was faith in the Pure Land (*Jōdo*) which imagined the existence, beyond the grave, of contrasting realms of utter bliss and total misery, the Pure Lands (Paradise) and the Hells. It claimed that one could attain rebirth in the Western Pure Land by total reliance on salvation by the Buddha Amida (Sanskrit: Amitabha). This Pure Land was a splendidly adorned world, a pure and wonderful abode where one could attain perfect peace, happiness and enlightenment. No one could justify failing to make every effort to gain admission to this Pure Land of unsurpassed bliss. Members of the nobility, therefore, performed those religious works that were considered important in Buddhism, such as building temples and pagodas, commissioning Buddhist icons, sponsoring ritual gatherings and copying sacred texts (the sutras). The concept also provided the incentive for the building of many beautiful Amida halls, dedicated to this Buddha. Such good works, however, were not within reach of any except the wealthiest. Therefore, they first made their appearance as the good works of aristocrats of the highest rank, and the customs then spread to powerful clans in other parts of the country. In spite of the strictly defined social stratification, all commoners were free to participate in these meritorious projects of the nobility.

The observance of the rites of esoteric Buddhism and the dissemination of the Pure Land faith required considerable economic resources. These were provided by donations from rich provincial governors (*kokushi*) and the income from private domains (*shōen*) belonging to the aristocracy or to large temples. The noblemen tried to acquire such private domains by many means, but they never gained full possession of them, since the domains were actually managed by local potentates and the noblemen merely received taxes in kind or in services from the holdings.

Unlike Shinto priests, who served as government officials, Buddhist priests lived ostensibly removed from the secular world. After the eleventh century, however, the management of the great Buddhist temples was almost exclusively in the hands of men who came from powerful noble families. The status of the high priests at the large temples was one of ecclesiastical officers, appointed by the government. These high priests should, therefore, be regarded as integral members of aristocratic society.

2) The Japanization of Culture

Around the third century B.C., agriculture was introduced into Japan giving rise to a culture called Yayoi. About this time we can speak of the emergence of a Japanese people. Life centered around agriculture, especially the growing of rice, while livestock-breeding never became a part. Soon after the third century A.D., Japan entered a period of powerful clans whose leaders were buried in tumuli and from the fifth century on, the unification of the country began to progress; after that, no large-scale immigration of foreign peoples occurred.

Around the late seventh century the culture of the continent, especially that of Tang China, penetrated into Japan with tremendous impact felt in many spheres: in the art of writing, religion, social systems, education, literature and everyday life. During the seventh and eighth centuries (Nara period) Japan endeavored to absorb these influences.

However, Tang China and Japan differed in their peoples and languages, as well as climate and customs. Whereas the Asian continent has vast plains and several of the largest rivers in the world, seventy percent of Japan's territory consists of mountainous regions and volcanic zones that are unfit for human habitation. Flatlands are scarce, and most of the rivers are short, rapidly flowing streams, while the climate is warm and humid, conducive to the growth of plants. There is great seasonal variation especially because the archipelago stretches long from north to south. In this setting from the tenth to twelfth century a courtly culture arose in the aristocratic circles of the Heian period. Without strong stimuli from abroad, maturing over a long period of time, Tang-style culture and traditional native culture merged. The result can be called *kokufu,* a native or Japanized culture.

An important aspect of that Japanization is the *kana* syllabary, a unique script (in fact there are two variants) for the Japanese language. The script that came to Japan, which had no writing system originally, consisted of Chinese texts written in Chinese characters (*kanji*). *Kanji* are ideographs, each with its own sound and meaning, and there are tens of thousands of different characters. To the Japanese whose language was totally different in structure from Chinese, it must have been exceedingly difficult to master them. The Japanese, therefore, devised a system in which each *kanji* was given the Japanese pronunciation of the word it represented. This reading called *kun* differed from the reading based upon the Chinese pronunciation, which was called *on*.

As a result it became common practice during the seventh century to read Chinese texts in *kun* pronunciation and in modified Japanese word order. In order to write Japanese proper nouns, the Japanese used *kun* readings of *kanji* phonetically, disregarding their meaning, one *kanji* for each syllable of the Japanese word. Examples of this phonetic use of *kanji* date back to the middle of the fifth century.

Kanji and Chinese texts constituted the foundation of knowledge. The great quantity of documents produced in the bureaucratic society were all written in Chinese. During the ninth century, three collections of Chinese-style prose and poetry by Japanese authors and poets were compiled at the order of the emperor. These were not works pronounced in the Chinese manner, but compositions in modified Japanese using Chinese script.

Poems or songs (*waka*) in pure Japanese were composed from early times. No useful purpose would be served to write them in Chinese. In order to write Japanese poetry, the Japanese poets came to use *kanji* phonetically. To render each Japanese sound by a character composed of many different strokes was a time-consuming process. The *Man'yō-shū*, a collection of about 4,500 (*waka*) poems, compiled in the eighth century mainly consists of this use of simpler Chinese characters for their phonetic sounds irrespective of meaning.

During the Heian period, a new type of writing was created. The approximately fifty basic sounds of the Japanese language were each rendered by a single *kanji*, selected to stand for a separate Japanese sound, and all abbreviated and simplified. The graphs of this new *kana* syllabary, called *hiragana*, differed greatly in shape from the *kanji* from which they were derived. They have remained in use to the present day. The *Kokin waka-shū*, a collection of *waka* compiled by imperial order early in the tenth century, frequently uses *hiragana*. The idea of *hiragana* originated and spread spontaneously among the aristocrats. Its use was not legislated by the government and there was no single inventor.

The Japanese thus succeeded in writing sentences, freely mixing phonetic syllables with characters used ideographically. In the beginning of the eleventh century, THE TALE OF GENJI (*Genji monogatari*) appeared, a lengthy romantic novel of fifty-four chapters, written by Murasaki Shikibu, a court lady. Composed in beautifully polished Japanese, it is a literary masterpiece, giving a vivid description of the life of idealized noblemen and women of the aristocratic society at the imperial court. Familiarity with THE TALE OF GENJI continued for later generations to be a criterion of education and Japanese culture. The novel served as a source of inspiration for not only the visual arts but many cultivated pastimes.

The Japanization of culture, typified by the creation of *hiragana*, is noticeable in all fields, especially from the the second half of the Heian period. Its effect was not limited to styles of painting, calligraphy, sculpture and the decorative arts, but it affected the noble life style, the architecture of dwellings, costumes, food, gardens, and rules of conduct. It is still felt in the cultural and spiritual life of Japan to this day.

Japanese courtly culture, nurtured in the aristocratic society of the Heian period, is often characterized by the word *yūbi* meaning graceful, elegant or delicate. In the thirteenth century, when warriors who had been local potentates took over the rule of government, these new masters readily accepted and assimilated the courtly culture while the aristocrats, even though they had lost nearly all of their power and income, were still held in high regard as the creators of the tradition and of the Japanese nation. The imperial and Kyoto aristocratic families remained the highest class of society and continued to transmit culture to later generations. Japanese civilization was to be enriched by the warrior (*bushi*) culture during the medieval period and by the contributions of merchants and other commoners during the early modern period; yet the courtly culture continued as a central current. From the mid-nineteenth century, Japan was flooded in waves of modern Western culture; living conditions and society underwent radical changes. Yet even today, many Japanese still feel an easy rapport with the arts of the courtly tradition dating from the Heian period.

Catalogue

This catalogue has been produced for the exhibition "Courtly Splendor: Twelve Centuries of Treasures form Japan" organized by the Japanese Agency for Cultural Affairs and the Museum of Fine Arts, Boston, and held from October 17th until November 25th, 1990.

The catalogue contains a complete list of objects. Because of the need to preserve fragile works from light and air, some pieces may not be on view the entire exhibition period.

The ordering of the plates and entries in the catalogue does not follow the placement of objects in the galleries, however the label and catalogue numbers correspond.

The following marks precede the title of the work when the art object, because of its quality and importance to an understanding of Japanese history, has been designated by the Japanese government:

⊙ A NATIONAL TREASURE
◎ AN IMPORTANT CULTURAL
○ PROPERTY
or   AN IMPORTANT ART OBJECT

All Japanese personal names are given in Japanese style, that is family name first, followed by the given name.

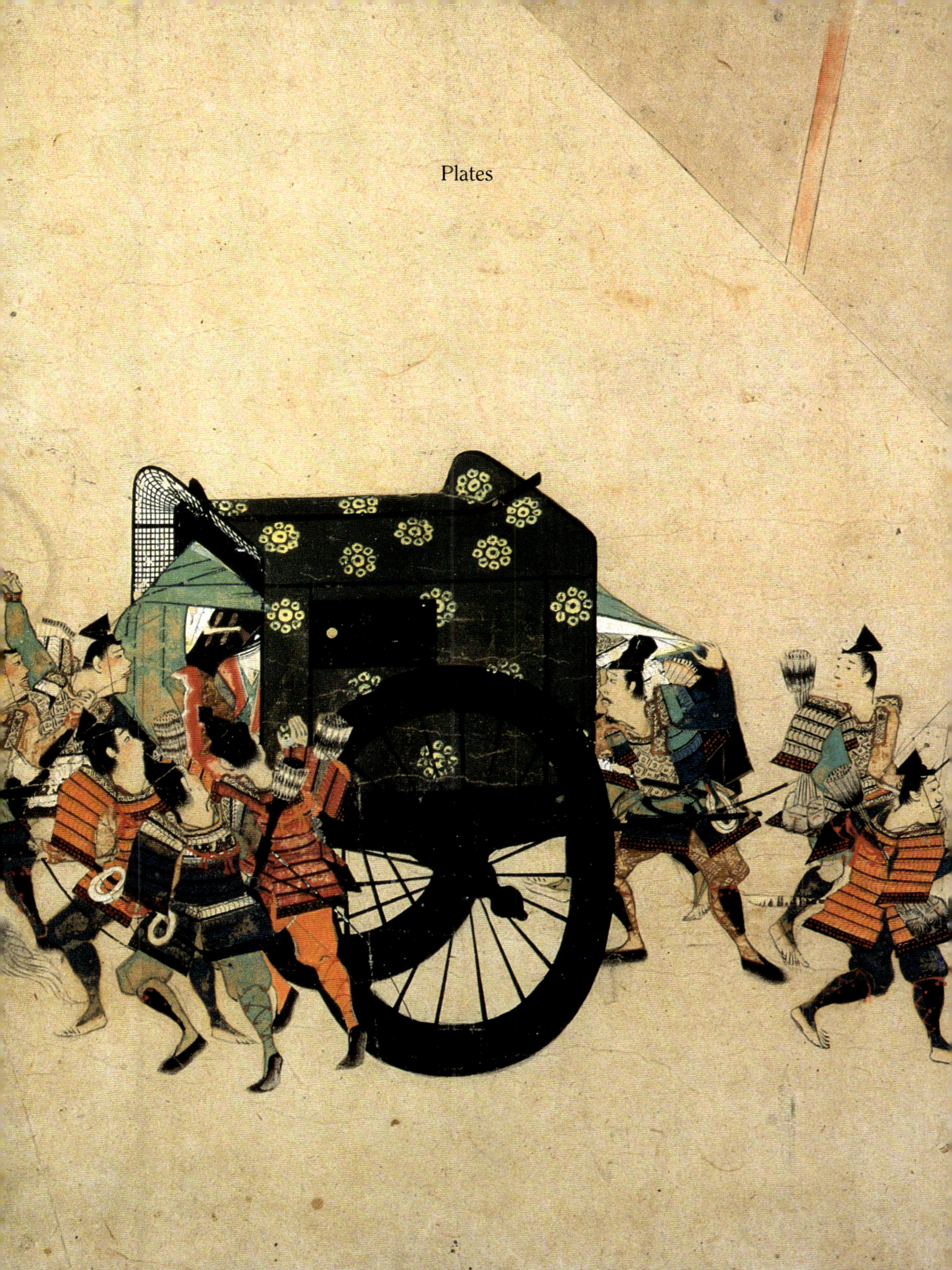

Plates

1 ⊙

Tobatsu Bishamon-ten
兜跋毘沙門天立像

China, Tang dynasty, 8th century
Wood, with gold-leaf
Height 189.4cm
Tōji (Kyōōgokoku-ji), Kyoto

Bishamon-ten (also known as Tamon-ten), Guardian of the North, the direction of greatest peril in Sino-Japanese cosmology, is the most prominent of the Four Buddhist Heavenly Guardian Kings (Jp: Shitennō). Although often found in the set of four fierce guardian images placed at the corners of an altar, as a giver of wealth and protector of towns and cities, he became the object of his own cult.

This particular iconographic version of the deity is known as Tobatsu Bishamon-ten in Japanese. The origin of the term is obscure. Characteristic are the high four-sided crown, decorated breast-plate and belt buckle, tortoise-shell pattern armor (here reaching below the knees), and the stupa (now missing) and spear (or club) which he carries. He stands supported on the palms of the Earth Goddess (Jp: Chiten) as though subduing the two demonic figures. Statues of this type began to be placed in city gateways of China around the mid-8th century, some sources suggest based on the legend that when the walled city of Anxi, in the Tobatsu kingdom of central Asia, was besieged, Bishamon-ten in this form appeared at the two-story gateway of the city to send the enemy fleeing.

Conclusive evidence is lacking, but this image of Tobatsu Bishamon-ten was probably brought from China in the 8th century and placed originally in the upper story of the gate Rashōmon (or Rajō-mon) guarding a major road into the Heian capital (Kyoto) from the south. It was transferred to the nearby temple of Tōji after the gateway was destroyed in a typhoon of 816.

Scholars agree that the image was not made in Japan and had arrived by the end of the 8th century. The statue is carved in a cherry wood native to China. Other Chinese technical aspects include the black stone inlays for the eyes and the high modeling in paste over wood for details such as the teeth, demon's hair and armor decoration. Although the image served as a prototype for several Tobatsu Bishamon-ten sculptures produced in Japan, certain stylistic features suggestive of images of the high Tang period (late 7th-early 8th c.), especially the large up-turned eyes, clinched waist and relatively elongated lower body, also were never adopted in other Japanese sculptures. The work survives however, as a fine example of the many cultural influences from China and the continent that would be sorted out, assimilated and Japanized as the Heian period progressed in the 10th-12th centuries. The flaming halo, most of both arms, and the spear are replacements.

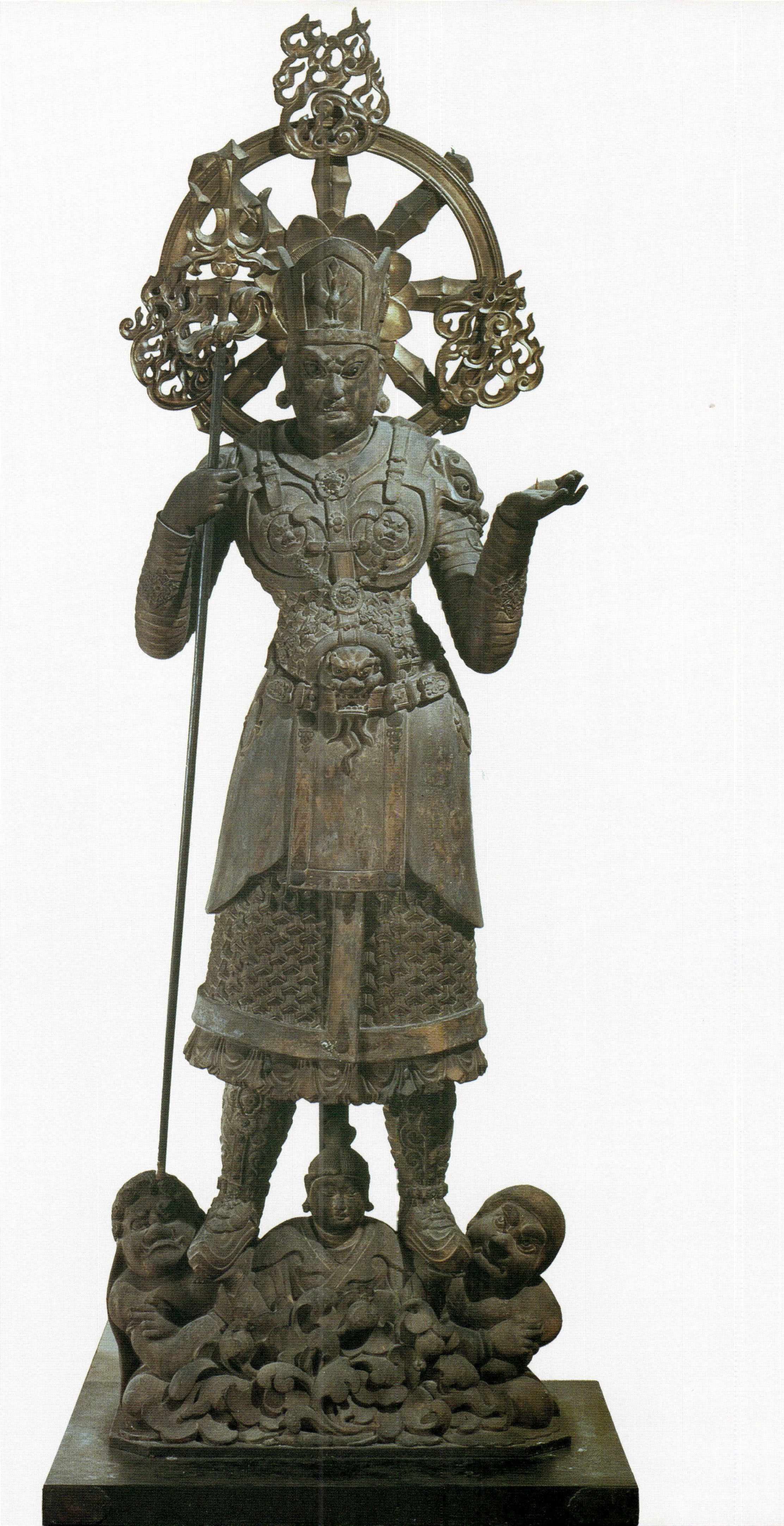

Image of Kichijō-ten
吉祥天像

Heian period, 1078
Japanese cypress, with polychrome and gold foil
Height 116.7cm
Hōryū-ji, Nara

Kichijō-ten (Sanskrit: Māhāsri), goddess of beauty, good fortune, and wealth, is one of the many Buddhist deities ranked as Heavenly Beings (Jp: Tenbu) who was an important Indian god (in this case Śri Laksmi) absorbed into Buddhism as a protector and benefactor by around the 8th century. She was popular in China and came to be particularly worshipped in Japan at a New Year's ritual for fortune and rich harvests in the coming year called the *Kisshō-keka*. A document states that the present statue was made together with an image of her consort Bishamon-ten (Guardian King of the North) for this ritual which was held in the Main hall of the temple Hōryū-ji in 1078.

The image is portrayed as a typical Chinese Tang court lady with hair pulled up into a topknot, and robes with long hanging sleeves. She holds a flaming "wish granting" jewel (Jp: *hōjū*).

The entire head and body were carved from one piece of Japanese cypress, *hinoki*, which was then split into front and rear halves and rejoined after being hollowed out. Arms and hands were carved separately and then joined to the figure. Although there is evidence of some later repairs these, as well as the independently carved pedestal, and the decorative crown and halo are thought to be original. After carving, the surface was covered with hemp cloth, primed with a coating of clay mixed with lacquer (*sabi-urushi*), and then painted. Cut gold foil (*kirikane*) decoration was applied to parts of the robes.

The carving of the gentle curves of the drapery folds and planes of the face is restrained and shallow. The graceful, rounded form of the figure and soft, yet ornate effect of the rich decoration and use of gold *kirikane*, is typical of late Heian sculpture. The feeling of ample weight and grave stability, however, are characteristics of the older style of Nara, rather than Kyoto, sculptors.

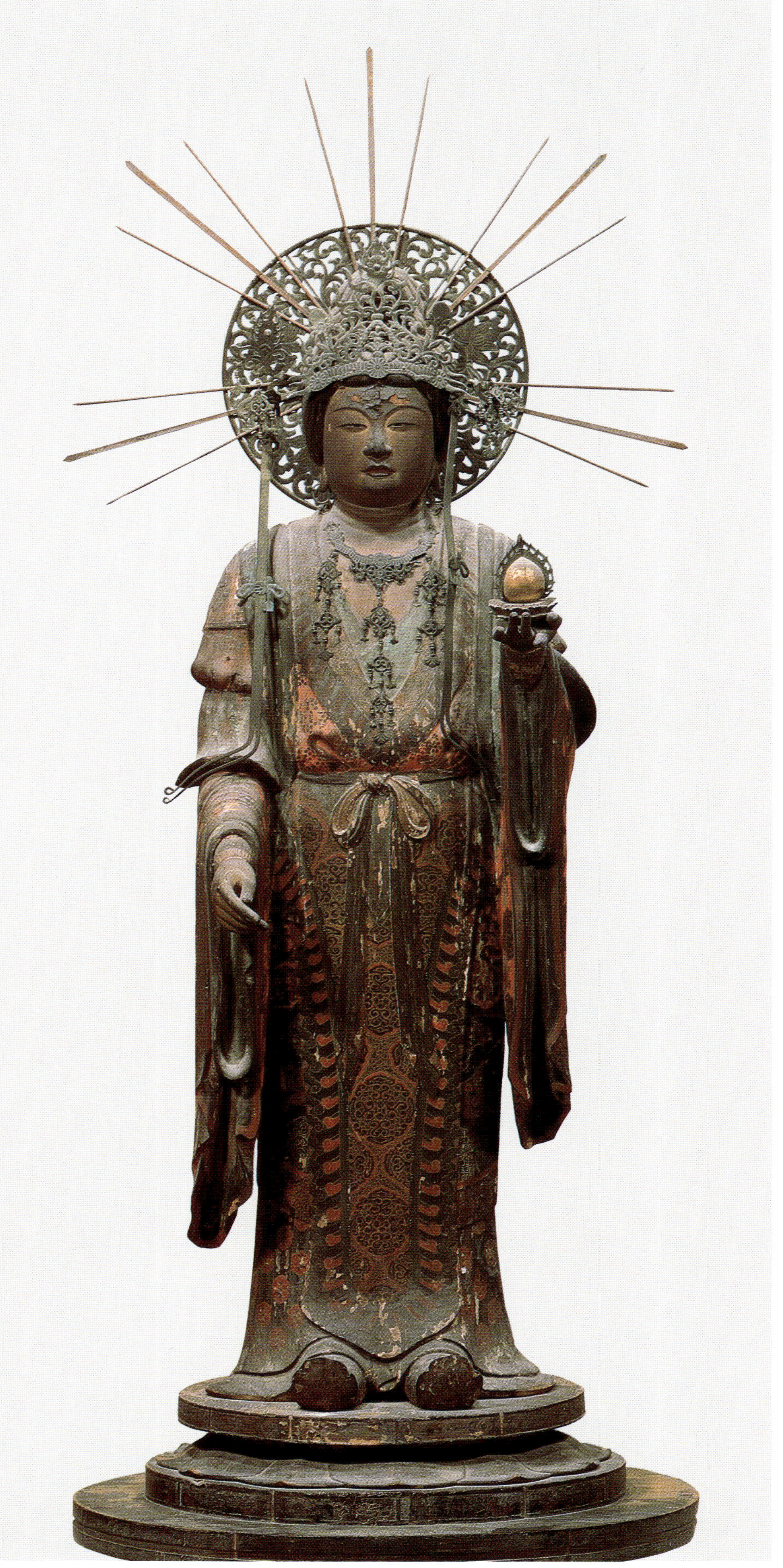

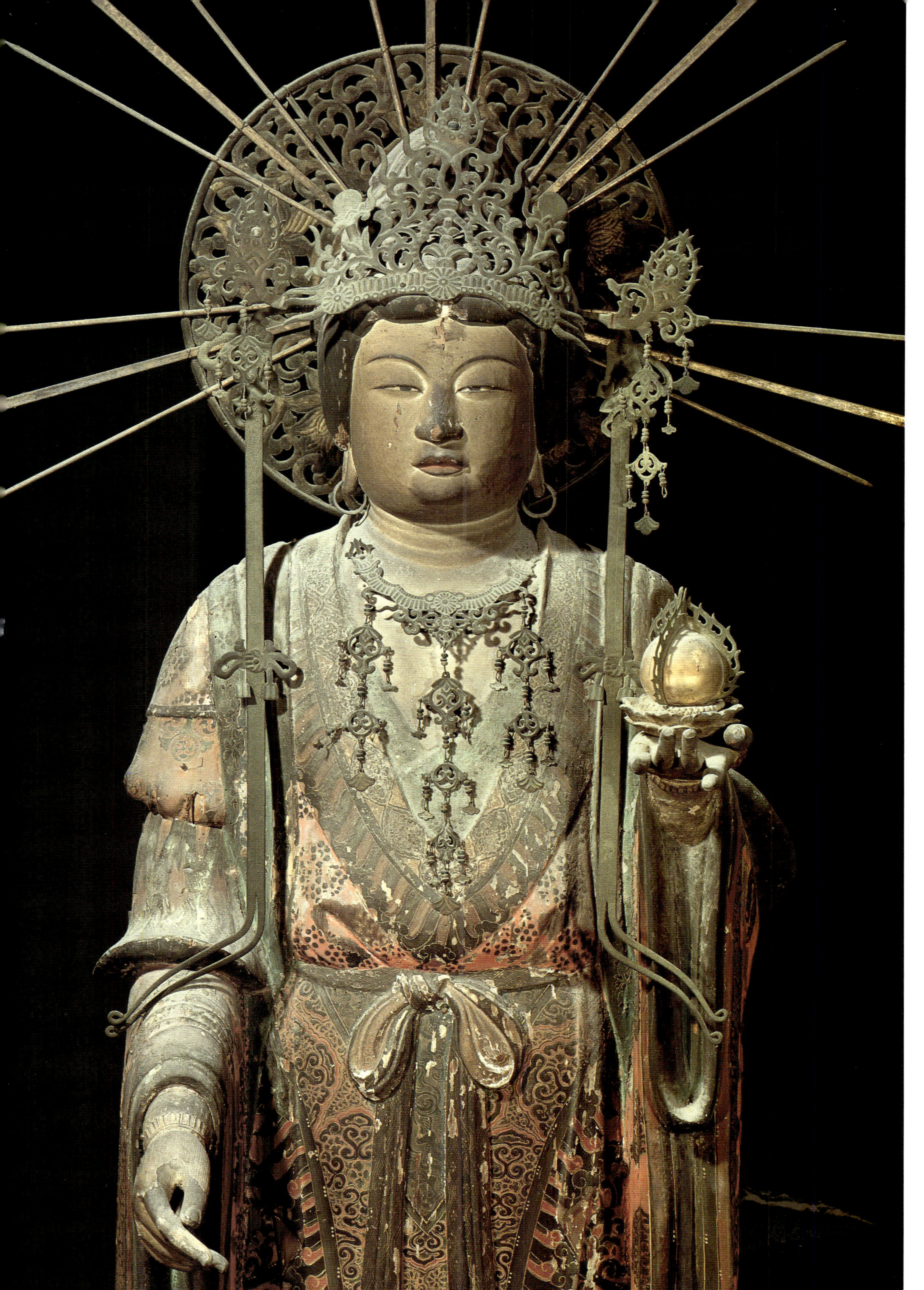

3 ⊙

Two of the Twelve Divine Generals:
Indara (Holding Battle Axe) and Kubira
十二神将立像のうち宮毘羅・因達羅

Heian period, 1064
Japanese cypress wood, with polychrome and cut
gold foil
Height: Kubira, 123.0cm; Indara 115.4cm
Kōryū-ji, Kyoto

The Twelve Divine Generals (Jp: Jūni
Shinshō) each personify a vow made by the
Healing Buddha, Yakushi, to cure humankind
of its physical and spiritual woes. They are
pledged to assist and protect all the faithful. A
set of images with fierce expressions and in
military regalia was often positioned on the
altar around an image of Yakushi. This Indara
(Sanskrit: Indra) and Kubira (Skt: Kumbhira)
are believed to be two of such a set mentioned
in records of the temple, Kōryū-ji, to have been
carved in 1064 by Chōsei. Chōsei was a
follower of the master sculptor Jōcho, who was
responsible for the epitome of late Heian sculpture—the Amida Image (dated 1053) in the
Phoenix Hall of the Byōdō-in, Uji.

The balanced forms and accomplished carving (seen especially in the armor and drapery)
do credit to the ability of Chōsei who was
the leading sculptor in the capital during the
second half of the 11th century. The figures
and the rock-like pedestals were each carved
out of a single block of Japanese cypress (*hino
ki*). The surfaces were decorated in bright
pigments and cut strips of gold foil (*kirikane*).
These technical features as well as the restrained poses and only modestly threatening
expressions for warrior guardians are characteristic of late Heian period sculpture of the
11th–12th centuries. The weapons they carry
are later replacements.

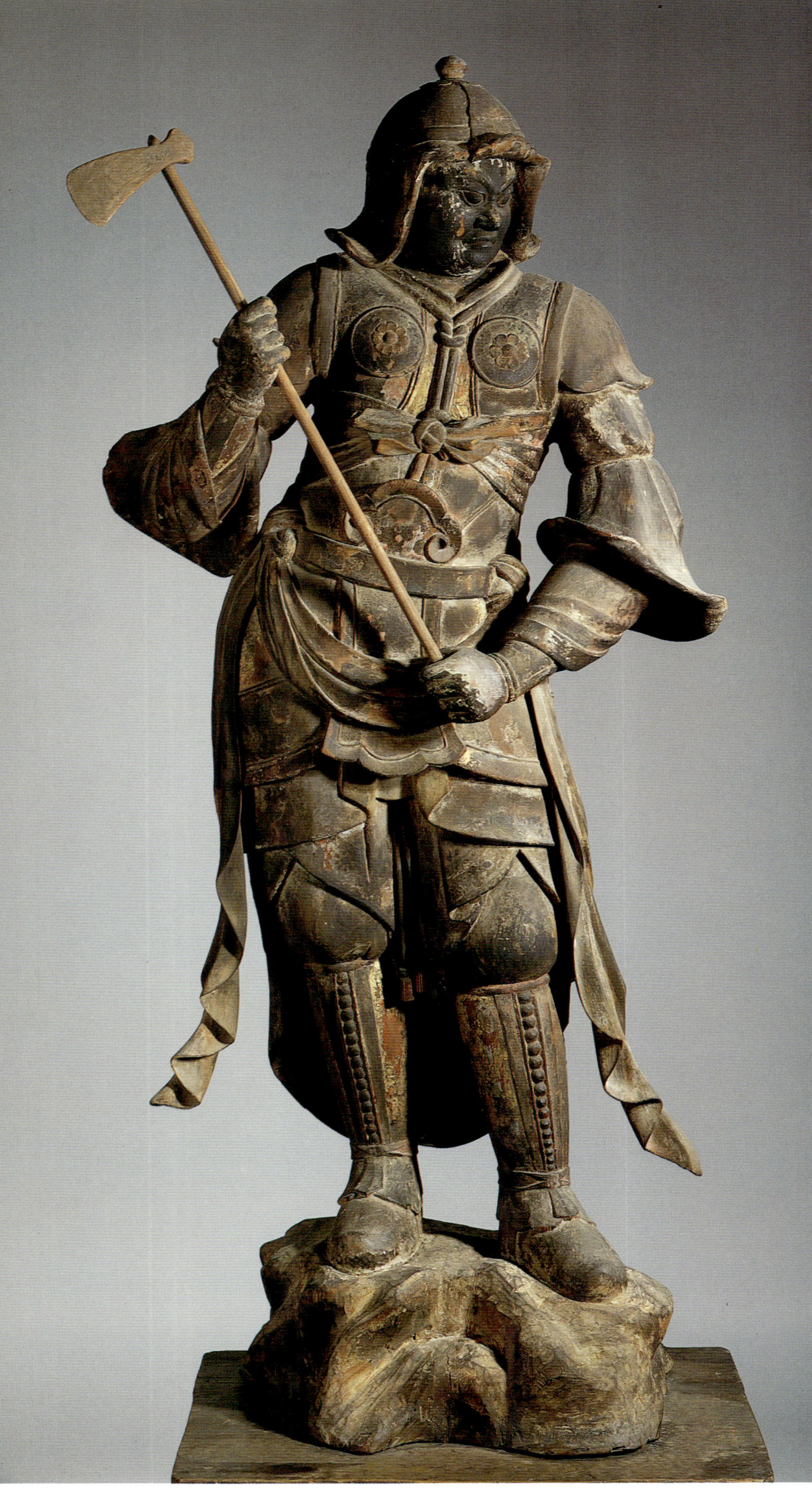

3-2 One of the Divine Generals: Indara

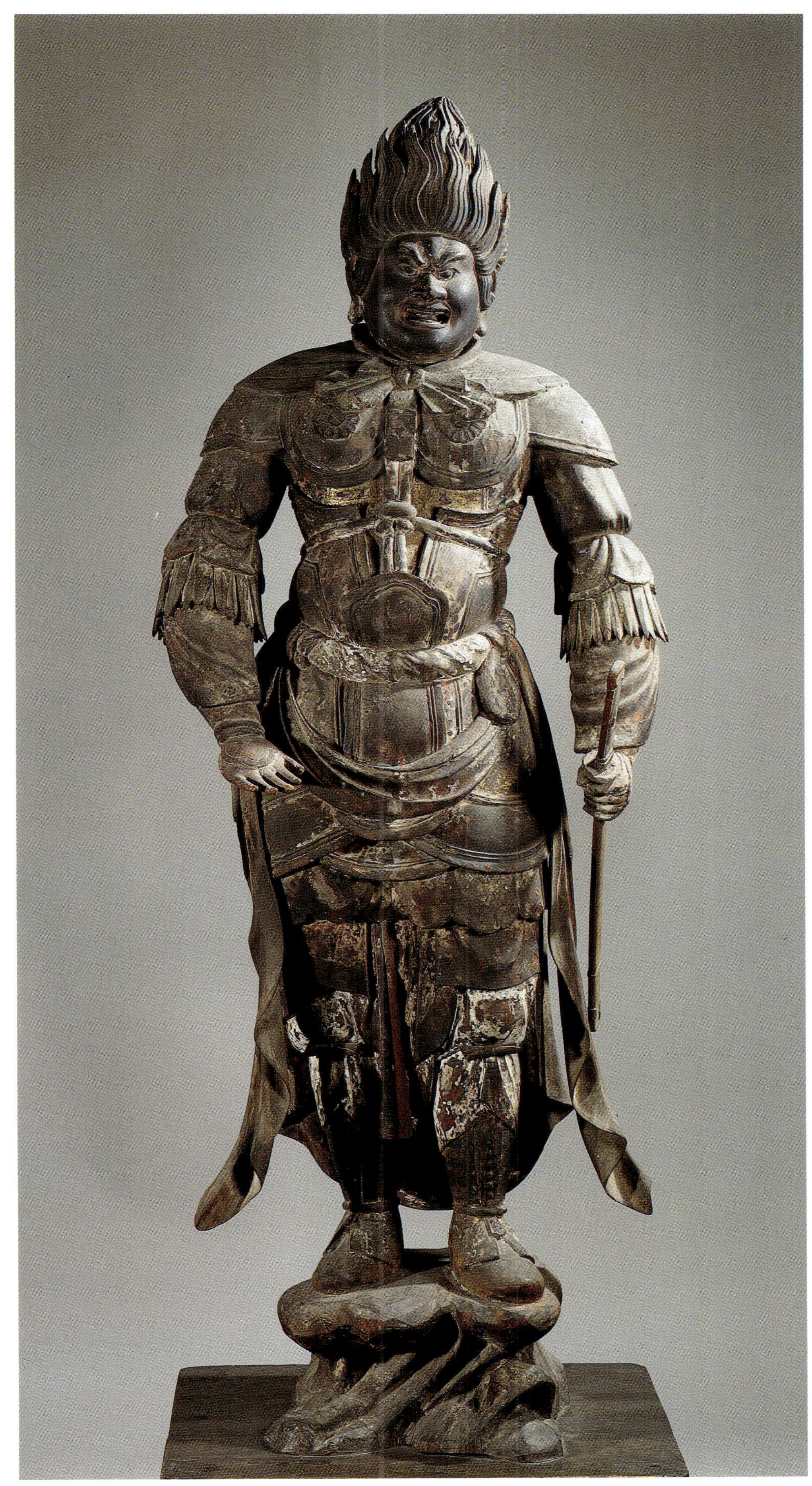

3-1　One of the Divine Generals: Kubira

4 ◎

Aizen Myō-ō
By Kaisei

愛染明王像

Kamakura period, 1256
Wood, with polychrome and cut gold foil and gilt
bronze ornamentation
Height 26.2cm
Nara National Museum

Aizen, one of the fierce Great Kings of Light
(Jp: Myō-ō) in esoteric Buddhism, symbolizes
the concept that illusion and human passions
are identical with enlightenment. In him passion (his Sanskrit name, Rāgarja, means "King
of Passion") is sublimated to combat profane
lust and destroy egotism and greed. Aizen
Myō-ō from the 9th–10th century was often
the object of independent worship in Japan.
He was believed to hold great powers of exorcism and protection from dangers. One peak in
popularity came in the 13th century with the
threat of Mongol invasions from the continent.

This small Aizen image displays standard
iconographical features based on sutras starting with the extensive red coloring. His fear-
some but sensuous three-eyed faced is domi-
nated by upstanding hair and a lion-headed
crown. In his arms he holds various esoteric
ritual objects (one missing), including a bow
and arrow (probably linked to the origins of
Cupid's bow in western mythology) and a lotus
flower. His round nimbus symbolizes the sun
and the lotus pedestal is supported by a vase
thought to yield rich treasures.

The figure was produced by joining separately prepared parts in the hollowed joined-
block (*yosegi-zukuri*) technique which was
well established by the mid-11th century. The
full-bodied modelling of the body and face
produces an impression of sensuous, real flesh-
and-blood that avoids exaggeration. Cut gold
foil (*kirikane*) patterns enhance the florid
beauty of the coloring. The eyes are crystal
inlay and the objects held in the hands, elaborate ornaments and flames on the halo are
added in gilt bronze, which complements the
effect of realism.

The bottom of the pedestal bears an inscription that the image was carved in 1256 by
Kaisei, at the request of a priest, Jakuchō, of
the temple Saidai-ji (Nara), from wood of an
old pillar which had been replaced during
repairs on the Great Buddha Hall of Tōdai-ji.
Kaisei was a sculptor in the line of Kaikei, the
master image-maker who at the beginning of
the 13th century had worked on the major
restoration of statues formerly enshrined at
Tōdai-ji which had been destroyed. Inside the
cavity in the sculpture was found a sutra
dedicated to Aizen Myō-ō that the sponsoring
priest had copied in his own hand.

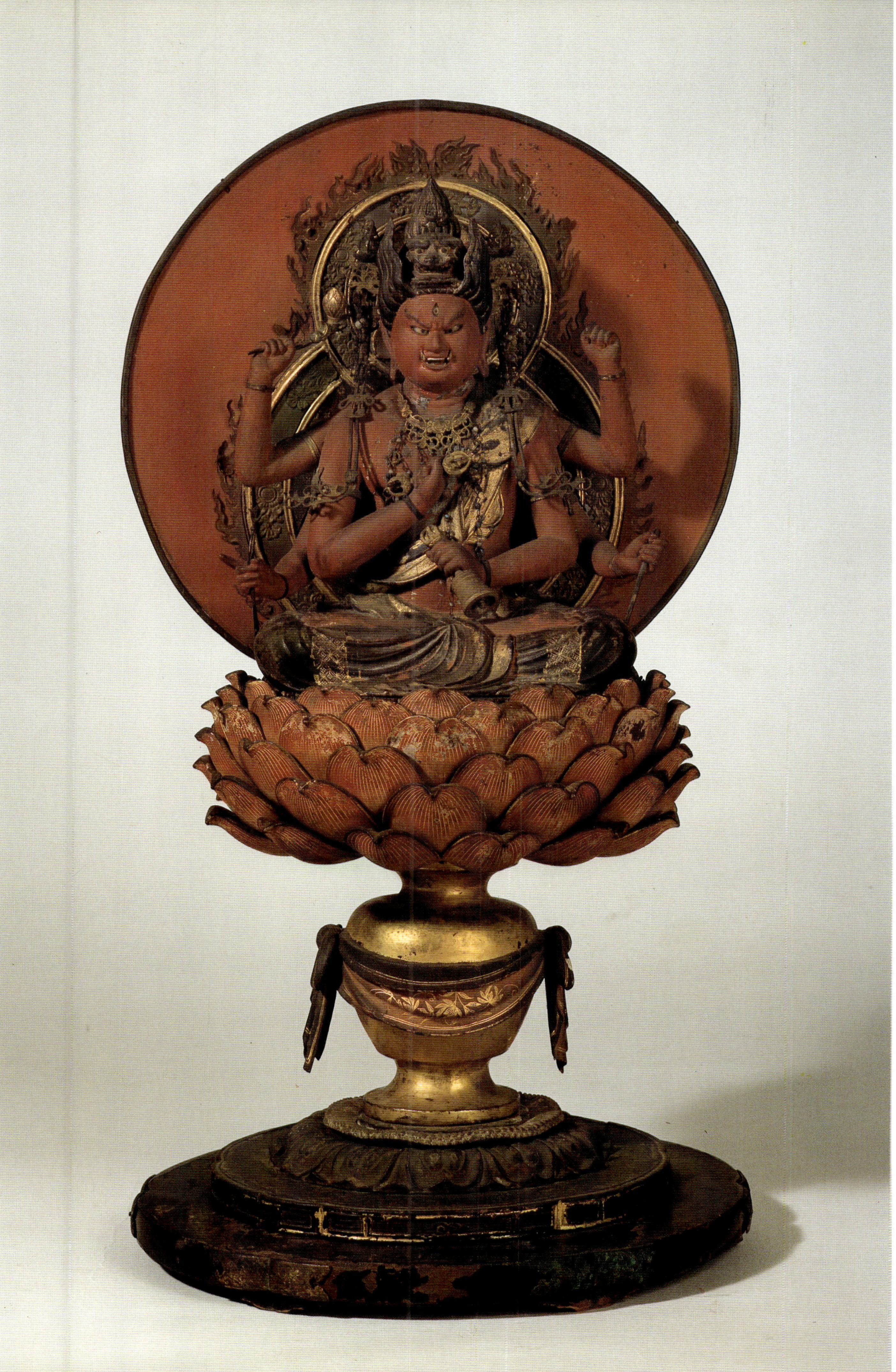

5 ◎

Thousand-Armed Kannon in a Shrine with Two Attendant Devas
千手観音及二天箱仏

Heian period, 12th century
Wood (probably sandalwood), partial polychrome
and gilt
Height of box: 12.5cm
Shitennō-ji, Osaka

The small shrine for private worship houses a Thousand-Armed (Jp: Senjū) Kannon protected by two devas (or demigods) in high relief attached to the insides of the two doors. The Thousand-Armed version was one of the most popular Sino-Japanese types of Kannon (Sanskrit: Avalokiteśvara) — the great bodhisattva, and agent of the buddha Amida, who embodies compassion. The multi-armed form was influenced by esoteric thought and the thousand arms and thousand all-seeing eyes symbolize Kannon's manifold powers to save or bring benefits to believers. Most images, as here, are abbreviated in actual depiction to have one main head (plus eleven smaller ones) or 24 eyes, and 42 arms.

A shrine such as this could have been carried on the person or always kept close at hand for private devotions. Small images in a shrine, often carved in lapidary-like miniature techniques from a single piece of sandalwood (Jp: *byakudan*) or other expensive and fragrant wood imported from distant India or S.E. Asia, were popular among the wealthy in China during and after the Tang dynasty. The fashion was adopted among members of the Heian nobility. Although this image is less than 10cm. high, the elaborate and finely detailed carving of the face and drapery, the minute decorative patterns on the flame halos and pedestal, as well as the use of rare imported wood reflect the high status of the aristocratic patron, probably a high-ranking priest or courtier living in the capital.

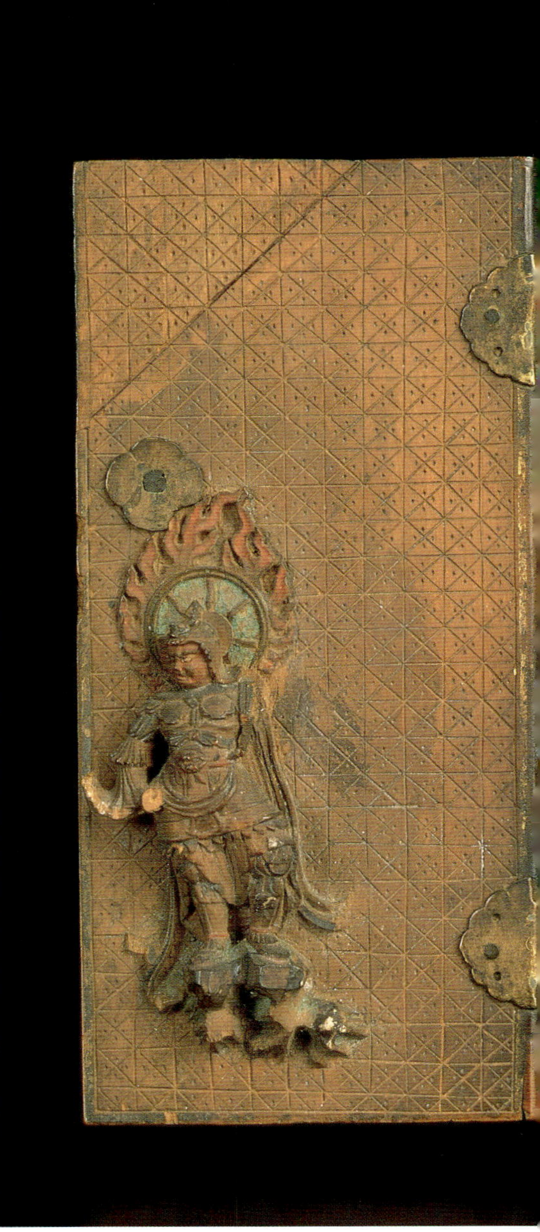

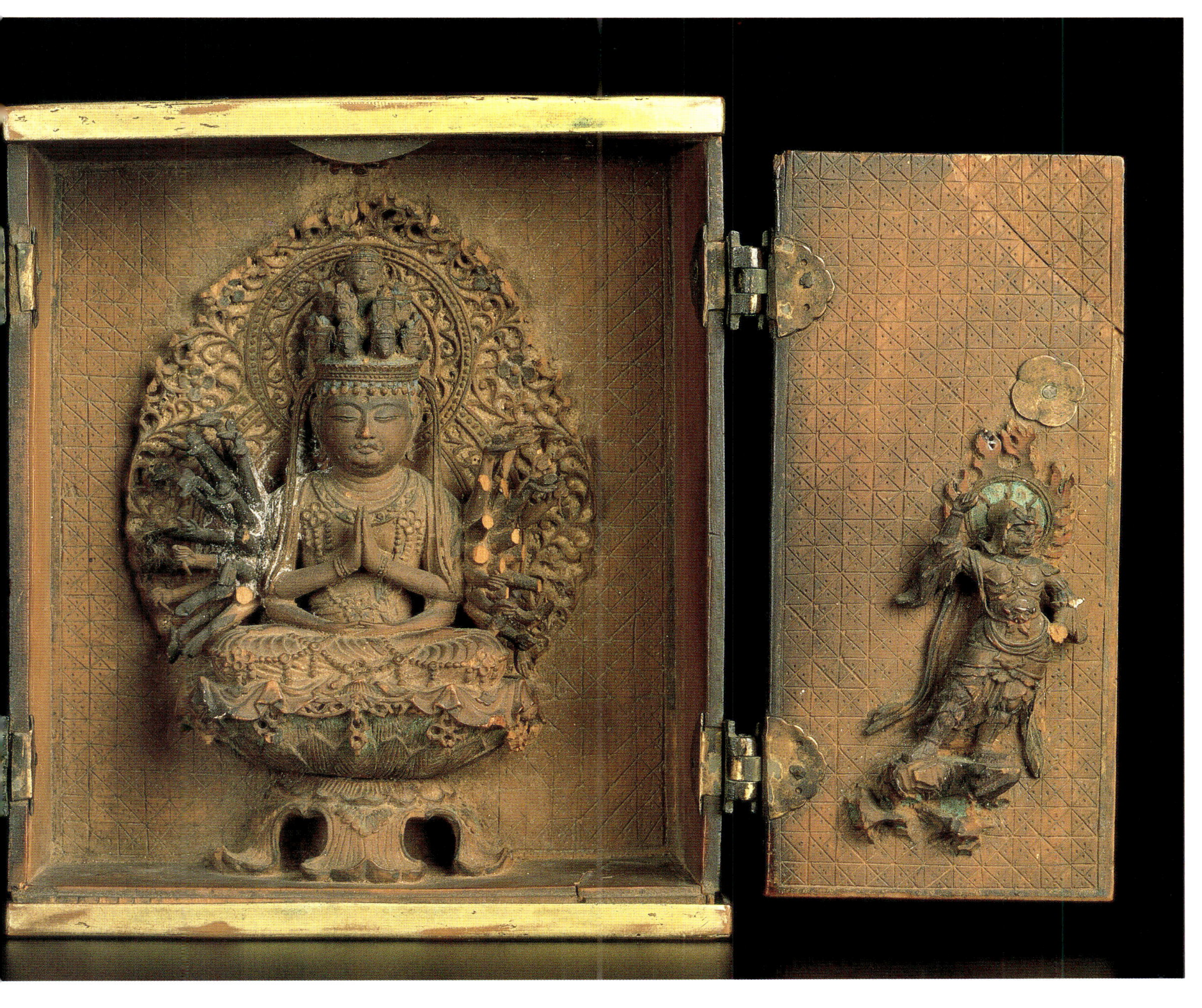

6 ⊙

Ritual Flower Basket
金銀鍍透彫華籠

Heian period, 12th century
Bronze openwork, with gold and silver plating
Diameter: 28.6cm
Jinshō-ji, Shiga

The shallow container (*keko*) was used in
the flower-scattering procession or ceremony
during Buddhist rites. The practice was early
adopted into Buddhism from the Indian
custom to scatter flowers on the floor for purification or in greeting honored guests. In
Japan, however, paper confetti of various
colors and often in petal shapes usually was
used instead of live blossoms. The *keko* was
carried suspended from the forearm on braided
ropes. The three rings (seen in photo) on the
reverse were for fastening similar decorative
ropes tied into an elaborate knot (*agemaki*)
which hung tassel-like from the bottom.

To create the complex circular repeat-
pattern of imaginary sacred *hōsōge* floral
scrolls the metalworker took a single sheet of
bronze, pierced-out the background and
hammered the leaves and flowers into prominent relief, to be embellished with line engraving and gold and silver plating. The lively
design belies the difficult medium. Earlier
keko, seen for example among pieces preserved
in the Shōsō-in repository dating from the
8th century, are done in easily-worked bamboo
basketry or lacquer. However, metalwork
largely superseded other materials by the
13th/14th century. This piece is probably the
oldest extant gold-or silver-plated bronze ritual
flower basket, and a superb example of late
Heian metal techniques and graceful stylistic
expression.

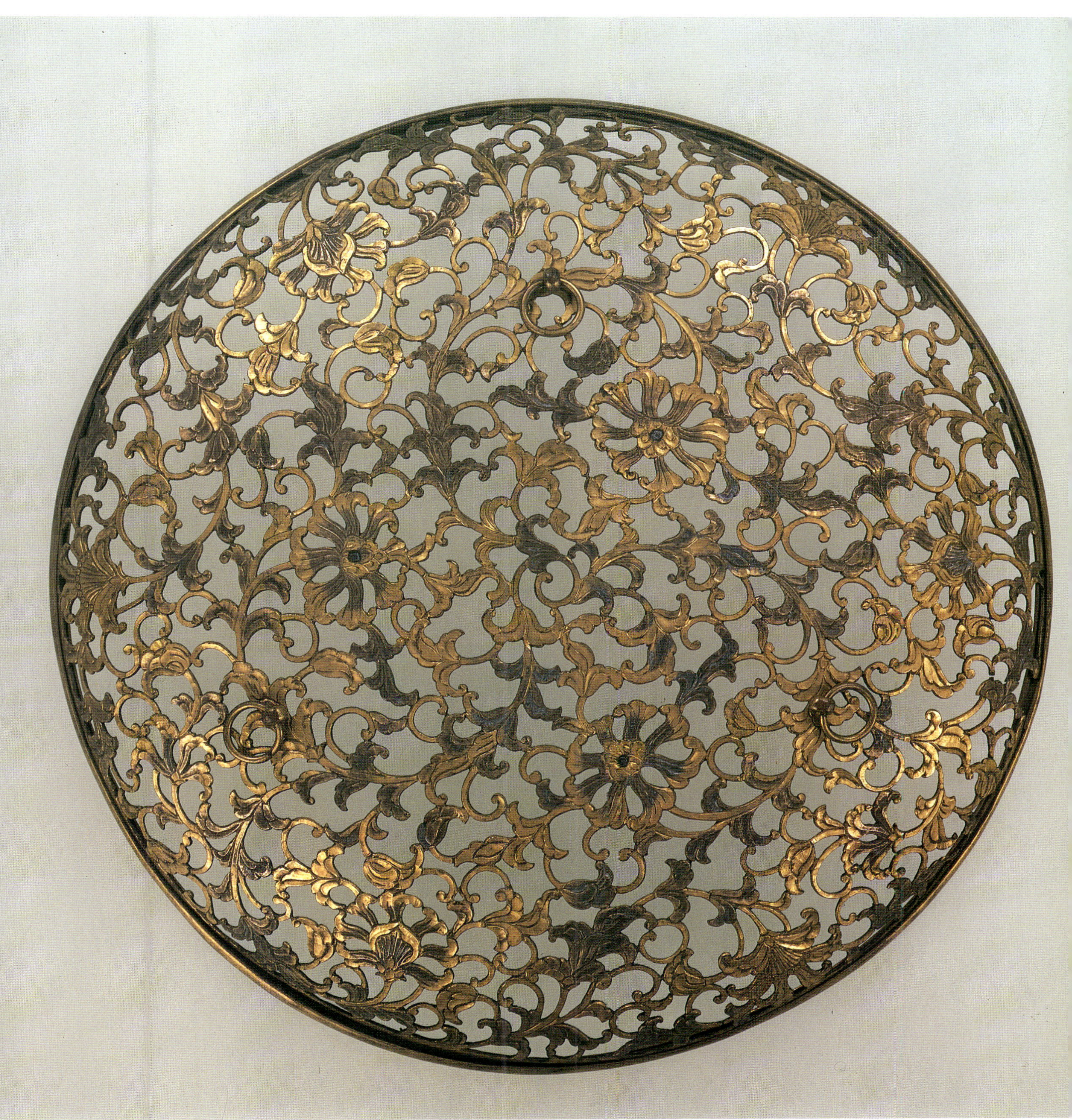

7

Ritual Flower Basket
紙胎漆塗彩絵華籠

Kamakura period, 14th century
Lacquer over a layered-paper base, with color
overpainting
Diameter: 23.9cm
Agency for Cultural Affairs

A similar Buddhist ritual basket (*keko*) to
Cat. No.6, but made by lacquering over a base
of layered paper, with simple cut-out sides.
Inside, mineral pigments and gold were used
to paint an alternating decoration of lotus
flowers and three-pronged thunder-bolt ritual
objects.

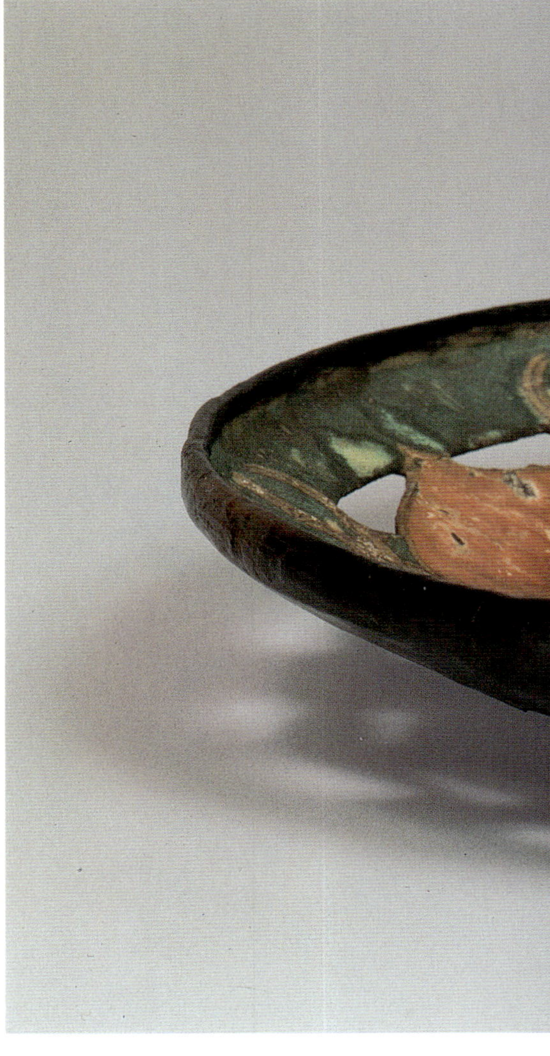

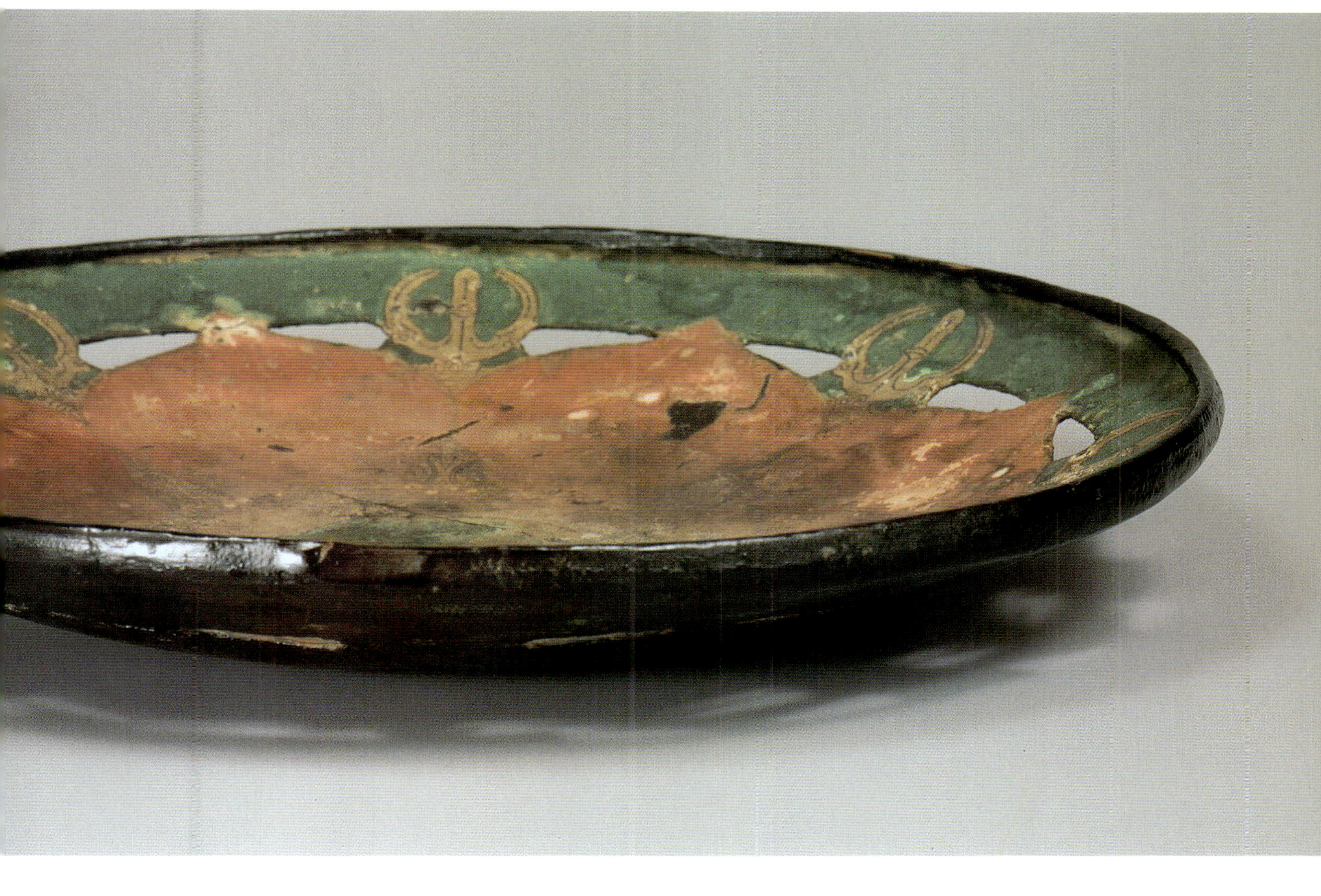

8 ⊙

Sutra Box
蓮唐草蒔絵経箱

Heian period, 12th century
Lacquer (over leather), decorated in *maki-e*,
with gilt bronze fittings
Height: 12.1cm
Nara National Museum

This box with a deep-fitting cover would have been secured by passing a braided-rope around the base, up through the two ring fittings, to be tied on top. Lotus flowers are emblematic of rebirth in Buddhist Paradise, especially the Buddha Amida's Pure Land, and are an auspicious motif frequently found on Japanese Buddhist ritual objects particularly after the 9th century. The delicate and graceful combination of lotus sprays with butterflies (the inside cover displays butterflies alone) typifies late Heian aristocratic taste.

The box is made of layers of lacquer (and decoration) over a base of deer or cow hide shaped and sun-dried, in a lacquer technique called *shippi*. The ground (termed *heijin*) was prepared by scattering relatively coarse gold filings in lacquer. The designs were then drawn in wet lacquer onto which were set fine filings of gold and a bluish alloy of gold and silver (*ao-kin*). Layers of clear lacquer were applied and then polished down to reveal the metal surface of the motifs, a technique known as *togidashi maki-e*. *Shippi* seems to have been more common in earlier periods, disappearing at the end of the Heian period, until a revival in early modern times. This is the only surviving box with *maki-e* lacquer decoration on leather known to date from the 12th century.

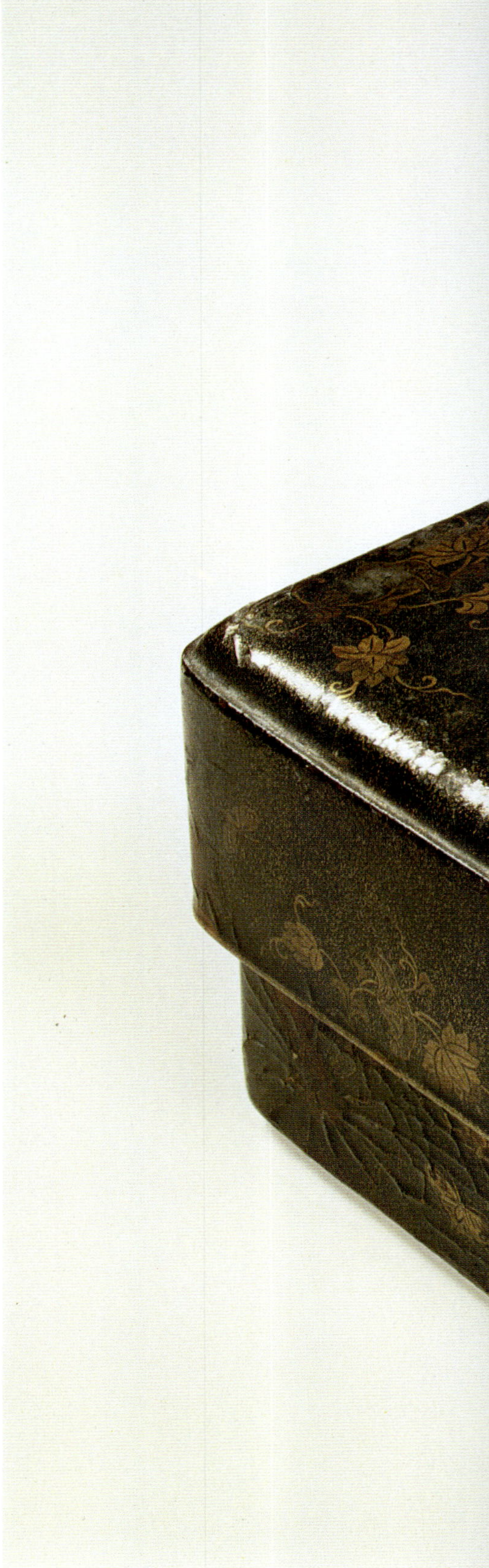

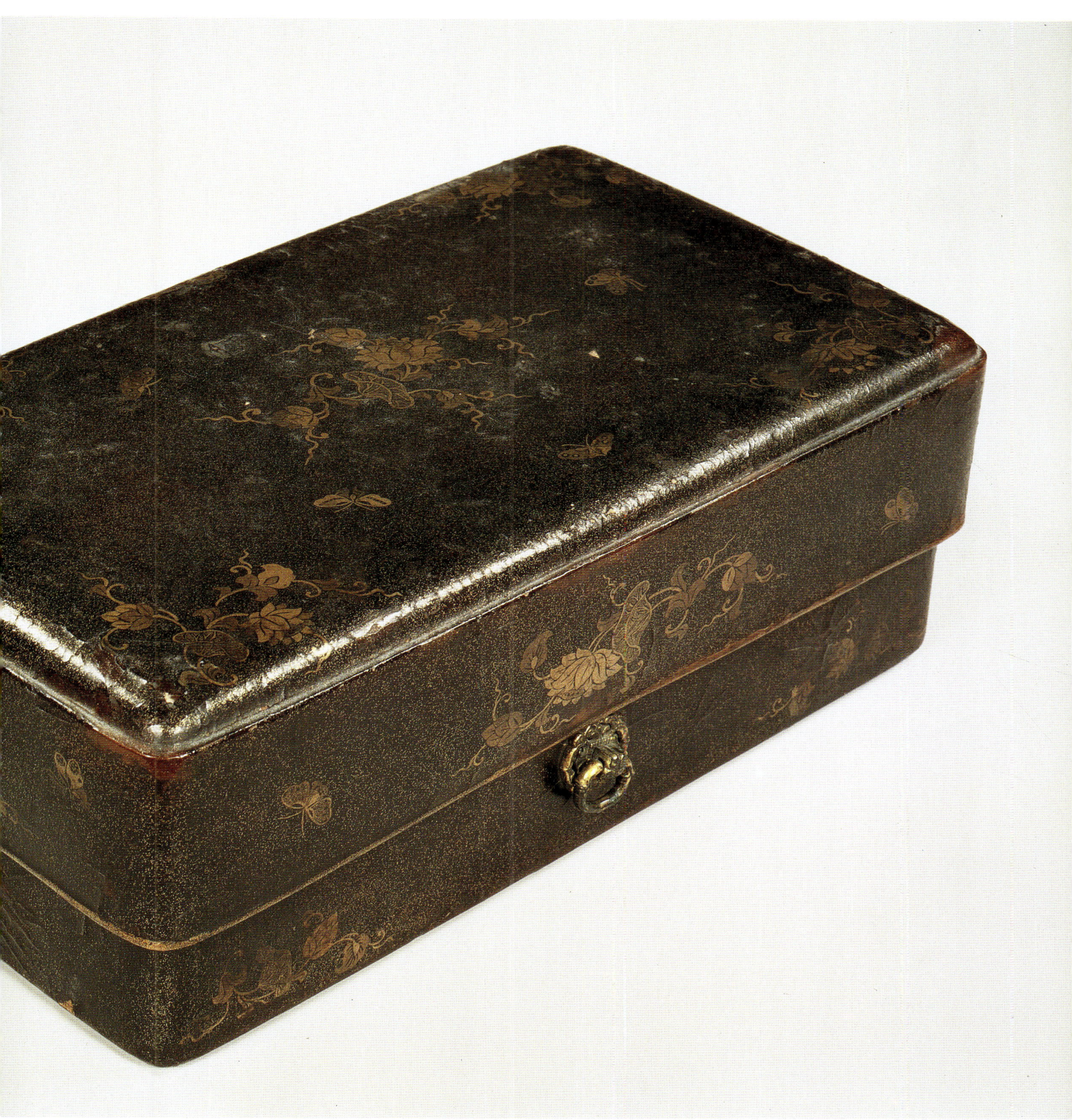

9 ◎

Openwork Sutra Scroll Container
(Together With Its Lotus Sutra
in One Volume)
金銅宝相華唐草文透彫経筒

Heian period, 12th century
Gilt bronze; height 22.0cm
Mantoku-ji, Aichi

The sutra case was made to display verti-
cally on an altar the accompanying handscroll
of the revered *Lotus Sutra* (Jp: *Hoke-kyō*),
written in gold on dark-blue paper. The pierced
openwork design hammered into low relief is
of *hōsōge,* the imaginary floral motif based
on the lotus sacred to Buddhism. The title:
Myōhō renge-kyō maki dai-ichi ("The Lotus
of the Wonderful Law Sutra, Volume One")
was hammered in relief on the front cartouche.
A raised-foot stand and cap at the top are
missing.

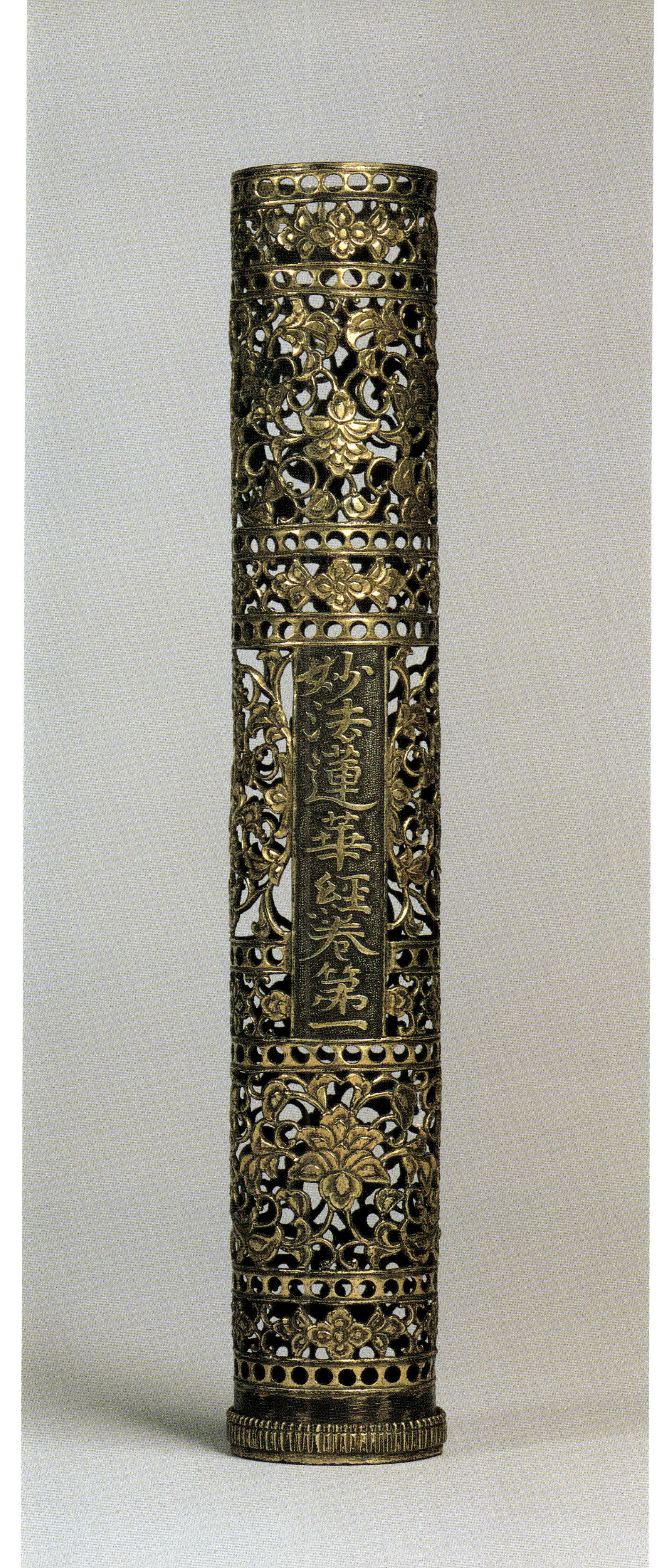

10 ◎

The Lotus Sutra, with Frontispiece
Painting
法華経

Heian period, 12th century
Fourth of 8 handscrolls; ink and colors on
decorated paper; w. 25.8cm
Matsudaira Koeki-kai, Kagawa

The fourth handscroll in an extant set of the *Lotus Sutra,* or more properly: *Lotus of the Wonderful Law* (Japanese: *Hoke-kyō*). This scroll contains Chapters 9, 10, 11, entitled "Receipt of Prophecy by 500 Disciples" (noted in the opening line next to the frontispiece painting), the famous "Preachers of the Law", and "Apparition of the Jeweled Stupa".

The *Lotus Sutra* was central in the teachings of the influential Tendai sect. Its message that all beings have a Buddha-nature and are guaranteed salvation (if one follows certain enumerated practices especially the copying, support, dedication or preaching of the *Lotus Sutra*) made it immensely popular among Heian period aristocrats. It continued to be revered through later periods and across many sects. Copying the sutra was widely practiced among noblemen and noblewomen. Copied sutras were then often dedicated at memorial services to assure the salvation of relatives or offered and displayed at recitation services held in supplication or thanksgiving for this-world benefits.

The calligraphy written in gentle, rounded characters is probably by a noblewoman living around the mid-12th century. Although there is no colophon, Scrolls 1, 6, and 8 bear the brief end inscription "Written by the woman, Shinjo."

The scroll is noted for the opening frontispiece painting in fine preservation which depicts in color pigments over silver on purple paper the appearance of a pagoda before believers above a landscape with a waterfall. Although Chapters 9 and 10 also mention pagodas, this probably illustrates the passage from Chapter 11 "Apparition of the Jeweled Stupa" that whenever the *Lotus Sutra* is preached a jeweled pagoda shall appear and bear witness.

The text was brushed in black ink between lines drawn in silver on paper made from *gampi (Wikstroemia sikokiana)* fibers called *hishi*. The paper had been painted with gold motifs such as grasses, birds, pines, set amid cloud or mountain shapes in the upper and lower margins, which carry auspicious or religious symbolism but have no direct relationship with the text passages. Heian aristocratic taste as well as some measure of the seriousness of purpose of the person dedicating the sutra are reflected in the beautiful embellished paper and the painting with their liberal use of expensive gold and silver. The title cartouche on the purple cover is written in gold and even the backing paper of the body of the scroll is decorated with scattered flecks of silver foil and designs of birds and butterflies.

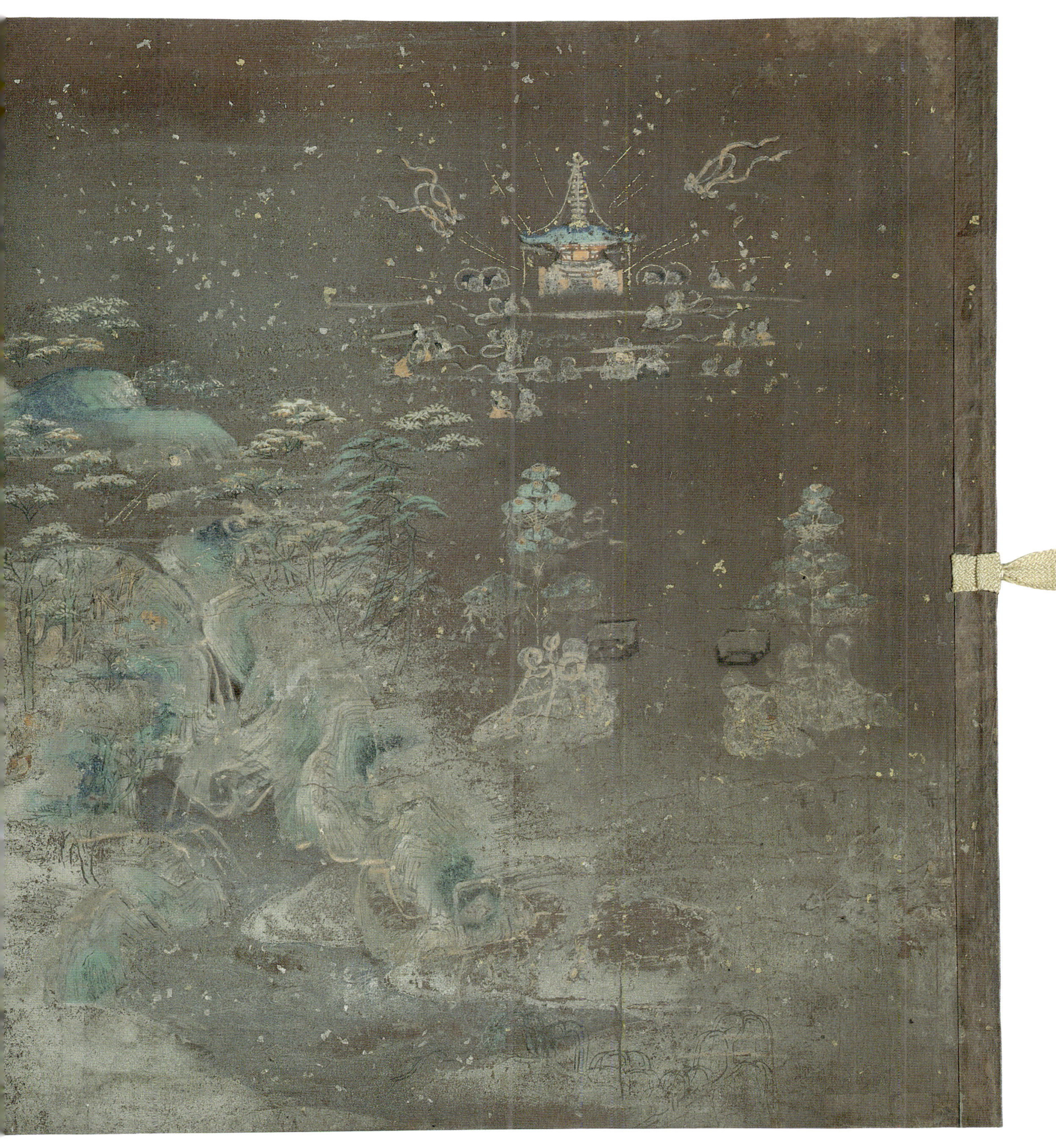

11 ◎
Ritual Implements of Esoteric Buddhism
金銅法具類

Kamakura period, 13th century
Gilt bronze
Iwaya-dera, Aichi

Footed-stand *(kongōban)*: d. 27.9cm, h. 3.6cm
Bell with five-pronged handle *(gokorei)*: l. 19.7cm
Thunderbolt (pestle) with one prong *(tokko-sho)*:
l. 18.0cm
    with three prongs *(sanko-sho)*: l. 18.0cm
    with five prongs *(goko-sho)*: l. 18.2cm
Incense Burner *(kasha)*: h. 10.0cm
Two Flower Vases *(kebyō)*: h. 12.4cm
Covered Holy-water Container *(shasuiki)*:
h. 9.8cm
Perfume Salve Container *(zukōki)*: h. 8.2cm
Two High-footed Food Containers *(onjikiki;* one is
later brass replacement*)*: h. 6.1cm
Set of Six Cups *(rokki)*: d. 6.7cm

These objects were used at the officiating priest's low table arranged in front of images or mandalas at Shingon or Tendai esoteric Buddhist ceremonies of exorcism and supplication. The esoteric teachings and rituals were introduced from China mainly in the 9th century and their sophistication and mystery found great favor at the court and among the Heian nobility. The implements all are made of bronze, decorated with incised floral *hōsōge* (on the bell) or lotus petal patterns and gold-plated. Owned by a Shingon temple in the provinces they conservatively preserve the high level of technique and dignified style of late Heian metalwork. The one-prong and three-prong thunderbolts although of the same style and period are not part of the original set to be designated Important Cultural Properties.

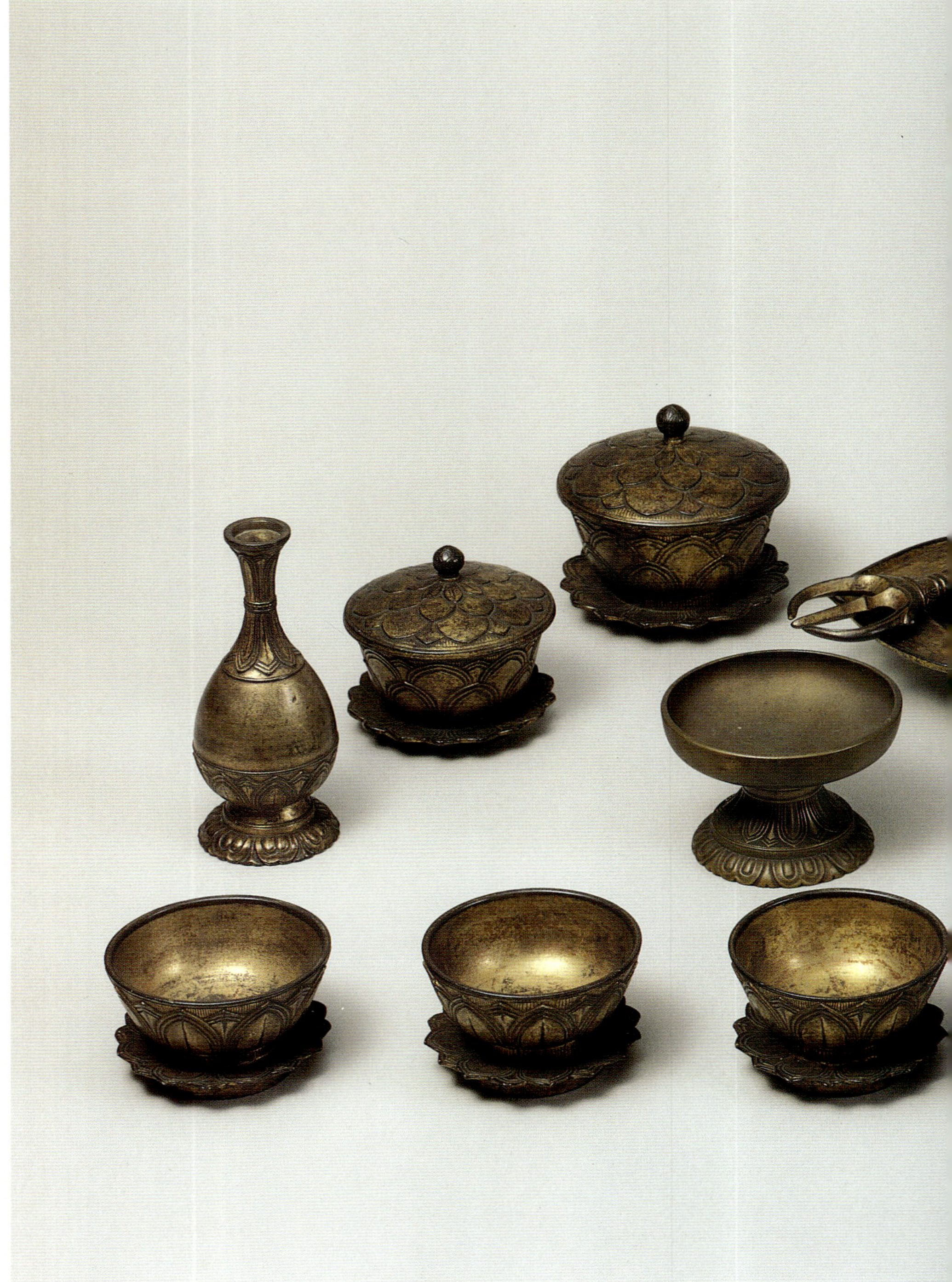

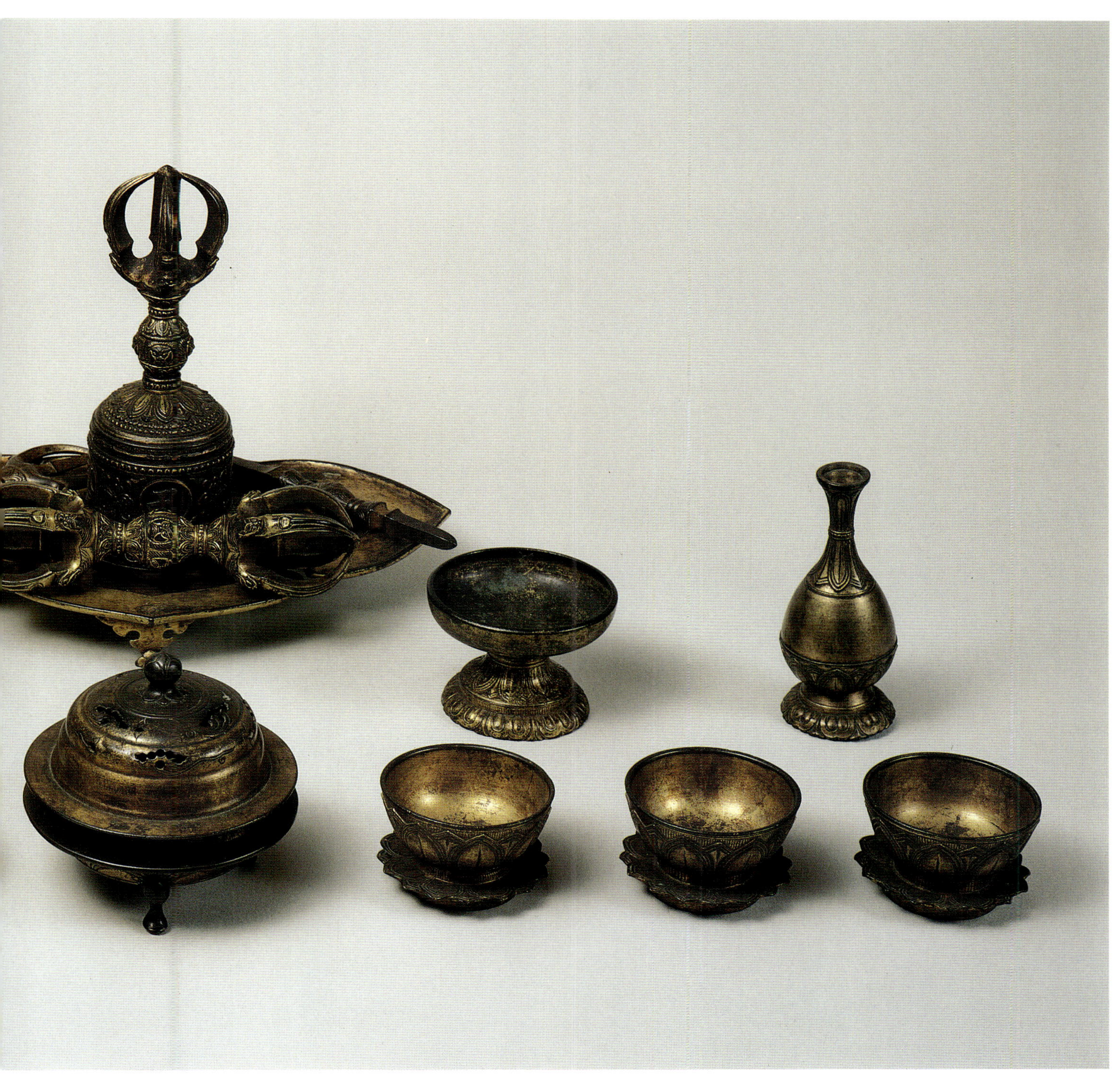

12 ⊙

Five Great Kings of Light
五大明王像

Kamakura period, 13th century
Five hanging scrolls; ink and colors on silk
Each 193.9cm × 126.2cm
Daigo-ji, Kyoto

The Five Great Kings of Light or Great Wisdom Kings (Jp: Go Dai Myō-ō) are powerful deities prominent in esoteric Buddhism, introduced to Japan around the 9th century. Ranking just below Buddhas (Jp: *nyorai*) and Bodhisattvas (Jp: *bosatsu*) they embody the teachings of Dainichi (Skt: Mahāvairocana), the supreme Buddha in esoteric thought. Their fearsome appearances manifest Dainichi's wrath against evil and their abilities to overcome and convert those hardened against Buddha's truth. Usually they are depicted, as here, in a group of five, but particularly Aizen Myō-ō (not part of the set, see Cat. No.4) and Fudō Myō-ō inspired independent worship.

When sculptured images on an altar the Five Great Kings are always positioned with Fudō Myō-ō ("The Great Immoveable One") at the center with the other four in their respective cardinal directions. Fudō (Skt: Acalanatha) is depicted here with two young attendants *(dōji)* Kongara and Seitaka. On the north is Kongōyasha Myō-ō (Skt: Vajrayakṣa) powerful deity of Indian folk demon origin with distinctive double-tiered eyes. Gundari Myō-ō (Skt: Kundali) on the south is readily identifiable by the coiling snakes symbolizing human vices such as prejudice, laziness, and passion. His power is to remove all obstacles. On the east is the eight-armed Gōsanze Myō-ō (Skt: Trailokyavijana) whose powers equal Fudō's. He tramples underfoot the Indian gods Daijizaiten (a form of Visnu) and his consort Uma. Riding on the buffalo is six-legged six-armed Daiitoku Myō-ō (Skt: Yamantaka) at the west. Thought to be a manifestation of the Bodhisattva Monju he was worshipped in Japan especially to bring victory in battle.

Strong ink outlines, clear, un-fussy detailing on robes and ornaments and the swirling, lively rhythms of the flaming halos rank this set among the most powerful of all painted depictions of Myō-ō. They are thought to date from early in the Kamakura period (13th century).

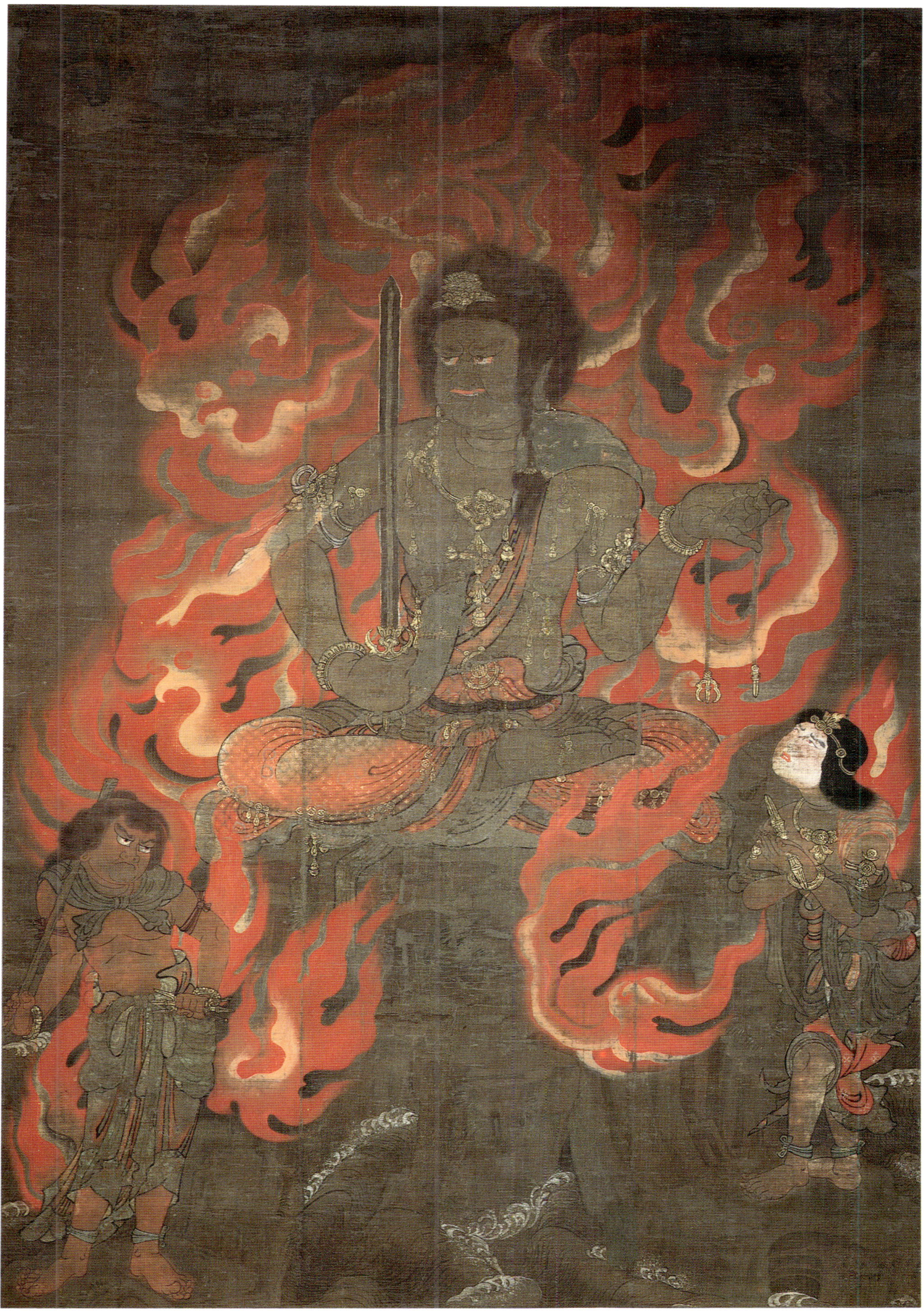

12-1 Fudō Myō-ō

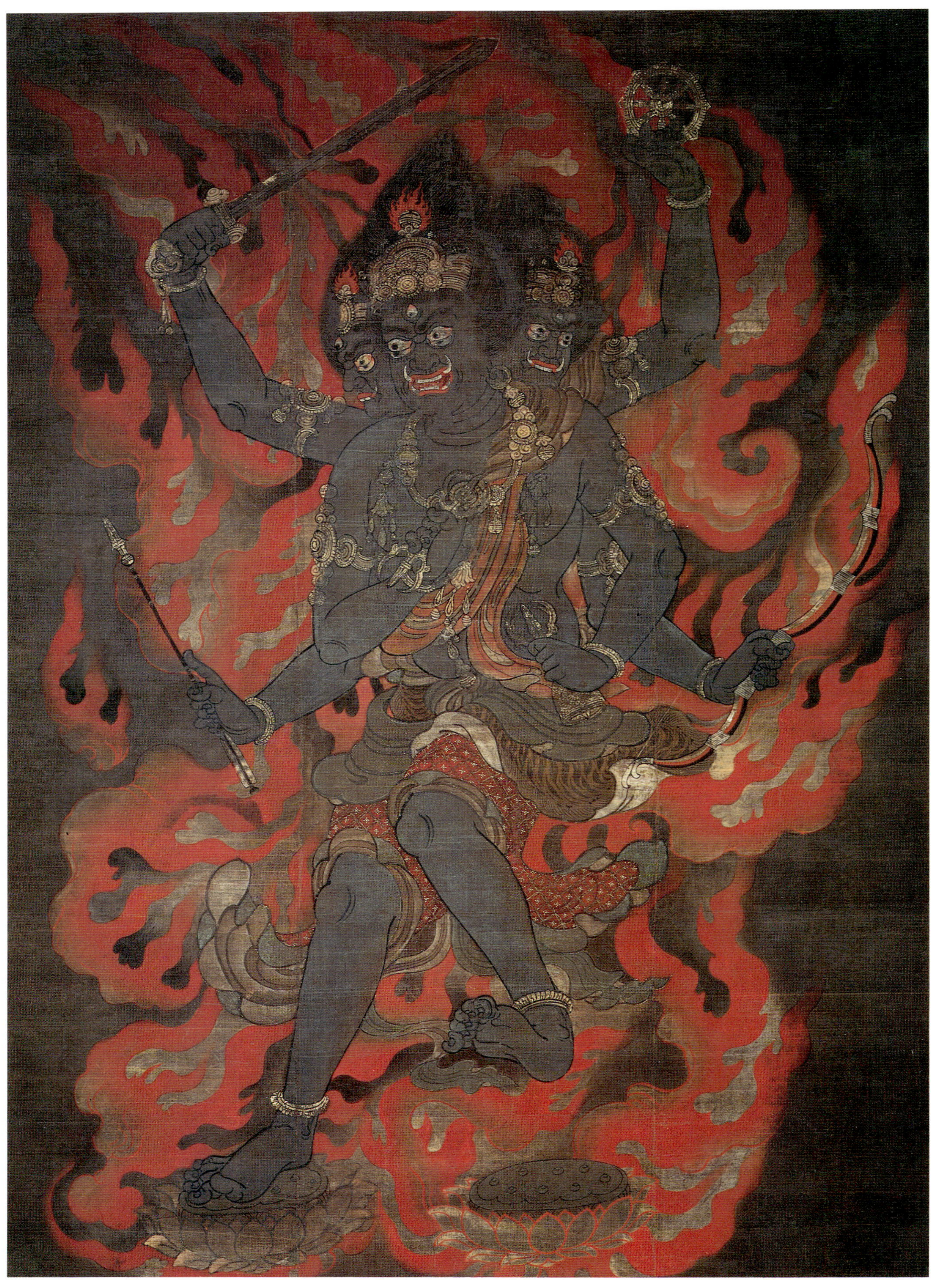

12-2　Kongōyasha Myō-ō

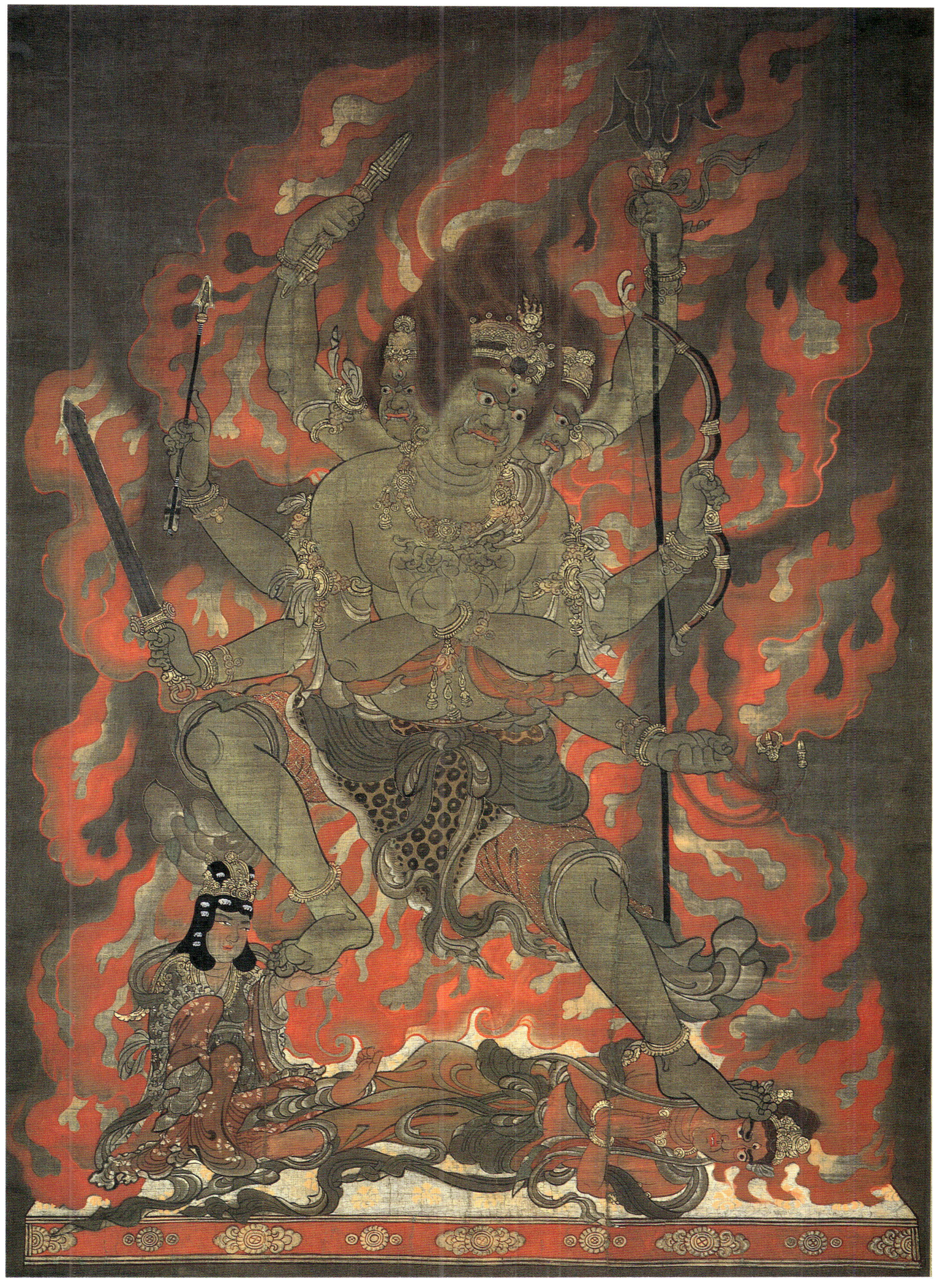

12-3 Gosanze Myō-ō

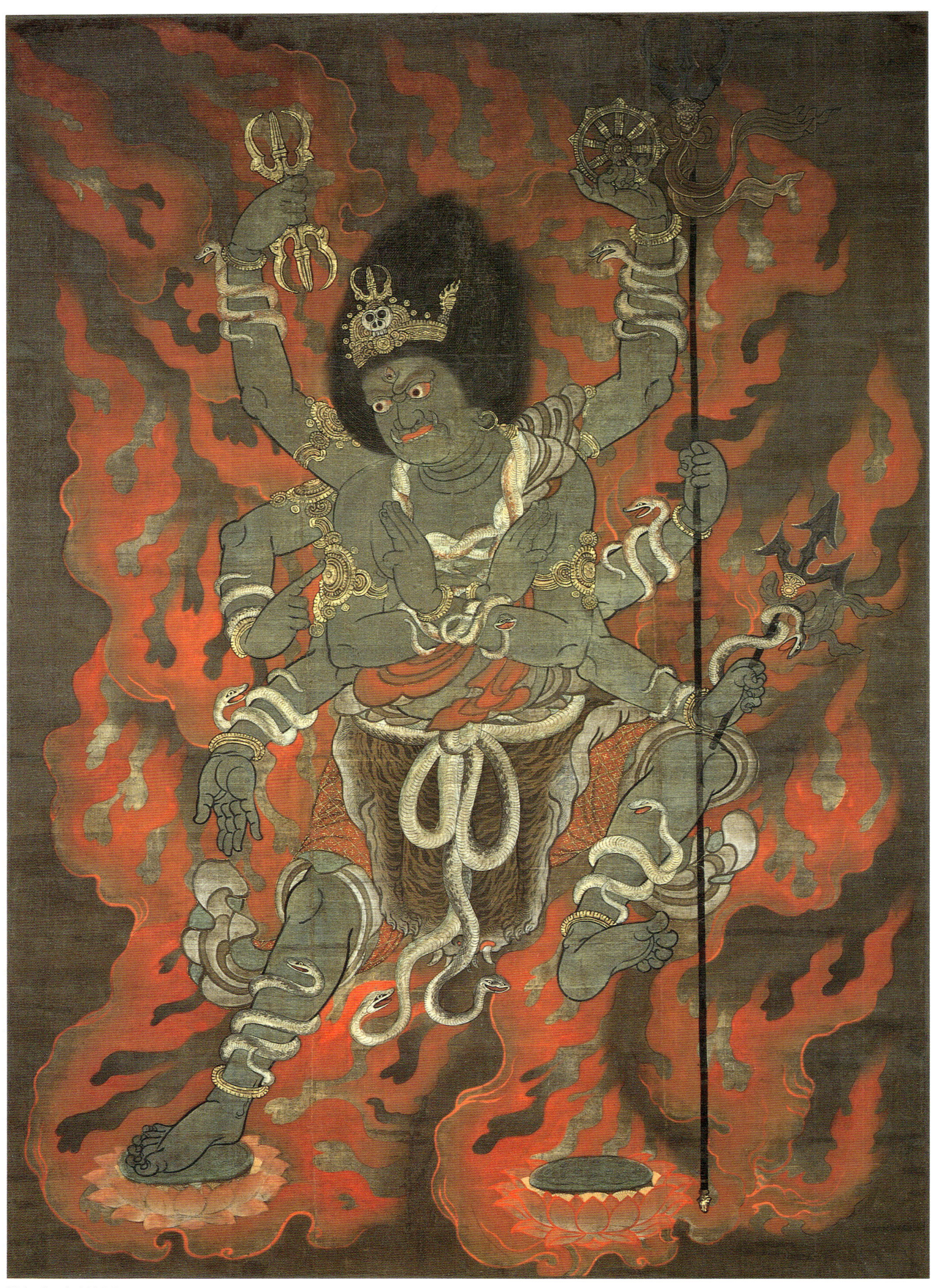

12-4 Gundari Myō-ō

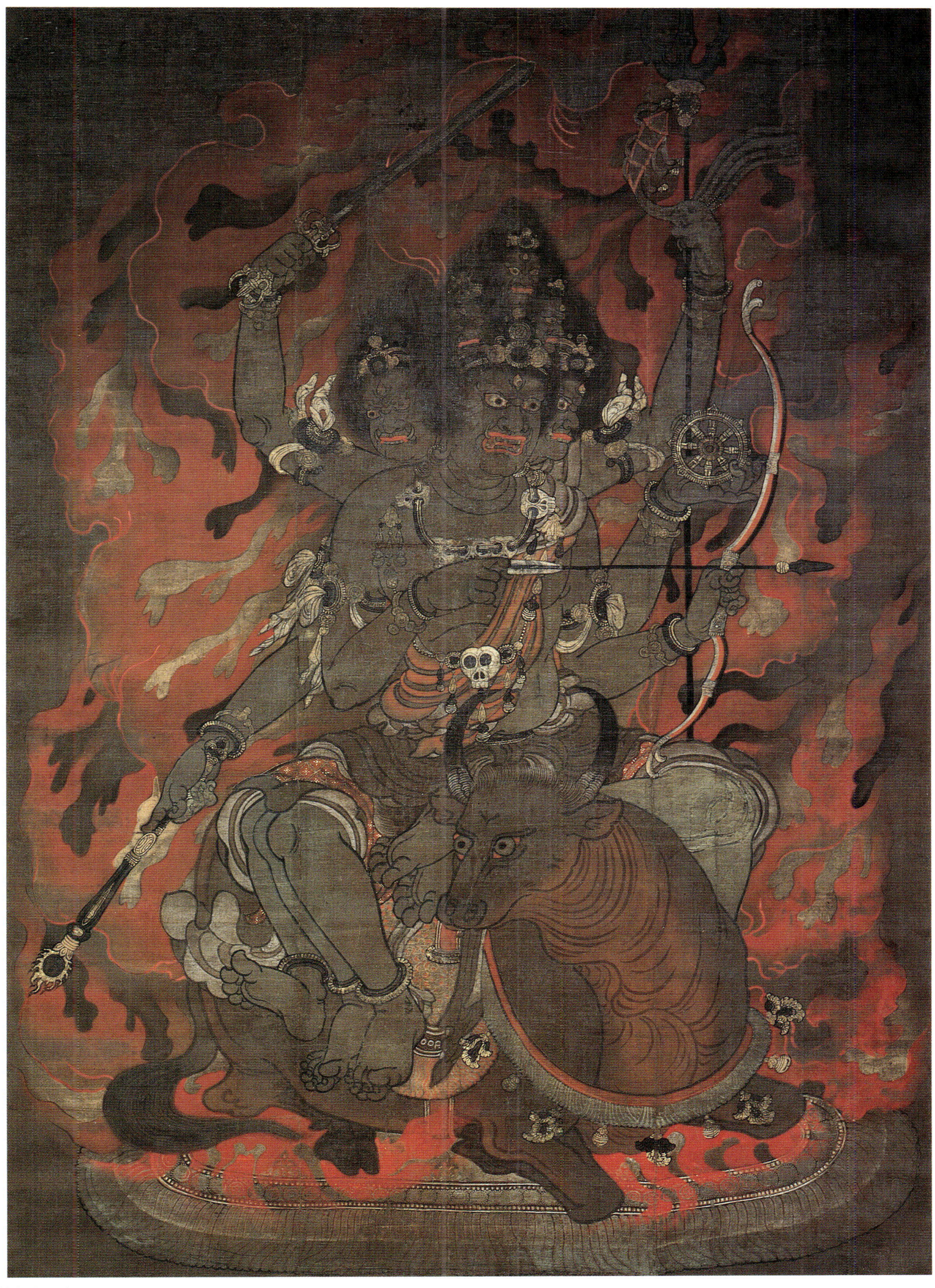

12-5 Daiitoku Myō-ō

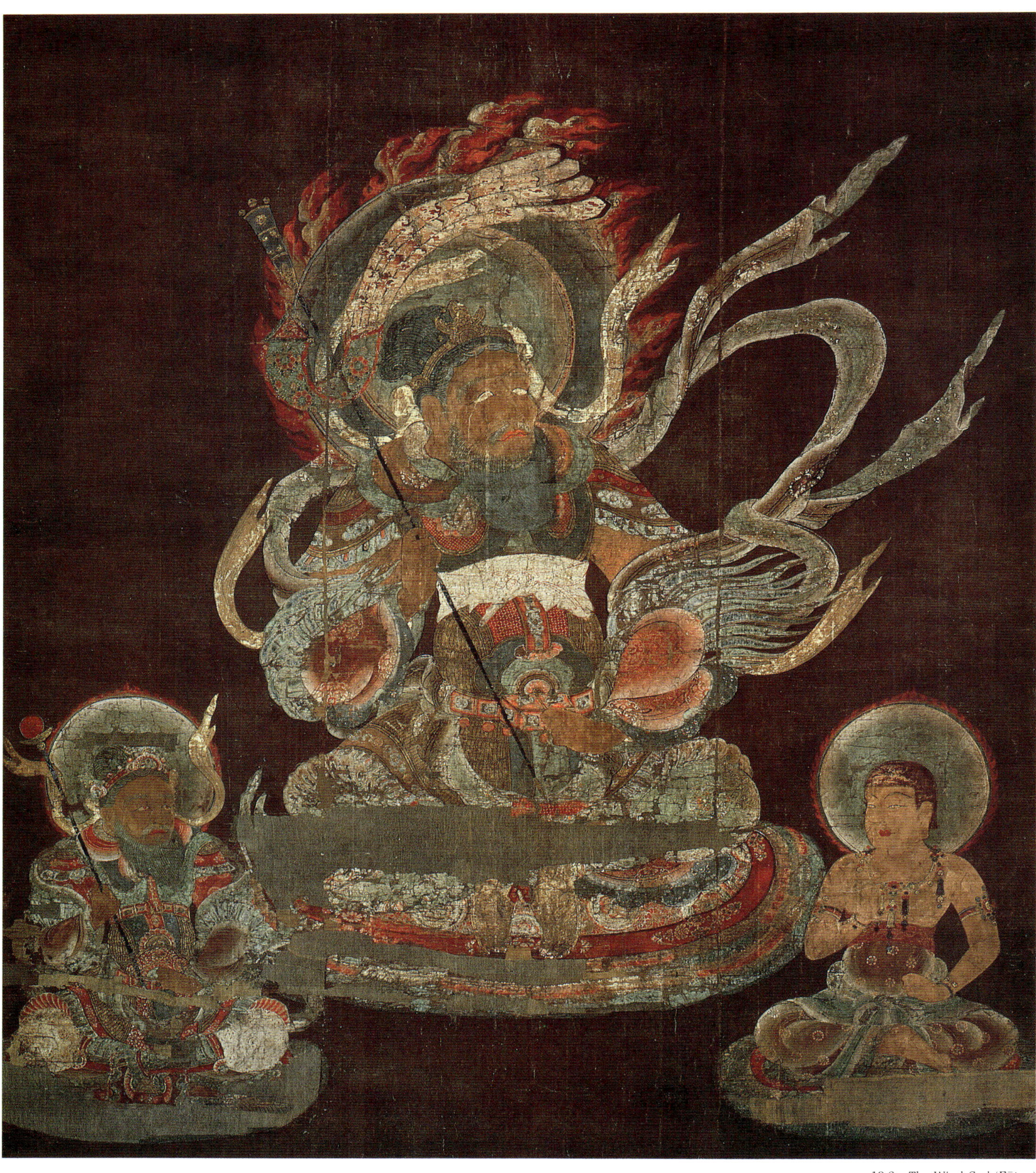

13 ⊙

Two of the Twelve Heavenly Beings:
The Moon God (Gatten) and The Wind
God (Fūten)
十二天像　12幅のうち　月天・風天像

Heian period, 12th century
Ink and colors on silk; each 144.2cm × 126.6cm
Kyoto National Museum

The group of Heavenly Beings (Japanese: Jūni-ten) were introduced to Japan with esoteric teachings around the 9th century. An auspicious combination of what were originally Indian Brahmanic deities, they guard the eight cardinal points, the zenith and nadir, the sun and moon. From the Heian period hanging scrolls or screens of the Twelve Heavenly Beings were displayed, along with a set of the Five Great Kings of Light (see Cat. No.12), in the Imperial Chapel (Shingon-in) within the Palace during an esoteric ceremony held early in the New Year to protect the nation. Other Shingon temples held similar ceremonies to protect their precincts..

These paintings belong to one of the earliest sets extant and were painted probably in 1127 for the Shingon-in because the set in use

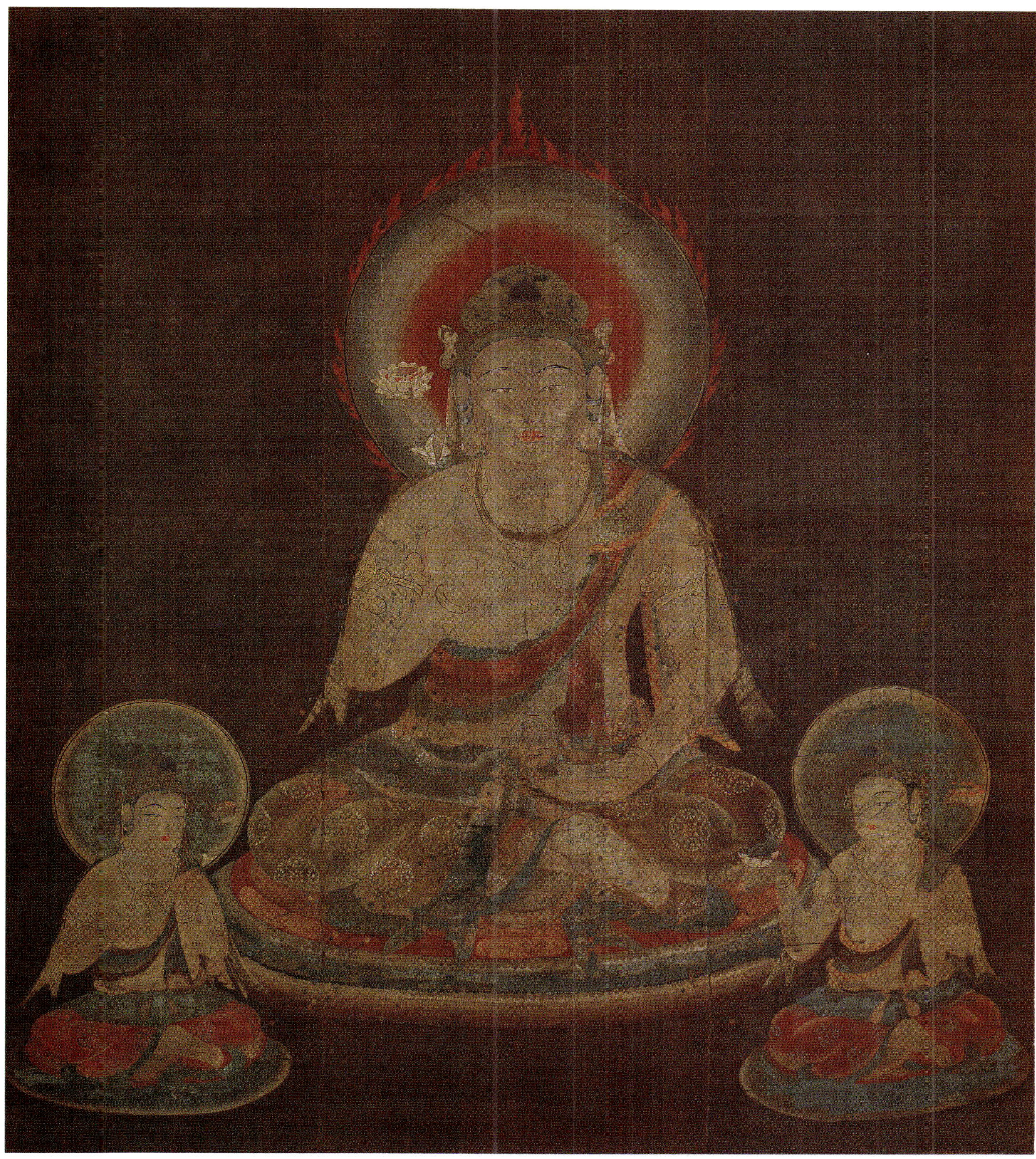

13-1 The Moon God (Gatten)

there was destroyed by fire. After the court fell on hard times and before coming to the Kyoto National Museum, they were handed down at Tōji (Kyōōgokoku-ji) the great temple built at the behest of the Shingon patriarch Kūkai (Kōbō Daishi) in Kyoto. All twelve of the paintings (of which two are in the exhibition) show the deities in seated postures flanked by attendants. The brilliant coloration which includes pigments applied from the back of the silk (*urazaishiki*) and the use of cut gold foil (*kirikane*) are representative of late Heian painting.

The Moon Guardian (Gatten) derives from the Indian moon god, Chandra. His attendants hold a crescent-moon shape and a rabbit, which long has been associated with the moon in Asian folk myths and Buddhist tales. The Wind God, Fūten, derives from the god Vayu, guards the northwest, and is shown here wearing a crown and holding a distinctive staff. Details of the technique and stylistic expression of the Wind God (along with one other painting in the set) have led some scholars to suggest it survives from an earlier series produced in the 11th century.

14 ◎

Fugen Bosatsu and the Ten Rasetsunyo
普賢十羅刹女像

Kamakura period, 13th century
Ink and colors on silk; 72.3cm × 39.1cm
Private collection

Fugen Bosatsu (Sanskrit: the Bodhisattva Samantabhadra) embodies goodness and personifies the teaching, meditation, and spiritual practices of the Buddha. He is often depicted, as here, riding on a white elephant. The *Lotus Sutra* (Jp: *Hoke-kyō*) discusses Fugen extensively, especially in the expanded version "The Three Books of the Lotus" (*Hokke sambu*) revered by the esoteric Tendai sect. This scripture (see Cat. No.10) which assures salvation to all — lay as well as cleric, women as well as men, was the sutra most often studied and copied by the nobility in the Heian period. It continued to be important in later periods. Fugen was considered the special patron and protector of believers in the *Lotus Sutra*.

The Rasetsunyo are women with superhuman powers (adopted into Buddhism from Indian folk demon origins) that are mentioned briefly in the *Lotus Sutra* as guardians of those who preach it. Although there is no direct scriptural basis for grouping the Rasetsunyo with Fugen, the links are obvious. The combination, which perhaps began in China although no examples are known, was depicted by Japanese artists from the 12th century. Part of the appeal of such paintings, especially for noblewomen of that time, may lie in the unusual appearance of women in religious depictions, either shown in Chinese attire or, as in this version, in the dress of Heian court ladies themselves.

This painting is dated to the 13th century, but it retains many of the features of late Heian (12th century) depictions. For example, the plump faces of the Rasetsunyo, with abbreviated lines rendering the eyes and noses, and the exquisite patterns of applied cut gold foil (*kirikane*) on the multilayered robes or the ornaments of Fugen and his elephant convey well the earlier style.

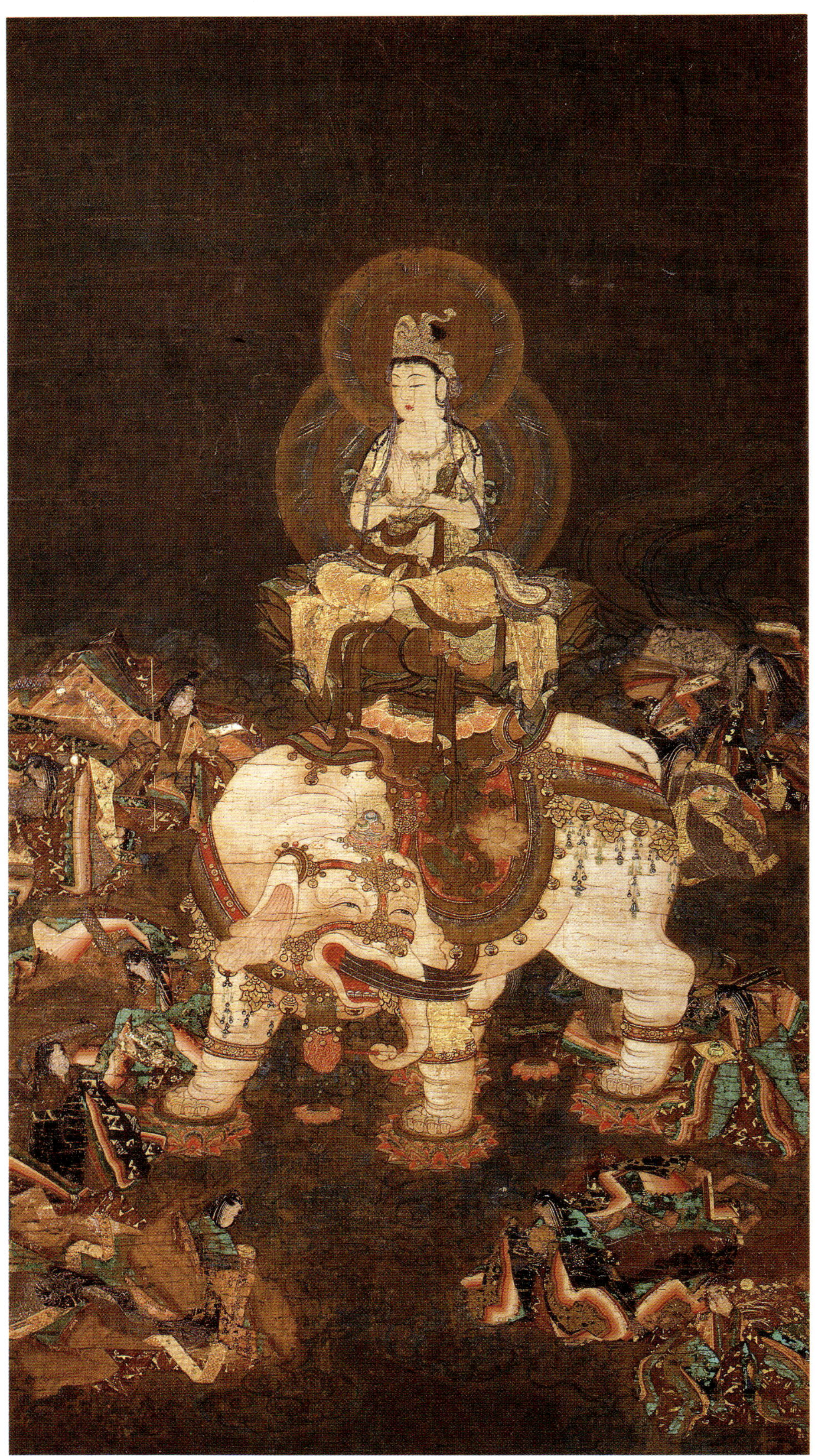

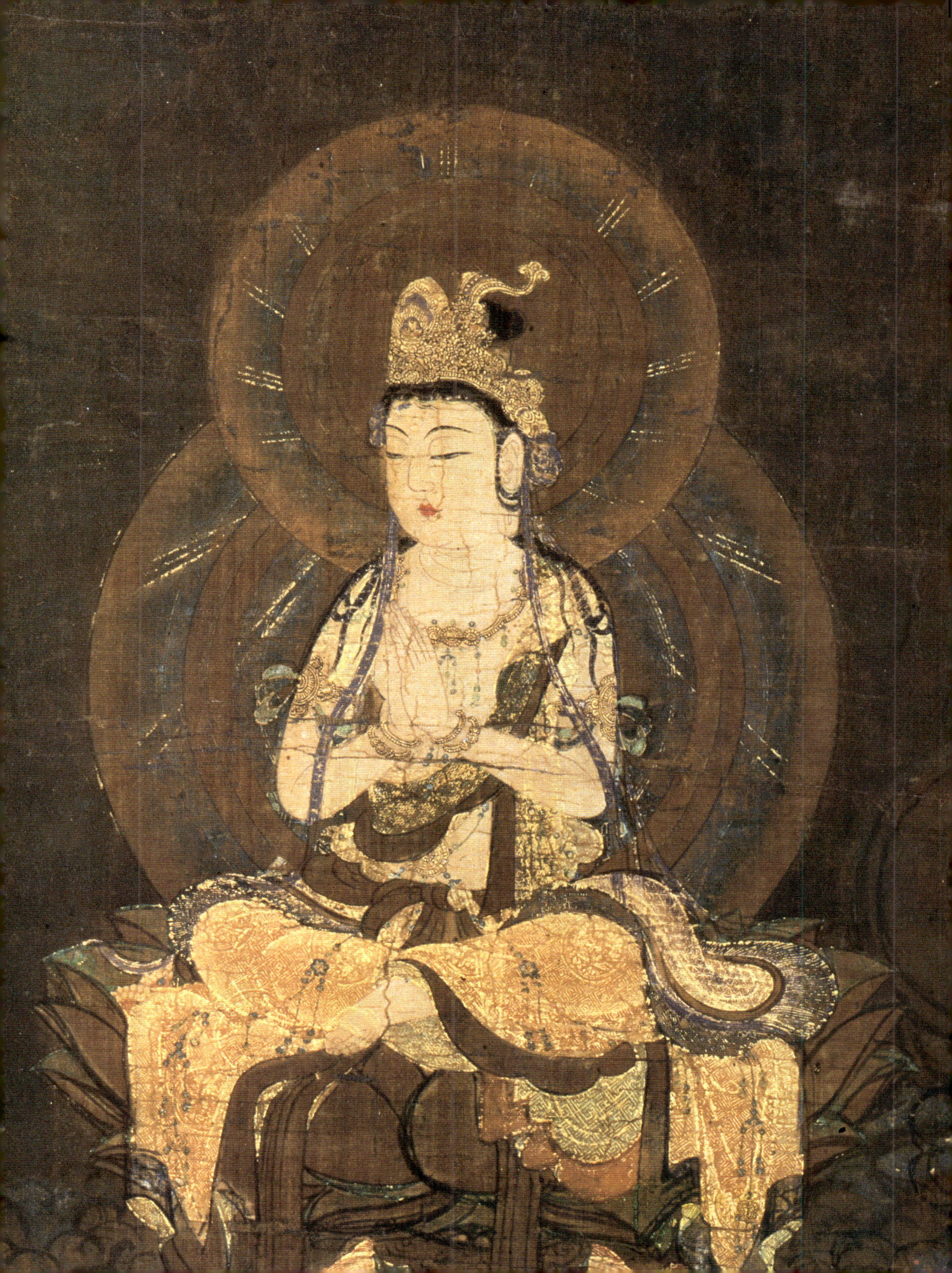

15
Welcoming Descent of Amida and His Heavenly Host
阿弥陀聖衆来迎図

Kamakura period, 13th/14th century
Ink and colors on silk; 180.3cm × 76.5cm
Fukushima Prefectural Museum

The buddha, Amida (Sanskrit: Amitābha), is depicted descending on a vapor trail of clouds with his heavenly host. He comes to welcome and escort the dying believer, shown inside the aristocratic villa with walled garden, back to his paradise, the Pure Land (Jp: Jōdo). There as promised in the sutras the faithful will be reborn to certain bliss and enlightenment. "Welcoming Descent" (Japanese: *raigō*) paintings seem to be a largely Japanese development and enjoyed great popularity starting in the early 13th century. *Raigō* paintings were intended to be hung or positioned as screens before the dying to ensure the proper thoughts in Amida at the moment of death.

The religious basis for the paintings can be found before the 13th century in the beliefs and practices of the Heian nobility. On the one hand, their sponsorship or attendance at awe-inspiring rituals of esoteric Buddhism was believed to ensure benefits and protection in the present life. Relying on the Lotus Sutra and such influential teachings as Genshin's (942-1017) *Essentials of Salvation* (*Ōjō yōshū*), however, most aristocrats on their deathbeds prayed that Amida would come and welcome them into his paradise. They practiced contemplative meditation to visualize this paradise, built temples and gardens in its image, and reaffirmed their faith by repeated invocation of Amida's name (the practice of *nembutsu*). Charismatic preachers especially Hōnen (1133-1212) helped to spread such beliefs in salvation through simple faith in Amida throughout all levels of society.

Although there are many variations in "Welcoming Descent" paintings this work displays many typical iconographic and stylistic features. Most basic is the idyllic, naturalistic landscape setting that sets off the conservative iconic images of golden Buddha and twenty-five bodhisattvas (Jp: *bosatsu*). The bodhisattvas Kannon and Seishi are shown at the head of the group, here preceded by two young attendants (standing before the veranda). It is unusual to find the heavenly deities given no musical instruments. The dragon and flying heavenly maidens (Jp: *hiten*), as well as the full moon at upper right, and the colorful painted borders added to frame the entire scene also are rarely seen in earlier examples, and suggest the influences of paintings such as the mandalas of the Pure

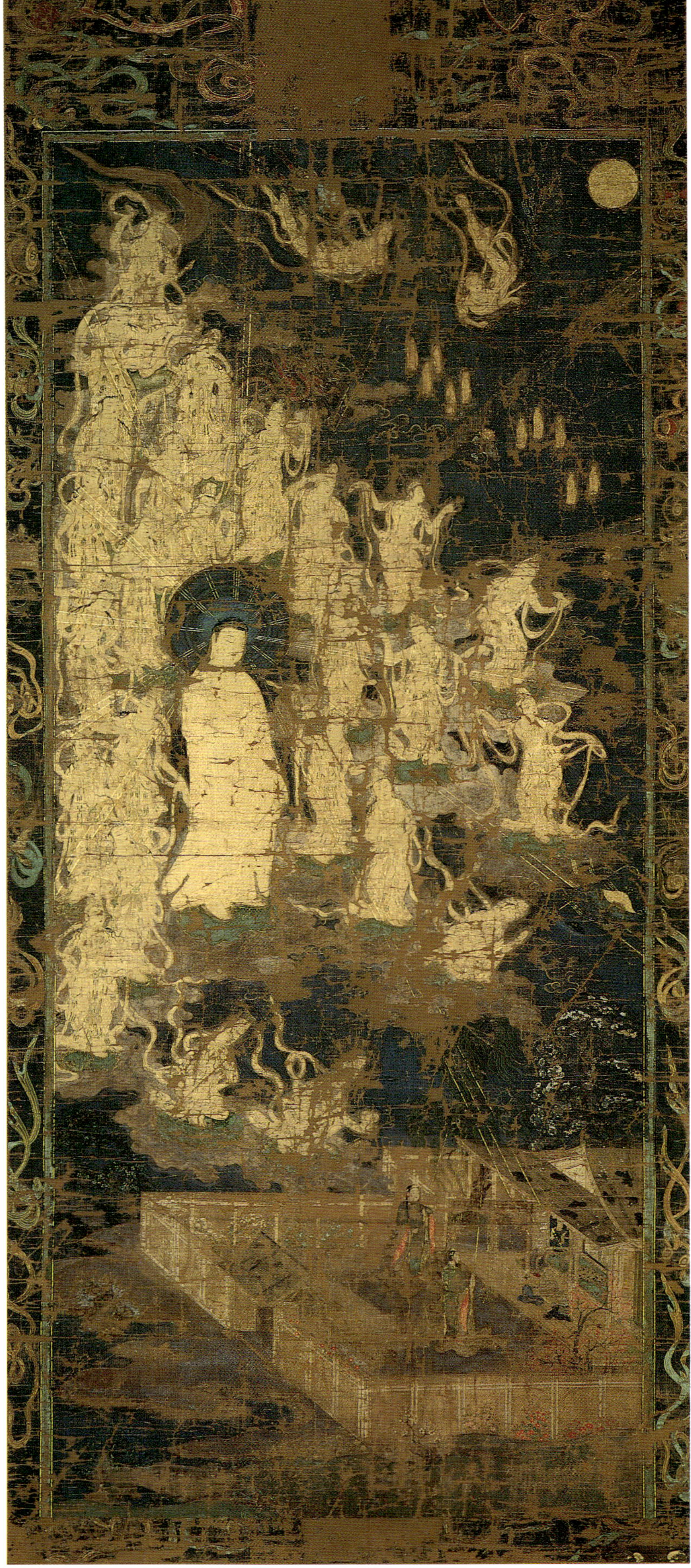

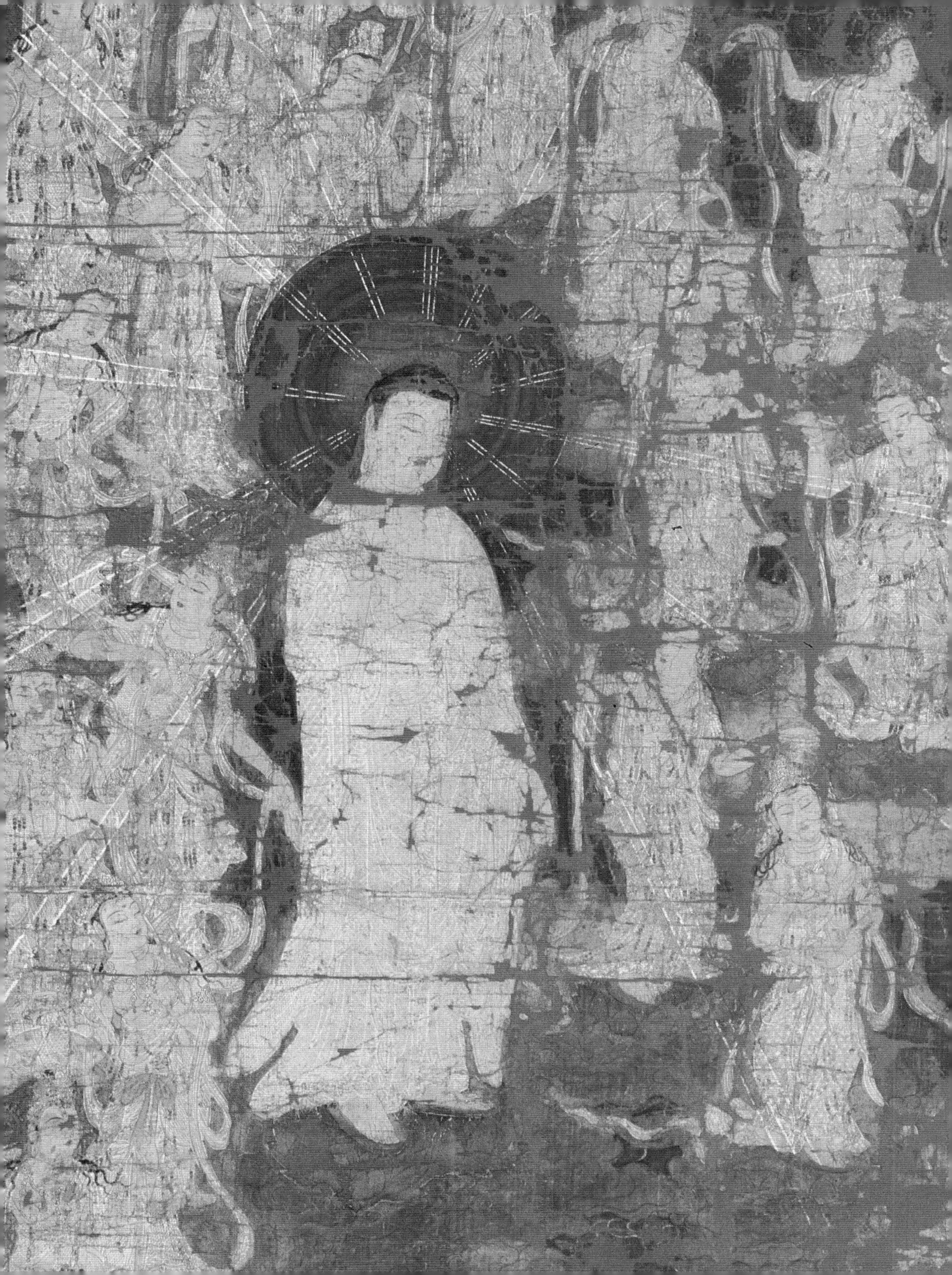

Land of the Kanmuryōjū-kyō. The vertical layout of this composition inhibits the impression of movement, but, enhanced by the extensive use of gold, it possesses a dream-like shimmering quality noteworthy among Pure Land paintings of its time.

16

Welcoming Descent of Amida and His Heavenly Host
阿弥陀聖衆来迎図

Kamakura period, 14th century
Ink and colors on silk
129.3cm × 158.4cm
Tokyo National Museum

The buddha, Amida with his heavenly host is shown descending to welcome the dying believer (depicted at right) back to his paradise. See Cat. No.15 for more discussion of "Welcoming Descent" (Jp: *raigō*) paintings. At the front of the group are the bodhisattvas Kannon, holding a lotus throne on which to receive the dying, and Seishi, hands clasped in prayer. At the right of the accompanying bodhisattva musicians and chorus stands a young boy attendant (*dōji*) in court dress. Damage to the silk has obliterated a second attendant figure. Barely visible in the sky above the background spring landscape are tiny Buddhas mentioned as one of the manifestations of "Welcoming Descent" in the sutra, *Kanmuryōjū-kyō*. Various stylistic devices such as the triangular hillock at left foreground, repeated in the triangular groups of the clouds and heavenly figures, or the golden rays emanating from the Buddha's forehead tuft of hair (signifying enlightenment), work together to draw the eye from left to right. This creates an impression of movement characteristic of the most impressive "Welcoming Descent" compositions.

The painting has suffered damage and retouching. However especially in the compositional layout it remains a representative example of earlier *raigō* paintings during the period of greatest creativity. It forms a pair with a painting of the Historic Buddha, Shaka (Sanskrit: Sákyamuni) and other divinities placed in a mountain landscape. This unusual pairing suggests that this painting too may have been associated with syncretic Buddhist-Shinto beliefs.

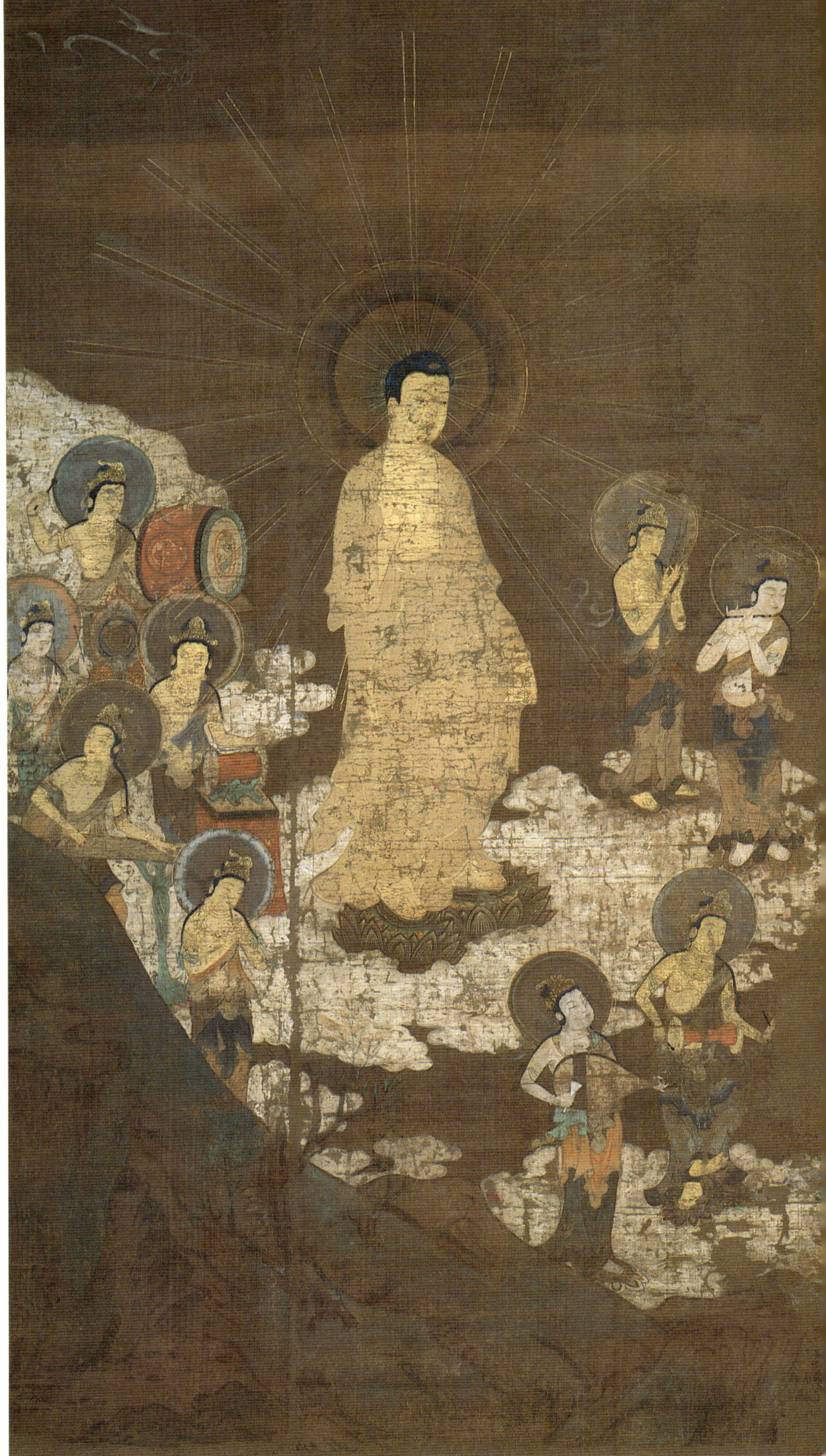

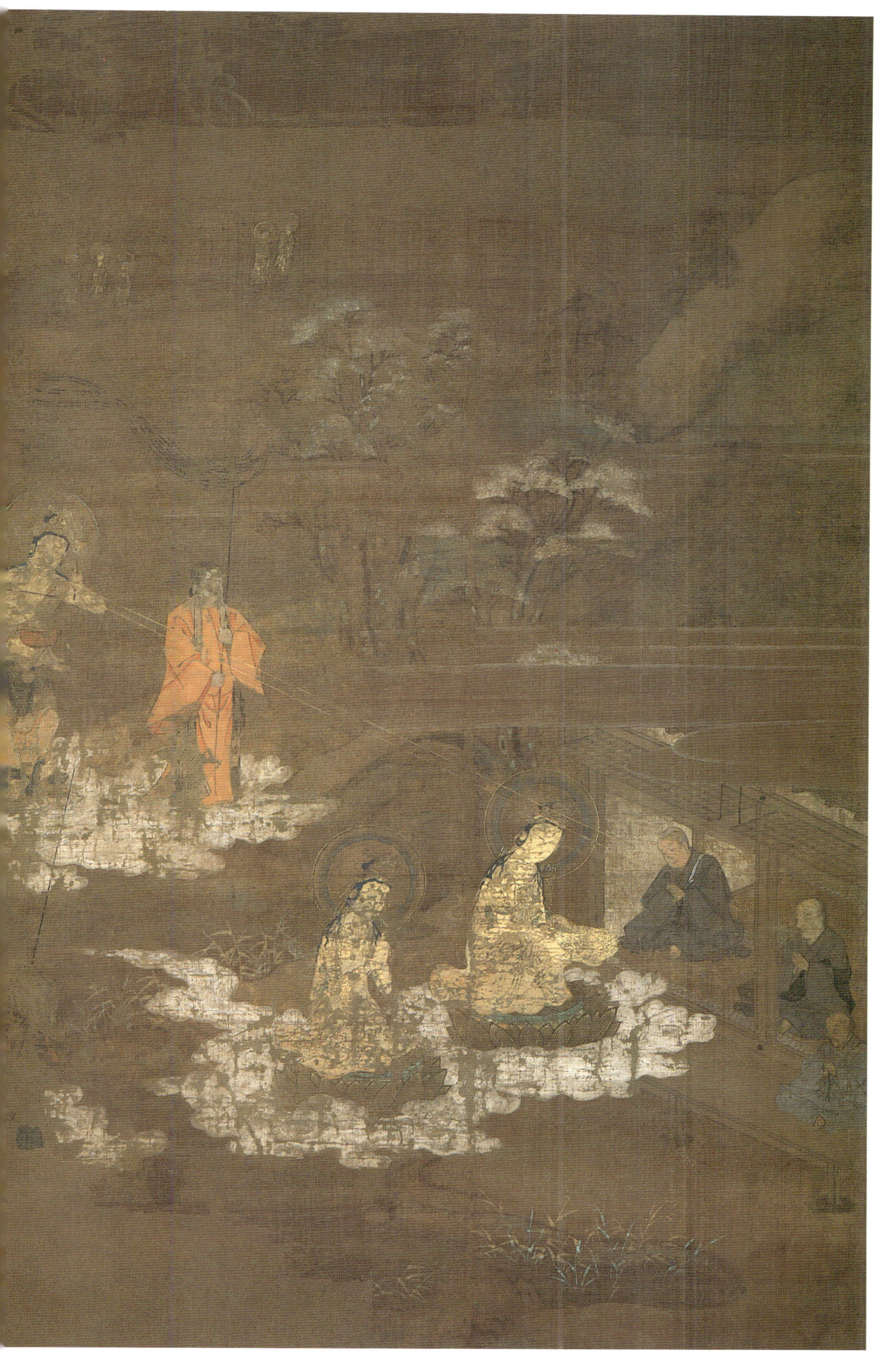

Hanging Plaque of the Gods of
Kumano In Their Forms as Buddhist
Deities
熊野十二社権現御正体

Kamakura period, 13th century
Gilt bronze; diameter 41.3cm
Private collection, Osaka

During the generations after the introduction of Buddhism to Japan in the 6th
century the ancient beliefs in various local
and ancestral gods were accommodated to the
doctrinally vastly more complex teachings of
Buddhism. Under the impact of Buddhist and
century the ancient beliefs in various local
and ancestral gods were accommodated to the
doctrinally vastly more complex teachings of
the Heian period one central concept to
emerge in the syncretic mingling of beliefs, in
part because of the sympathetic approach to
Shinto ("the Way of the Native Gods") taken by
the esoteric sects, was that the *kami* were not
competitors or enemies of Buddhism but
simply more easily approachable and under-
standable manifestations of universal Buddhist gods. An elaborate pairing of a god, the
native incarnation (*suijaku*), with its respective original form as a Buddhist deity
(*honjibutsu*), was in place by the 11th century.
This assimilation served to strengthen and
enrich the traditions of both religious systems,
and closely linked temples with particular
shrines.

Here, in the center row of the plaque,
slightly larger than the rest, we find (from left
to right) the Buddhist deities: Thousand-Arm
(Jp: Senjū) Kannon, Amida and Yakushi. They
correspond to the main gods of the three
Kumano Shrines — the Nachi Waterfall,
Hongū, and Shingū or Hayatama. The ten
other Buddhist images, also cast separately
and attached to the plate with nails, represent
the original Buddhist forms of minor gods or
sub-shrines in the area (now Wakayama pref.)
southeast of the Heian capital (Kyoto). The
beauty of Kumano's mountains, its mild climate and accessibility near the sea, helped to
make the area a favorite pilgrimage of emperors
and nobles down through the years. Indeed
sacred Kumano was considered a paradise
(Jōdo) on earth.

This type of hanging plaque with Buddhist
images is known as a *kakebotoke*. It probably
was hung in or outside one of the shrine buildings, offered by a worshipper for the fulfillment
of a request.

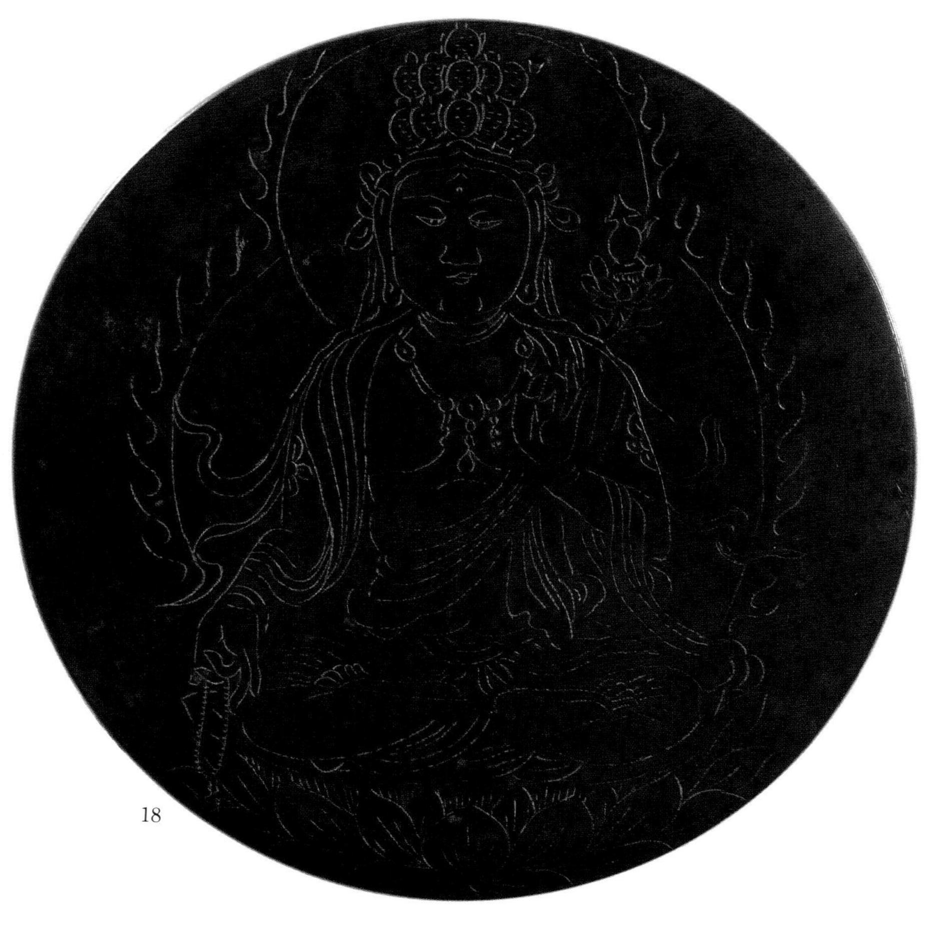

18

18

Sacred Mirror With Incised
Eleven-Headed Kannon Image
線刻十一面観音御正体

Heian period, 12th century
Bronze; diameter 11.2cm
Agency for Cultural Affairs

A cast mirror of a silver-ish alloy of mostly
copper and tin called *hakudō* (literally "white
bronze"). The face of the mirror bears the
incised figure of a seated bodhisattva, the
Eleven-Headed (Jp: Jūichimen) Kannon. On
the reverse side are cast relief designs of bushclover, birds, and butterflies and an incised
dedicatory inscription which includes the

date: "25th Day of the Intercalary Fifth month
(1159) ... Priest Kokaku". The flowing fine-
line image of Kannon was presumably made at
the time of dedication on a mirror intended for
cosmetic use.

Mirrors from early times were placed inside
shrines as the embodiment or medium
through which a Shinto god (*kami*) was given
visual form. By the 11th-12th centuries
mirrors came to be actually incised with the
figures of Shinto deities, or more often, their
corresponding Buddhist deity forms (see Cat.
No.17). These mirrors are known as *mishōtai*.
Extant examples usually served as the object
or repository of the god's spirit in smaller
family and branch shrines. The Shinto god or
shrine of this mirror remains uncertain.

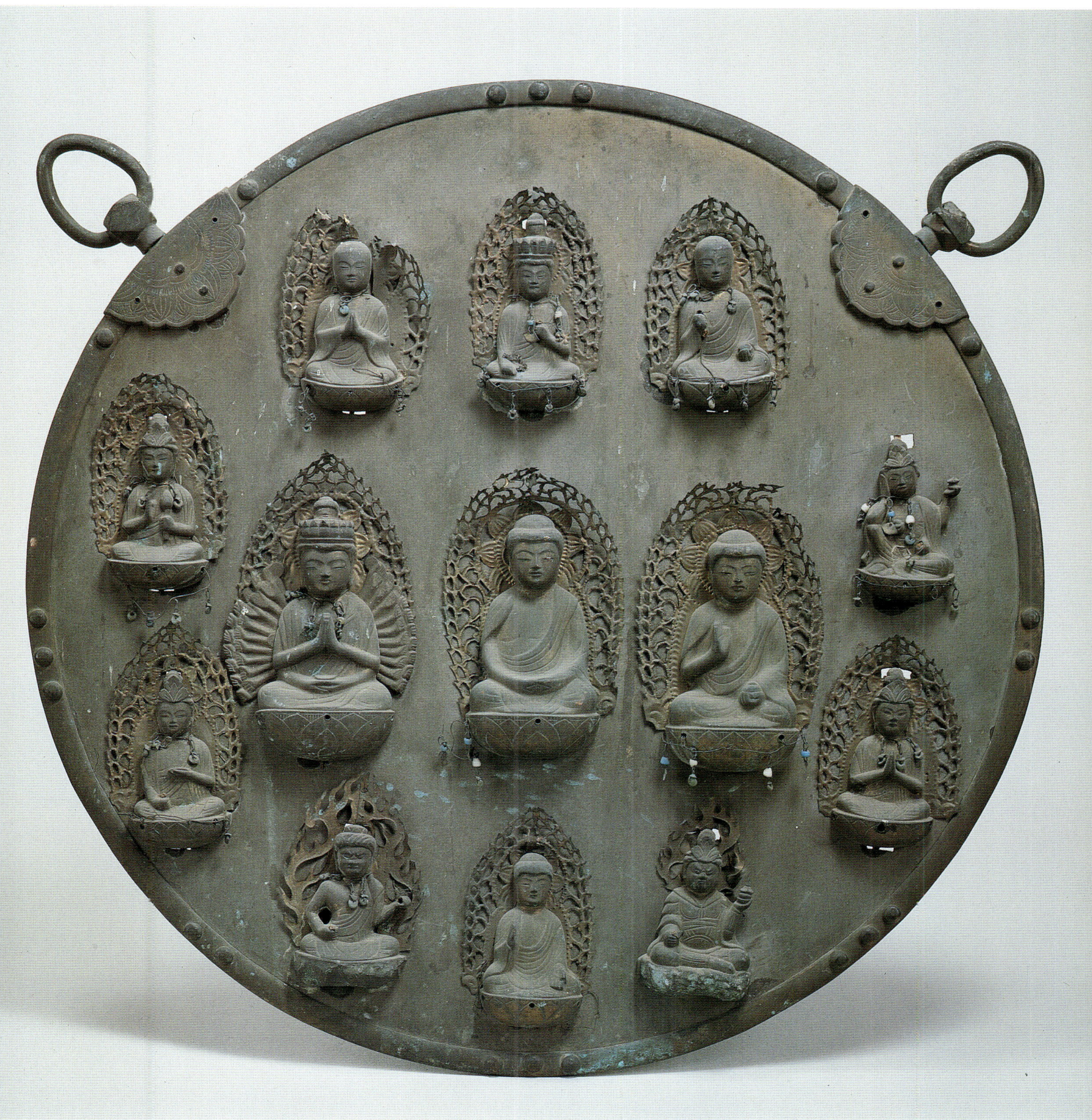

17

19

Kasuga Deer Mandala
春日鹿曼荼羅図

Kamakura period, 13th century
Ink and colors on silk; 76.5cm × 40.5cm
Agency for Cultural Affairs

The deer is the messenger or vehicle of the Shinto gods of the Kasuga Shrine. It was established at Nara in 709 as the tutelary shrine of the Fujiwara clan, the dominant aristocratic family, holding the real power behind the throne until the end of the Heian period (12th century). Although the fortunes of the Heian aristocracy were eclipsed in later periods the Kasuga Shrine managed to attrach a broad base of popular support.

Here, as in most of these schematized paintings (hence the title "mandala") of the deer, a branch of the sacred *sakaki* tree stands upright on the saddle. It supports, enclosed in a circle of light suggestive of the sun or sacred mirror, the five main Kasuga deities in their Buddhist forms (*honji*). From left to right: Eleven-Headed (Jūichimen) Kannon, who represents Hime-gami, the consort of Ame no Koyane no Mikoto represented next by Jizō Bosatsu, then the buddhas Yakushi and Shaka who stand for Futsunushi no Mikoto and Takehikazuchi no Mikoto, and finally, Monju Bosatsu who represents various agricultural deities subsumed under Wakanomiya. The deer floats over the Kasuga plain shroud in mist except for the first *torii* gate with pilgrimage path and a few of Nara's ubiquitous deer in the foreground. Above Mt. Mikasa and the distant silhouette of Mt. Kasuga rises the morning sun.

Gold leaf was affixed to the back of the silk to produce the subdued gleam of the golden circle. The coloration and the meticulous detailing, for example on the deer's hide or trees in the landscape, are representative of the *yamato-e* stylistic tradition.

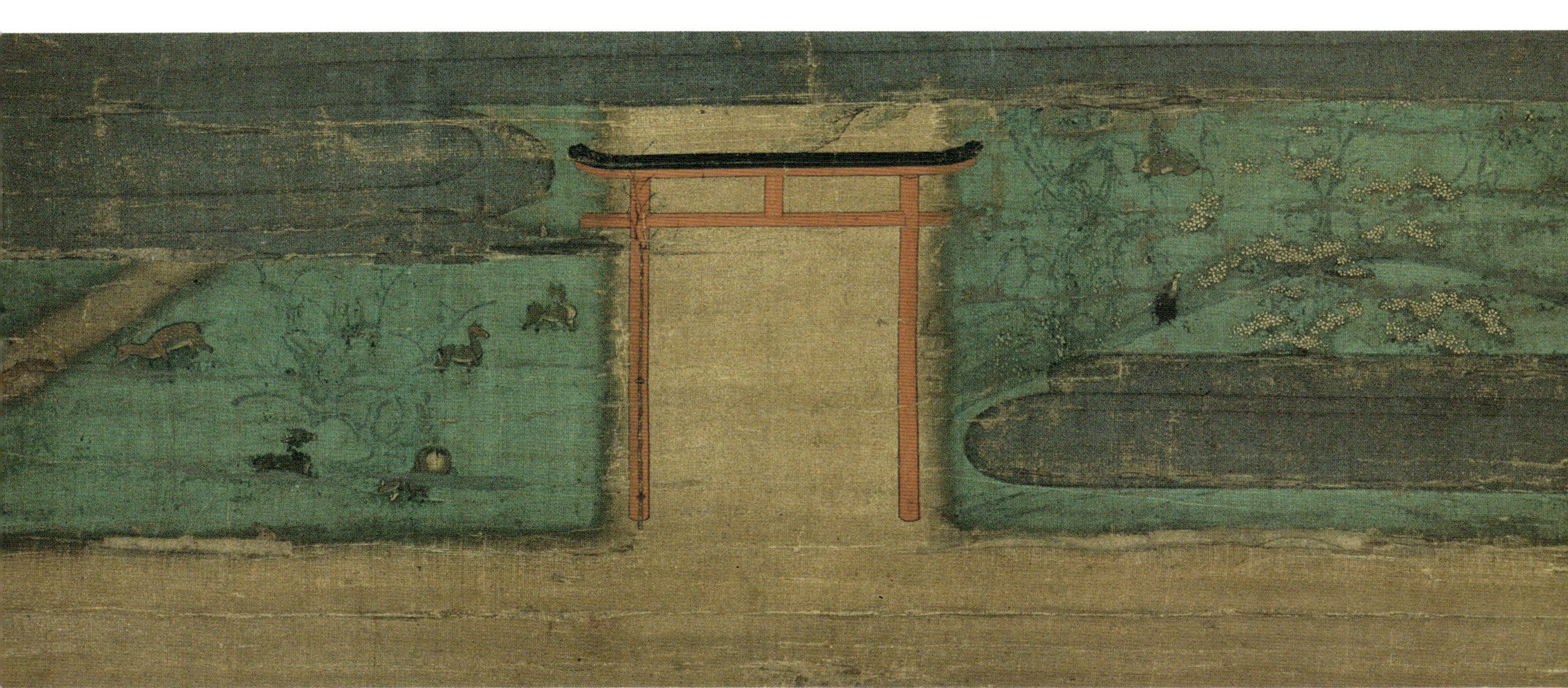

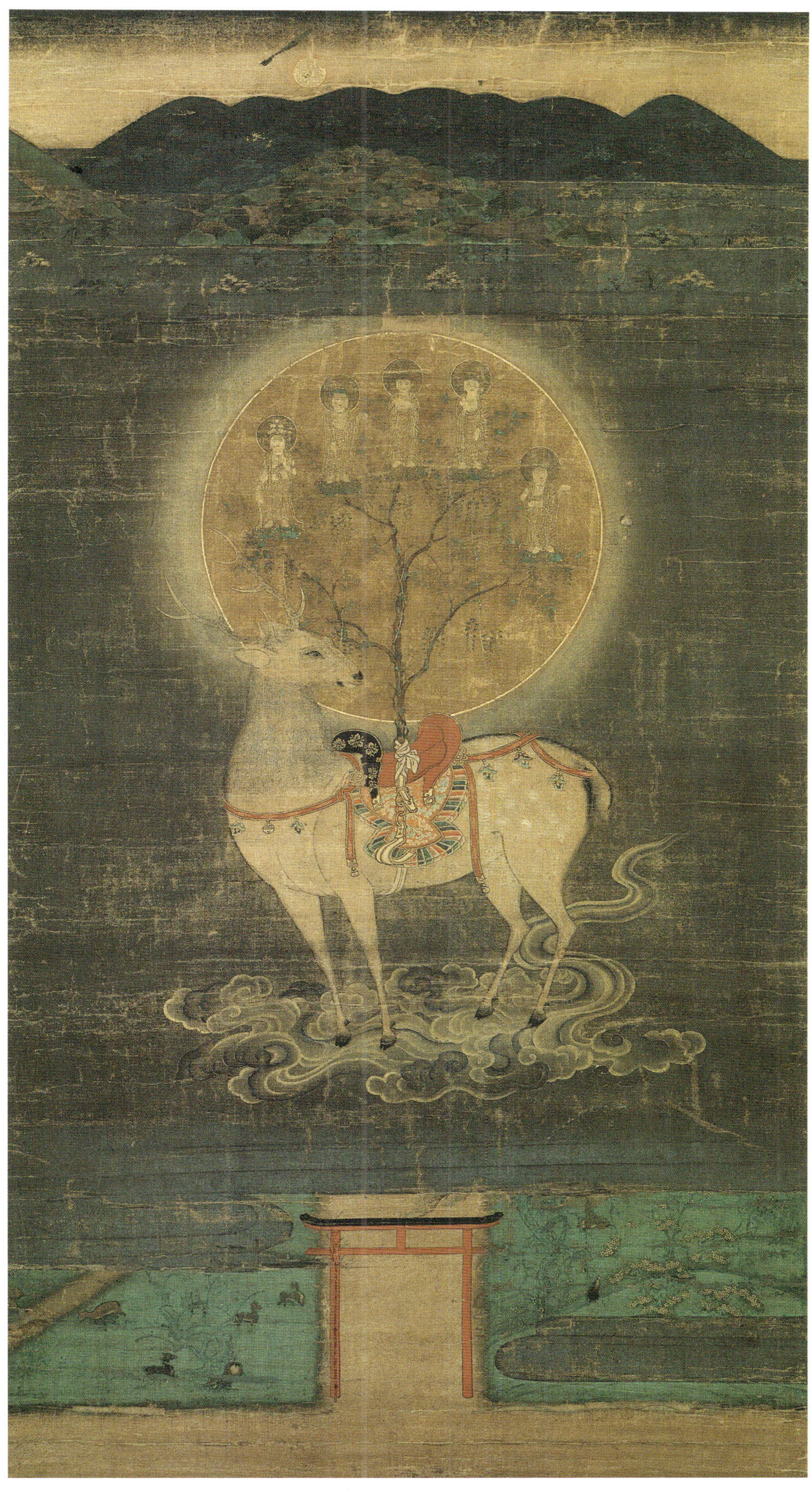

20 ◉
Shrine Mandala of the Otokoyama Hachiman-gū
男山八幡宮曼荼羅図

Kamakura period, 14th century
Ink and colors on silk; 140.0cm × 64.0cm
Agency for Cultural Affairs

A schematized rendering (hence the appellation "mandala") of the Buddhist forms of the Shinto deities at the Otokoyama Hachiman Shrine, popularly known as Iwashimizu Hachiman. The Iwashimizu shrine was founded in 859 a short distance southeast of Kyoto by a Buddhist priest to whom it had been revealed that the gods wished a sanctuary near the Heian capital to offer it protection. Buddhist connections, especially with the Shingon sect, remained particularly strong at this shrine until modern times.

Below a poetic inscription and a representation of three doves (the messengers or symbols of the shrine), the top register depicts, from a straight frontal viewpoint, an Amida Triad. These three correspond to the main gods: Hachiman, flanked by the female Ōtarashi-hime and Hime-gami. Hachiman and his two associated female deities were originally worshipped by clans in Kyushu and identified with the mining and metallurgy of mercury. In the Heian period Hachiman assumed the role of protector in battle and war.

Flanking the path, shown obliquely from above with no concessions to receding one-point perspective, are representations of four lesser deities, the Wakanomiya, and possibly including Takeshiuchi no Sukune, an ancestral god of the founder

According to an inscription affixed in 1479 to the back of the painting at the time of repairs, the figures on the path are the noble-man Kuga Nagamichi, members of his family, and retainers. The Kugas, it states, had donated the painting to the shrine where it was used at ceremonies held by an association of shrine workers.

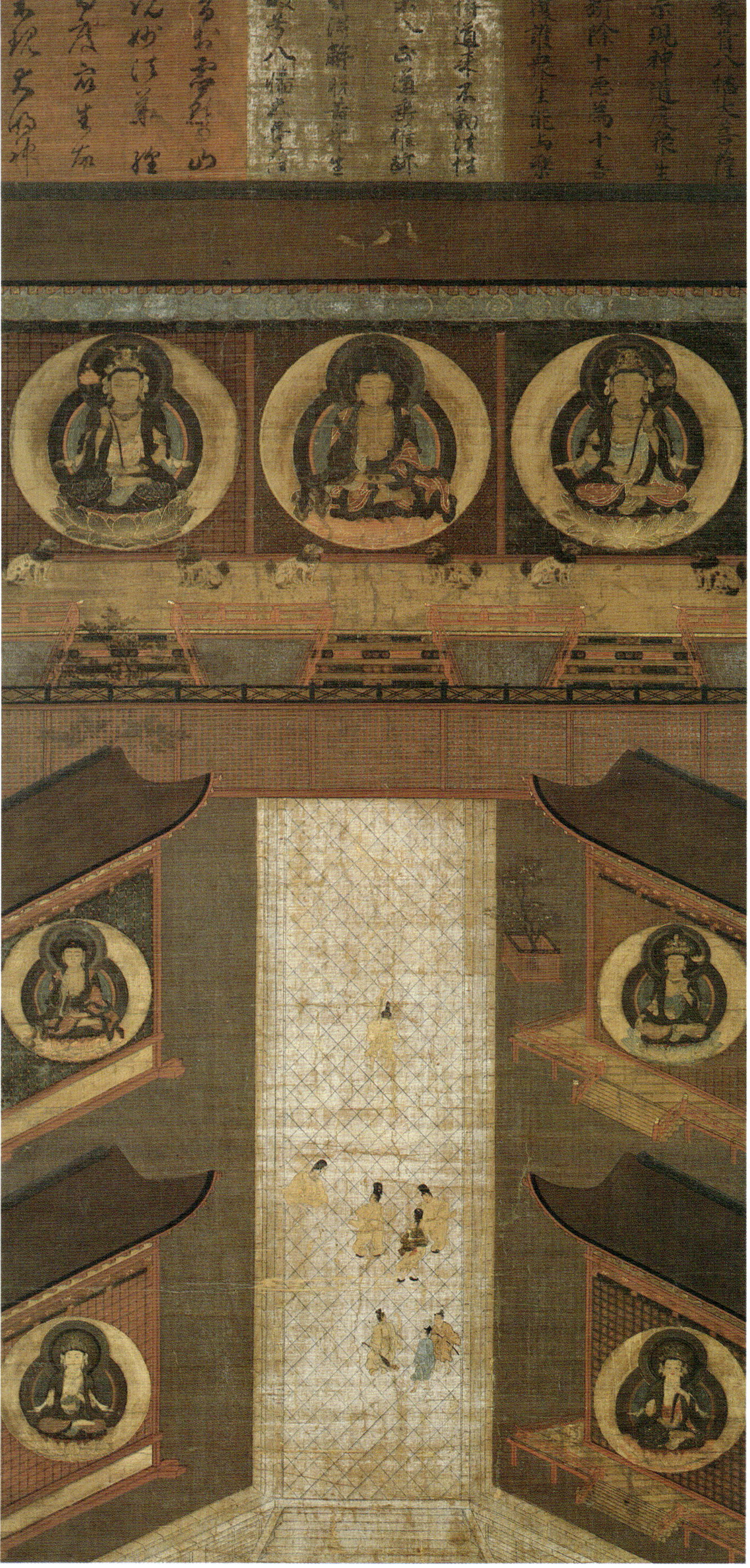

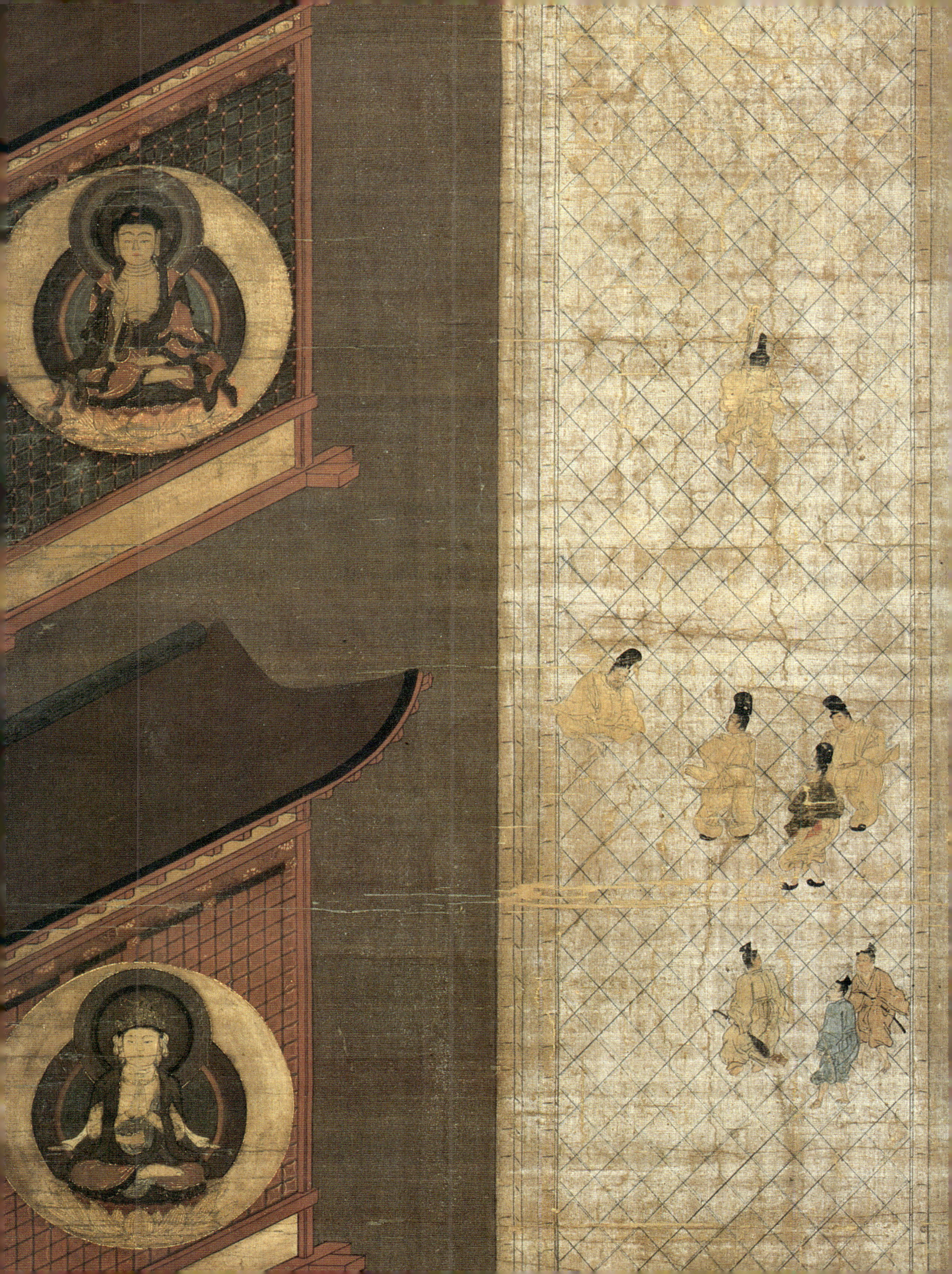

21 ◎

The God of Kasuga Shrine
春日明神影向図

Kamakura period, 1312
Ink and colors on silk; inscription: ink on paper
59.8cm × 32.7cm
Fujita Art Museum, Osaka

This is another painting (see Cat. No.19) associated with the deities (*myōjin*) of the Kasuga Shrine, Nara. According to the brief inscription (on paper attached to the lower edge of the painting) written in the Ninth month of 1312 by the courtier and imperial advisor Takatsukasa Fuyuhira (1275-1327), Kasuga Myōjin had appeared to him the previous year in a dream. Fuyuhira, it continues, commissioned Takashina Takakane (active early 14th c), head of the court painting atelier, to record the experience in this painting. The Myōjin is depicted here, presumably in Fuyuhira's garden, attired in court dress, having arrived in an aristocrat's ox-cart. The carriage is propped to a stop and the Myōjin is seemingly about to alight to give Fuyuhira a rolled scroll. The god's face is concealed in mist, a common convention in representations of *kami* and emperors. The five main Kasuga gods appear as seated Buddhist deities (*honjibutsu*) in roundels at the top.

A 1283 record mentions that a painting of Kasuga Myōjin was hung at a Japanese-style (*waka*) poetry gathering held at the Takatsukasa mansion. The rolled scroll depicted here may have a connection to the inspiration of poetry and the painting itself may have served at similar functions.

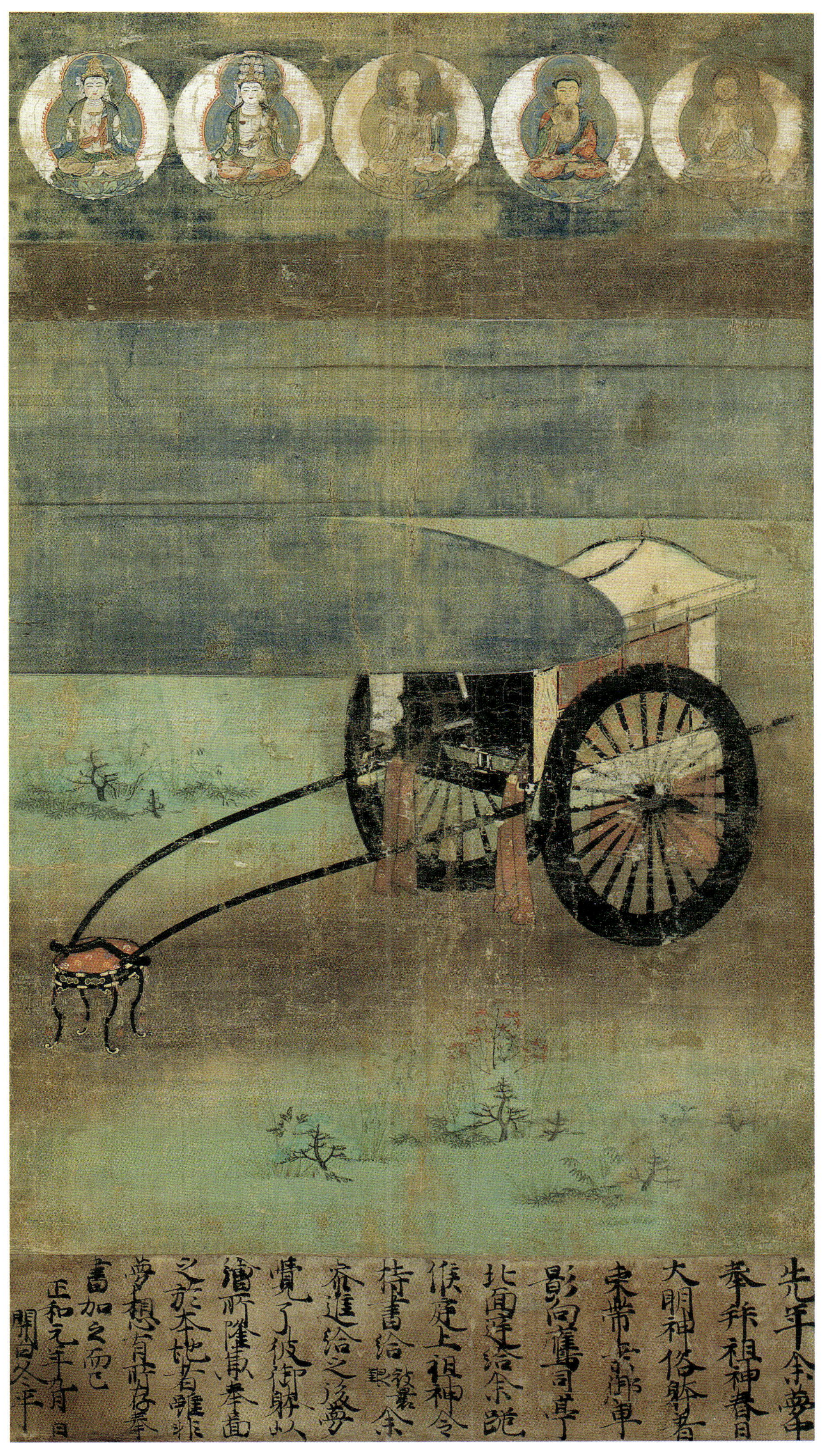

先年余夢中
奉拜祖神春日
大明神俗躰ヲ者
束帯兵衛車
影向鷹司其
北面庭上給余跪
候庭上祖神令
持書給彼裏余
疾進給之後夢
覚了彼御射山
繪所隆康奉畫
之於本地者雖非
夢想有所存奉
畫加之而巳
正和元年十月日
開白久平

22 ◎

Portrait of the Emperor Godaigo
後醍醐天皇像

Nambokuchō period, 14th century
Ink and colors on silk
93.9cm × 30.9cm
Shōjōkō-ji, Kanagawa

Godaigo (1288–1339) was an unusual emperor who endeavored to reassert the authority of the imperial house and restore direct rule. In his desire to eliminate the warrior government based in Kamakura he shared an agenda with warriors of central and western Japan, notably with Ashikaga Takauji, who in the end used the emperor as a pawn to further his own rise to power. Godaigo's hopes of a restoration came to an ignominious demise in 1336 when he was forced to flee to the mountain fastness of Yoshino (south of Kyoto). There he established the so-called "Southern Court" (Nanchō). This initiated the Nambokuchō period. Powerless imperial heirs alternating from the Southern and Northern (the branch that had remained in Kyoto) courts, were permitted to assume the throne by the ruling Ashikaga shoguns who themselves decreasingly were able to govern, until the country dissolved into more than a century of civil warfare.

The Ashikaga treated Godaigo very differently in death than in life, partially motivated by fears of his lingering malevolent spirit, and went to extraordinary efforts to look after his eternal welfare. Godaigo was made the posthumous founder of various Zen monasteries. The Ashikaga also commissioned portraits in which Godaigo is essentially apotheosized.

In the present portrait produced probably not long after Godaigo's death, he is installed on a priest's dias and framed, as if an icon, by curtains and *koma-inu* guardian dogs. He is depicted wearing the Chinese-style imperial headwear (*benkan*) and a Buddhist clerical cassock (*kesa*) over court ceremonial dress. He holds ritual implements of esoteric Buddhism (see Cat. No.11). The Buddhist accoutrements suggest the intention to show Godaigo having received the ritual of initiation *kechien kanjō* that formally identifies the individual with a Buddha. At the top of the painting are three cartouches with the bold characters proclaiming (l. to r.) Kasuga Daimyōjin, [The Sun Goddess] Amaterasu Ōkami, and Hachiman Bosatsu, major Shinto deities.

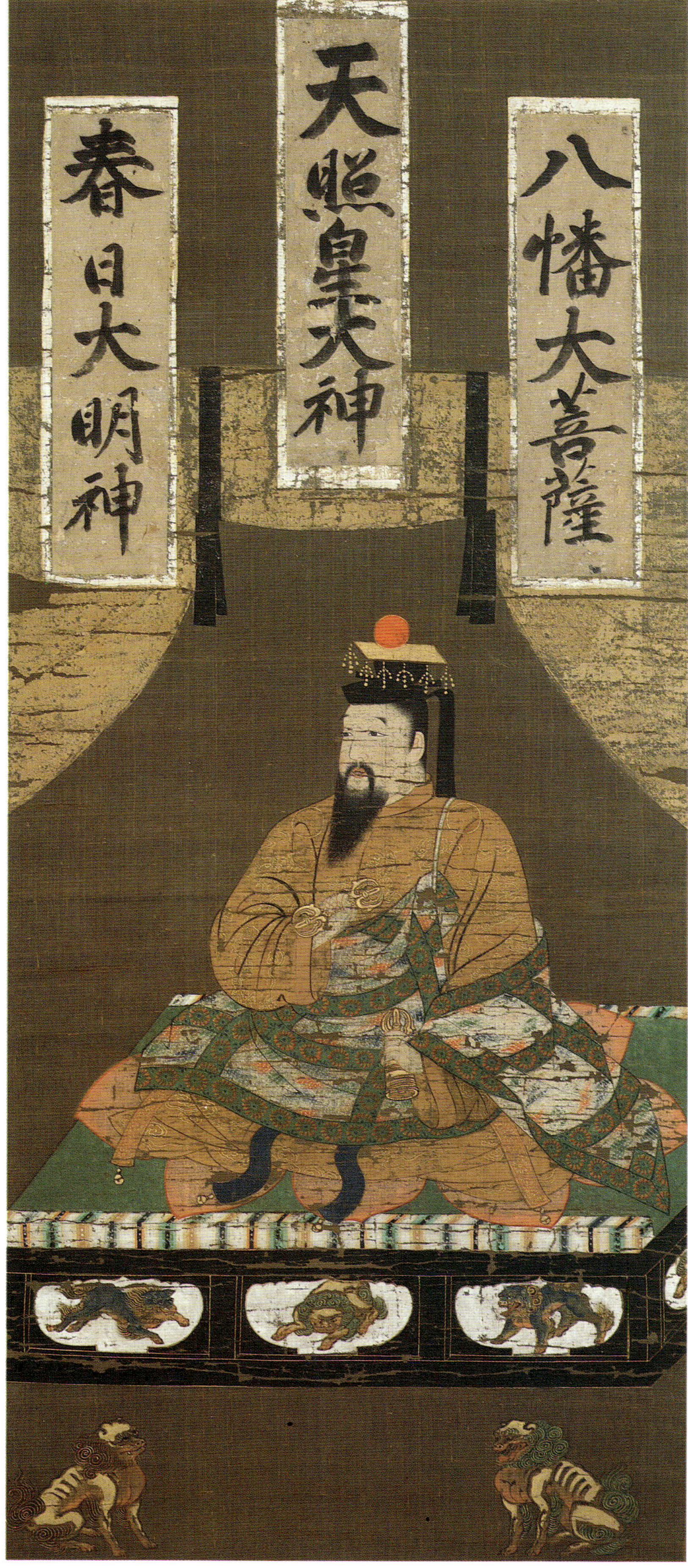

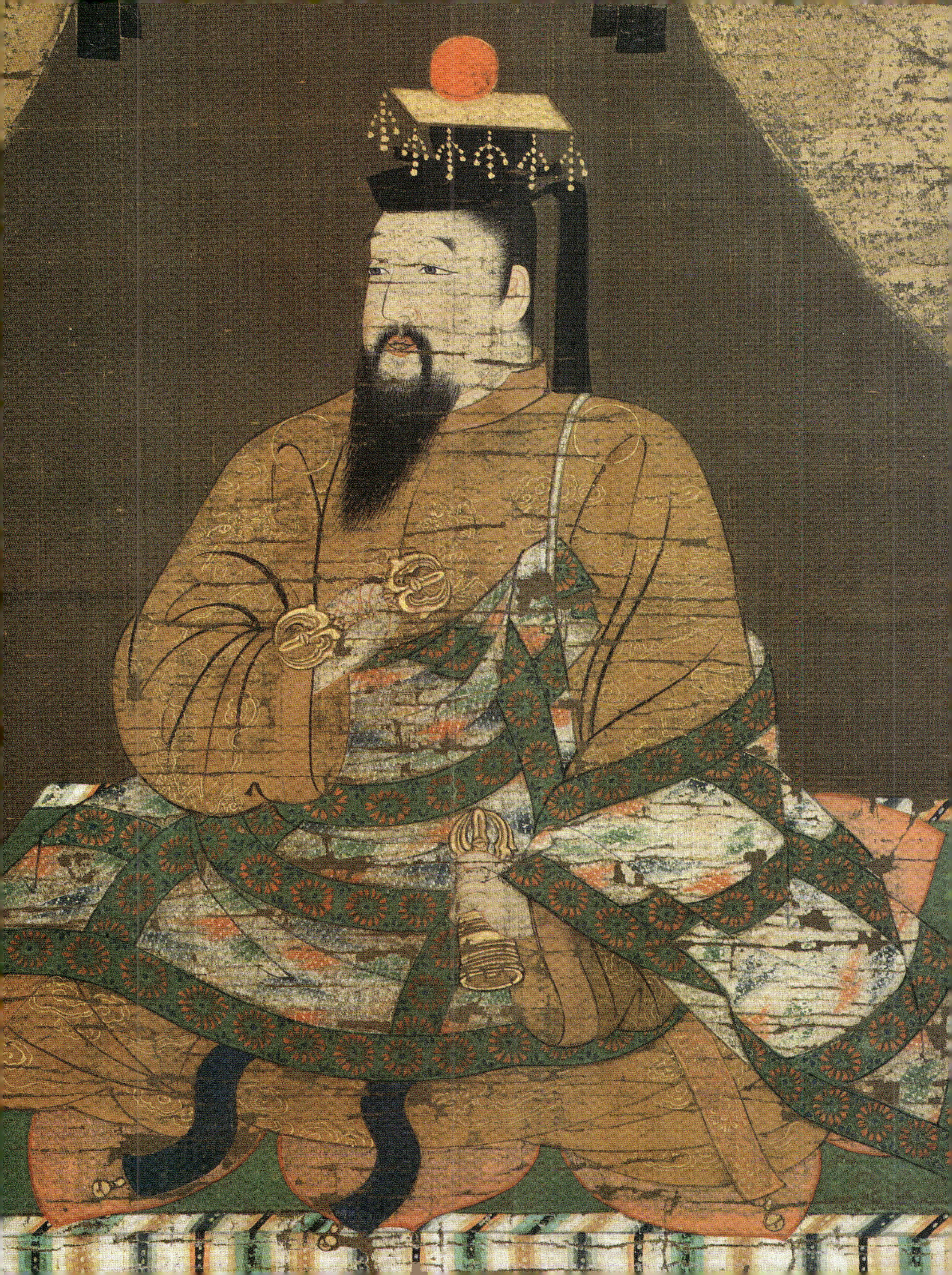

23

Portrait of Fujiwara no Tōyori
藤原遠賴像

Kamakura period, 13th century
Ink and light colors on paper
53.0cm × 33.7cm
Private collection

Little is known about the public life of the
subject of this portrait, identified as [Fujiwara]
Tōyori by an inscription written to the left of
the figure, other than that he was a function-
ary in the court bureaucracy of women officials
(*nyokan*) in the years 1211 and 1235. This
portrait concerns itself not with Tōyori's
apparently minor role at court but with a more
private matter: Tōyori is shown as a pious lay
Buddhist, pausing in the act of copying out a
Buddhist sutra. Tōyori is known to have been a
follower of Myōe (1173–1232), the charismatic
monk who practiced his own idiosyncratic
blend of esoteric and Kegon (Skt: Avatamsaka)
Buddhism at Kōzan-ji, a temple on the
northwest outskirts of Kyoto. The seal of
Kōzan-ji at the upper right of the portrait
confirms that it was once in the Kōzan-ji
archives.

To date the Tōyori portrait has received
little scholarly scrutiny, but it raises important
questions. First, how are we to interpret the
sketch-like technique and the color notations
marked on parts of the costume? Is this a pre-
liminary drawing—one that may have been
done from life and then forwarded to a professional artist as the basis for a more polished
painting; or is it a copy done after the painting,
perhaps as a reproduction for temple records?
Second, what artist might have executed this
sketch? Kōzan-ji under Myōe's leadership was
the site of an important painting atelier,
producing the famous "Myōe Portrait" and the
"Tales of Gishō and Gangyō" (*Kegon engi*)
scrolls, as well as innumerable copies of
imported Chinese iconographical drawings.
But in technique and composition the Tōyori
portrait bears little in common with the known
output of the Kōzan-ji studio. Instead it calls
to mind the secular portrait style developed
by the courtier Fujiwara Nobuzane (1176?–
1266?), the putative artist of the *Scroll of
Thirty-Six Immortal Poets* (see Cat. No.30).
Nobuzane is thought to have frequented
Kōzan-ji in the early thirteenth century.
Although the Tōyori portrait differs from those
in the "Thirty-Six Immortal Poets" in details of
execution, Nobuzane's relationship to the
Tōyori portrait merits further investigation.

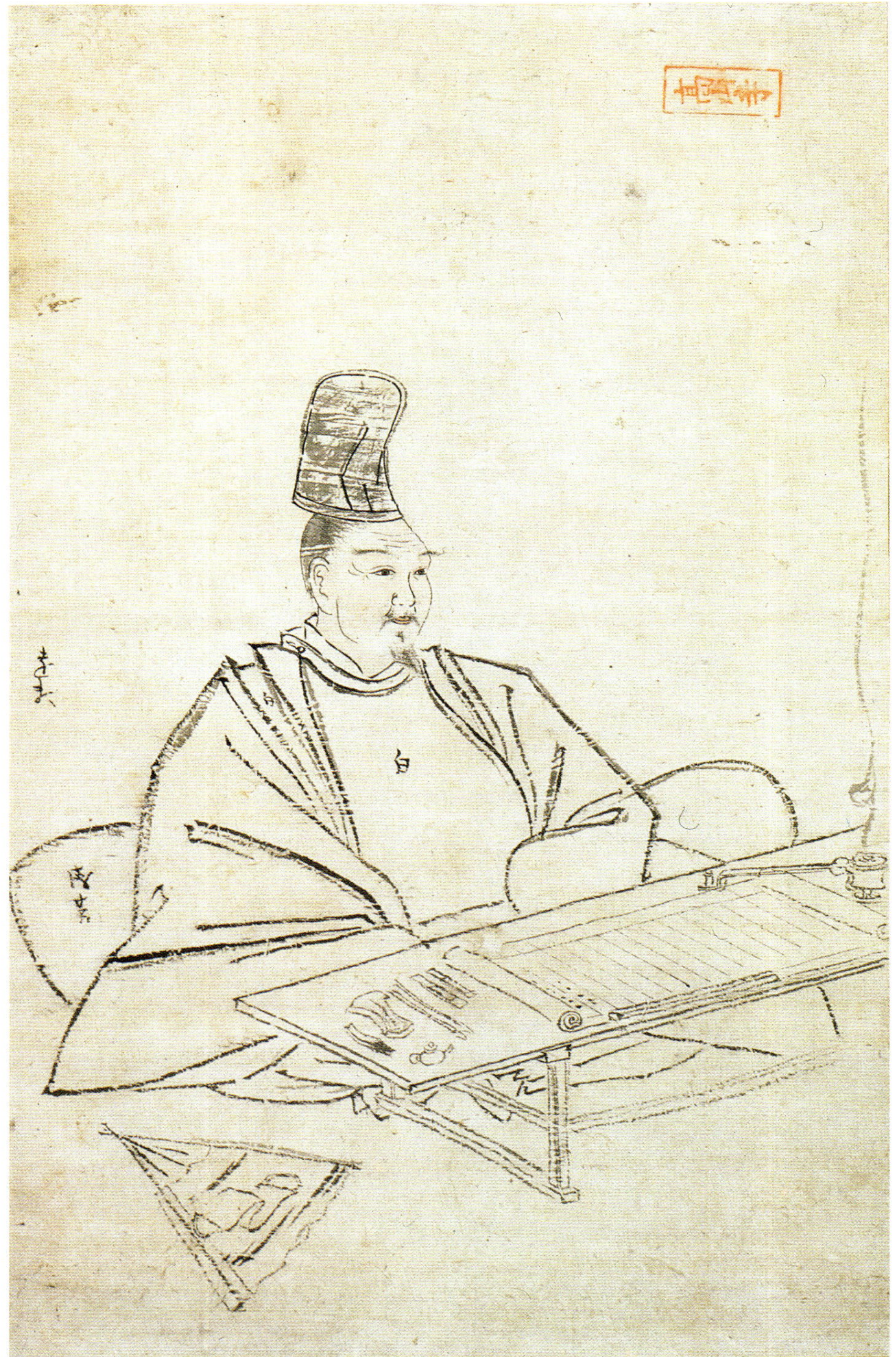

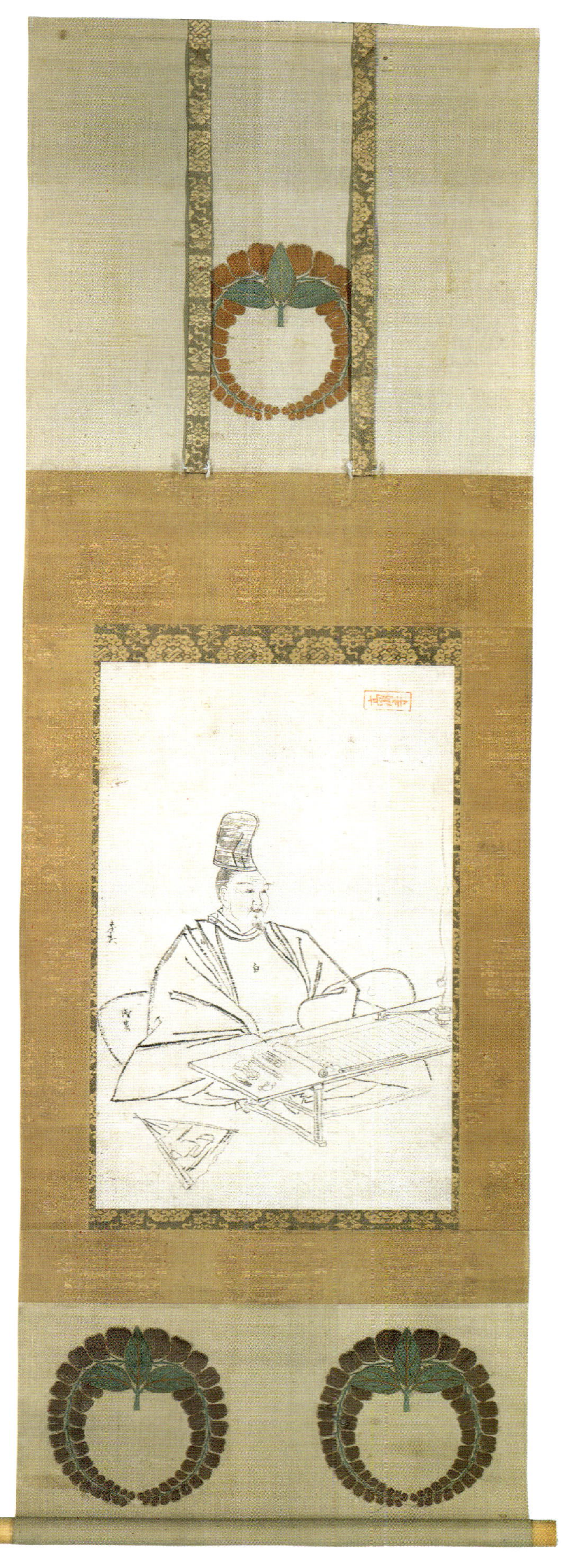

24

Imaginary Portrait of Ono no
Michikaze
小野道風像

Kamakura period, 13th century
Ink and colors on paper, with later inscriptions
71.5cm × 28.7cm
Imperial Household Agency

In this imaginary portrait of Ono no
Michikaze (894-966; better known as Ono no
Tōfū), the great calligrapher is depicted with
knee raised and brush poised about to write.
The animated profile and almost caricature-
like facial features are unusual for a formal
portrait. Beside him on the *tatami* mat is a
maki-e lacquer writing utensil box (see Cat.
No.51).

Michikaze was called on by emperors for
calligraphy in his own lifetime and by the
period of this painting had come to be known
as one of the "Three Great Masters" (Sanseki)
in the history of Japanese calligraphy. He was
revered as one of the founders of the Japanese-
manner, *wayō*, which relied on flowing, elegant *kana* script rather than Chinese characters. *Kana* had developed in the 9th and
10th centuries to write the vernacular Japanese, especially *waka* poetry and the letters
and diaries of aristocratic women who were
outside the government and Buddhist
hierarchy that still used Chinese as the written
language. By the early 11th century (witnessed
in the TALE OF GENJI) noblemen as well

as women were practiced in the combination of *kana* with some abbreviated Chinese
characters for private writing and poetry. A fine
hand was of course esteemed in the Heian
period. The remnants of the old Kyoto aristocracy moreover, after the rise of the warriors
in the 13th-14th centuries, and even later into
early modern times, managed to survive in
measure because many of them, respected for
their continued accomplishments in the traditional arts of calligraphy and poetry, could
teach parvenu samurai or merchants.

Although this portrait is un-iconic, even
humorously unflattering, it may very well have
been hung to inspire calligraphy practice, or at
ceremonies in Michikaze's honor, perhaps as
a founder, through influence on Fujiwara no
Yukinari (972-21027), of the conservative,
aristocratic Seison-ji calligraphy lineage, a
school which tenaciously survived until the
16th century.

Two sheets of paper have been added above
the painting at a later date. The square on the
right is inscribed with a *waka* poem taken from
the *New Anthology of Ancient and Modern
Japanese Verse* (*Shin kokinwaka-shū*). The
poem is not by Michikaze and is not in his hand.
However, a later admirer of the painting's
subject may have wished to give the ambiance
of elegant "Heian" calligraphy and so added it
here. The narrow *tanzaku* paper on the left
bears the title "Portrait of Ono no Michikaze"
and that it was done by "Raiju". No details of
an artist using this name are known.

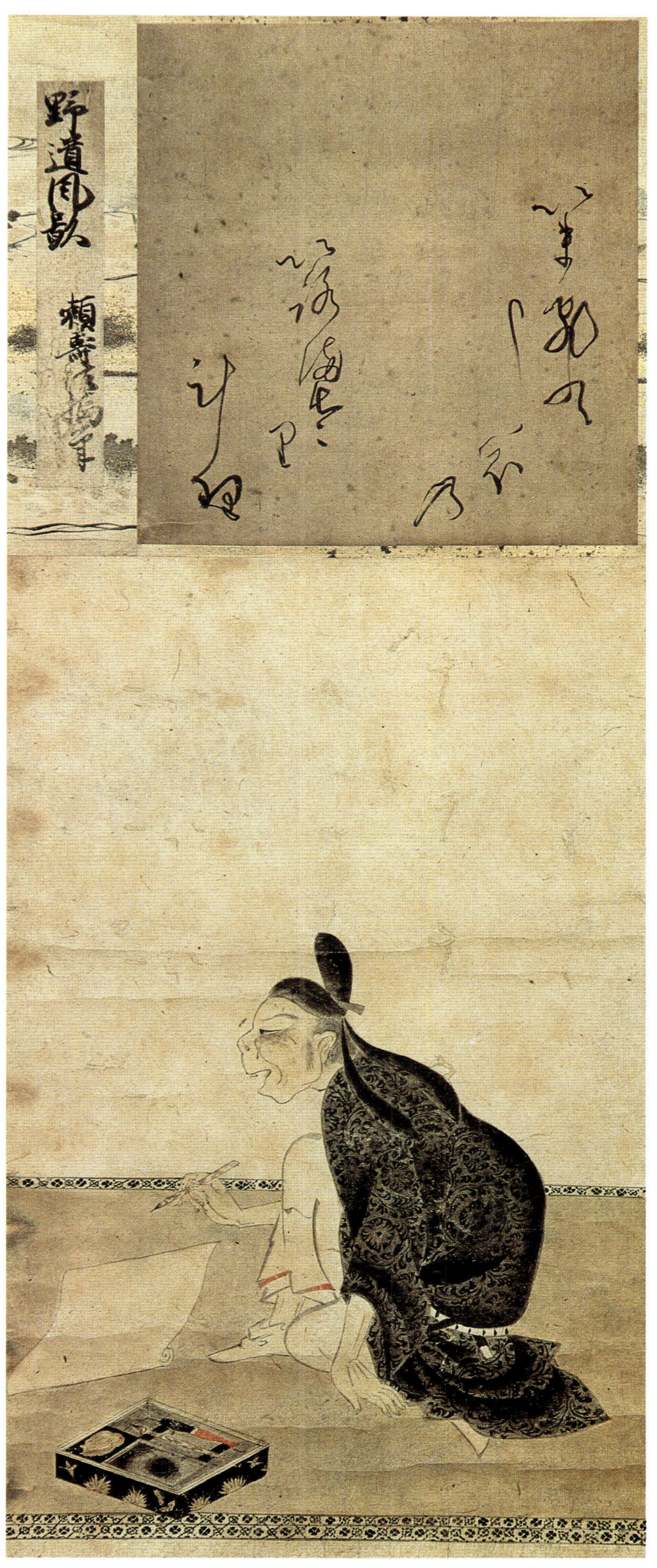

25

Section of the Poetry Anthology, *Man'yō-shū*
Known as the *Katsura-bon*
桂本万葉集

Heian period, 11th century
Ink on decorated paper
Handscroll (16 joined sheets)
29.2cm × 850cm
Imperial Collection

This scroll forms one of the oldest extant transcriptions (although incomplete) of the *Man'yō-shū*. The *Man'yō-shū* is the earliest collection of Japanese poems, compiled originally in the 8th century, which contains around 4,500 verses by many poets, both nobles and commoners, arranged in 20 books or volumes. A few other fragments from this same transcription (that presumably originally was in 20 scrolls) are extant, but this is by far the most extensive section and includes 109 poems, about one-third of the Fourth volume. The scroll acquired the appelation "Katsura-bon" when it passed into the collection of Prince Katsura-no-miya (or Hachijō) Toshihito in the 17th century.

The text consists of short headnotes (including the poet's name and circumstances when known) which start above the main body of text. Then follows a poem (or sometimes more than one) written first in the discrete Chinese characters of *man'yō-gana*, where the early Japanese (lacking a script) used Chinese ideographs irrespective of meaning to represent syllables in the native language. This usually one line or two is followed by a re-writing of the poem in connected, flowing Heian period script which predominately used the phonetic syllabary of *hiragana*. The overall effect is a visually interesting alternation of the darker lines of headnotes and *man'yō-gana* with paler, delicate script. In some cases there is no re-writing of the poem, which indicates that by the 11th century some of the verses in *man'yō-gana* probably could no longer be deciphered. Although opinions differ about the identity of the calligrapher, most now attribute the hand to Minamoto no Kaneyuki, who worked in the mid-11th century.

The sheets of (*hishi*) paper used here were dyed in eight different colors and then painted with gold and silver pigments in elegant motifs of birds, butterflies, flowing water and flowering plants. The scroll was gracefully remounted in the 15th century and given a cover of ink-painted quails and plants, and an opening frontispiece decorated in cloud and mist patterns, typical of the Muromachi period continuation of courtly taste, done with grains and flecks of gold and silver leaf.

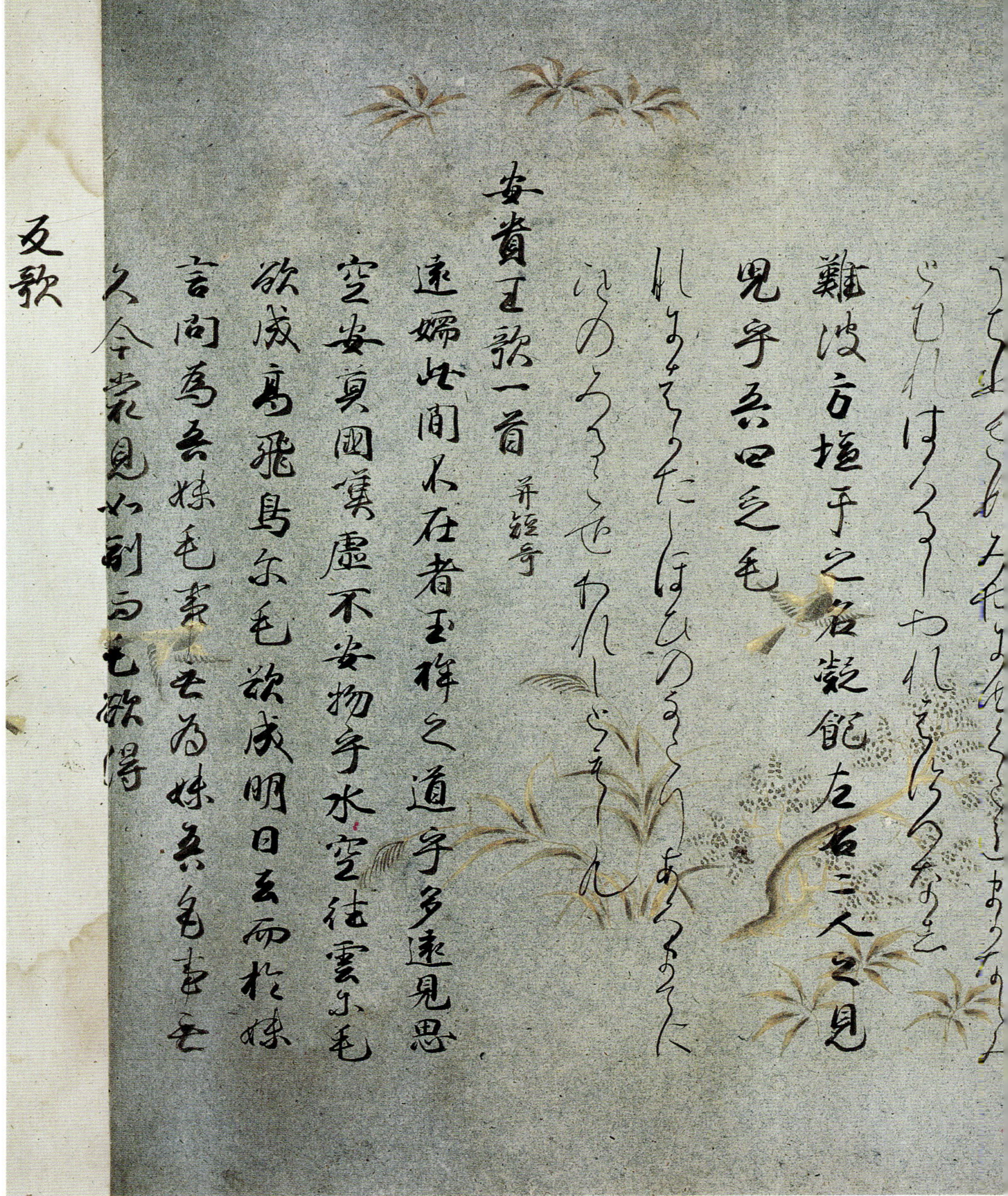

On the back is the written monogram (*kao*) of Emperor Fushimi (1265–1317), a scholar and noted calligrapher (see Cat. No.48), that serves as evidence the scroll was in his imperial collection at the end of the Kamakura period. The scroll is known to have been owned later by Matsuko (1547–1617), wife of Lord Maeda Toshiie, ruler of the Kaga domain, before passing into the hands of Prince Toshihito.

佐保河乃涯之官能　小歴木莫刈為在

作毛張之末者　立隱金

天皇賜海上女王御歌一首　宇樂言昌伝
　　　　　　　　　　　　　天皇也

赤駒之越馬柵乃織結師　妹情者記毛奈思

あかこまのこゆまきのしめゆひしいもがこゝろはのどもあるかも

右今案此歌擬古之作也　但此時當便

賜斯哥歟

海上王奉和歌一首　志貴皇子之女也

椋弓爪引夜音之遠音不毛吳之衛幸

乎聞之好毛

あつきみつめひくよるのこゑのとほごともきそのゆめさけさけほうたけれ

大伴宿祢麻呂宿祢哥二首　佐保大納言册之
　　　　　　　　　　　　第三子也

打日指宮乎行見乎真悲見面者苕聽

26 ⊙

Segment of the Poetry Anthology
Kokin waka-shū
Known as a *"Hon'ami-gire"*
古今和歌集第十二残巻（本阿弥切）

Heian period, early 12th century
Handscroll (8 joined sheets)
16.7cm × 317cm
Kyoto National Museum

This handscroll is a segment of an early 12th century transcription of the *Kokin waka-shū* ("Anthology of Ancient and Recent Times"). The collection assembled *ca* 905 was the earliest and most influential of the poetry anthologies compiled at imperial behest. Divided into 20 volumes or books, this segment is a large section of Volume 12, one of five volumes devoted to the major category of love poems. The scroll, narrow in width, largely retains the intimate original form of the 12th century. Only 13 poems (corresponding to 2 sheets of paper between the present 4th and 5th sheets) are missing along with the last two poems in the volume.

Although traditionally attributed to the hand of Ono no Michikaze (894–966), the calligraphy is now accepted to be by someone still uncertain, at the beginning of the 12th century. Each poem is written in two or rarely three lines, following a brief headnote with the name of the poet, sometimes starting at the top, sometimes dropping down to indent a line. The masterly ease reflected in this placement is continued in the free combinations of run-together with discrete characters, and the modulation of darker ink (where the brush was rapidly re-dipped) with paler tones. The sure, crisp brushwork plays against the bold rosebay (Jp: *kyochikutō*) flowers. The floral sprays were printed in mica on imported white paper, *karakami,* with a subtle textile-fabric pattern.

Besides this segment, Volumes 11 and 16 (mounted together) are preserved in the Imperial Collection, and various fragments are known. Many of the fragments, like this section, are referred to as *"Hon'ami-gire"*, because a large part of the transcription was treasured in the early 17th century collection of the artist and designer, Hon'ami Kōetsu. From the surviving fragments it appears that each of the volumes was written on dyed paper of a different color and decorated in a sumptuous variety of motifs.

Sometime after Kōetsu the present scroll passed to the Sakai family where it was handed down.

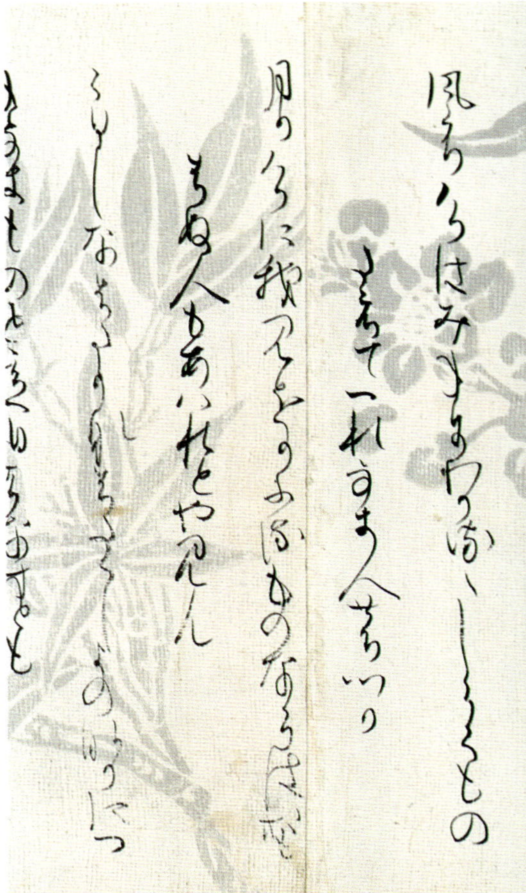

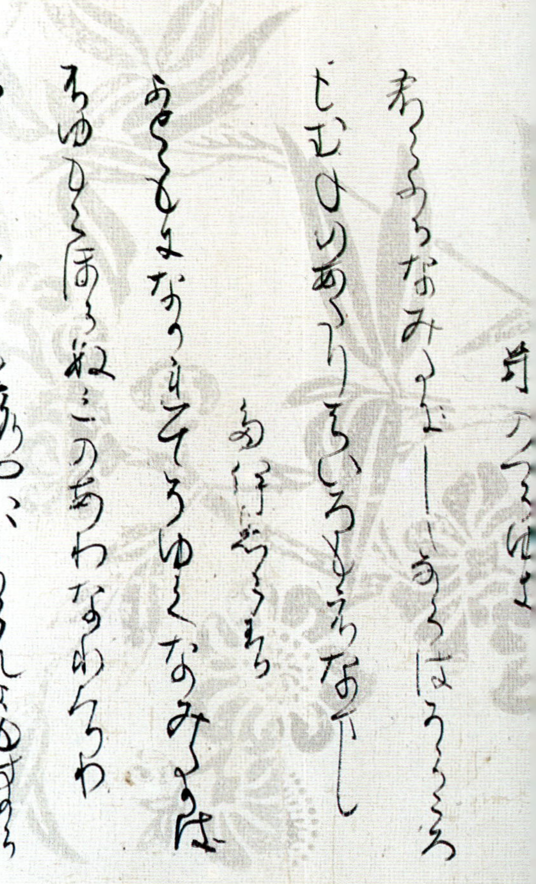

27

Segment of Extracts From the Poetry
Anthology, *Wakan rōei-shū*
Known as the "Large Characters Version"
Calligraphy by Fujiwara no Sadanobu
和漢朗詠集巻下断簡

Heian period, 12th century
Ink on decorated paper; handscroll (5 joined
sheets)
28.1cm × 94.4cm
Kyoto National Museum

The *Wakan rōei-shū*, or "Anthology of
Japanese and Chinese Poems for Recitation",
was originally compiled by Fujiwara no Kintō
(966–1041) at imperial order probably around
1013. Recitation, or intoning of poetry, often
to musical accompaniment, was an art cultivated at the Heian court. The anthology was
arranged under many topics with at least one
Japanese-style (*waka*) poem and one verse
composed in Chinese by Japanese as well as
Chinese poets. This is the longest extant section of a transcription of selected verses made
in the early 12th century known as the "Large
Characters Version" ("*Daiji-bon*") from the
prominent size of the ideographs, compared
for example to the writing in the contemporary
Kokin waka-shū, Cat. No.26.

This section consists of the first five
Chinese poems (or couplets from longer
poems) in Volume 2 under the topic "Poems of
the Imperial Dynasties" (so titled in the first
line at far right). Most lines consist of seven
Chinese characters brushed rapidly in the
semi-cursive (*gyō*) or cursive (*sō*) style. The
rapid tempo and energetic abbreviation of the
characters mark the style of the famous calligrapher in the Seison-ji lineage, Fujiwara no
Sadanobu (1088–1156?). The stylistic attribution to Sadanobu is attested by the insertion
at the end of the scroll of a sheet of *kōzo* paper
with the three line inscription: "Copying
begun at the Hour of the Sheep on the same
day/Finished at the Hour of the Monkey/
Sadanobu". This is considered to be a later, but
faithful, copy of an original postscript which
had been pasted to the spindle (*jiku*) of the
handscroll.

The paper of the main text is elegant
"Chinese-style" *karakami,* with three types
of printed designs: double tendrils, imaginary
hōsōge blossoms and tendrils, and roundels
of vis-à-vis lions and *hōsōge* tendrils.

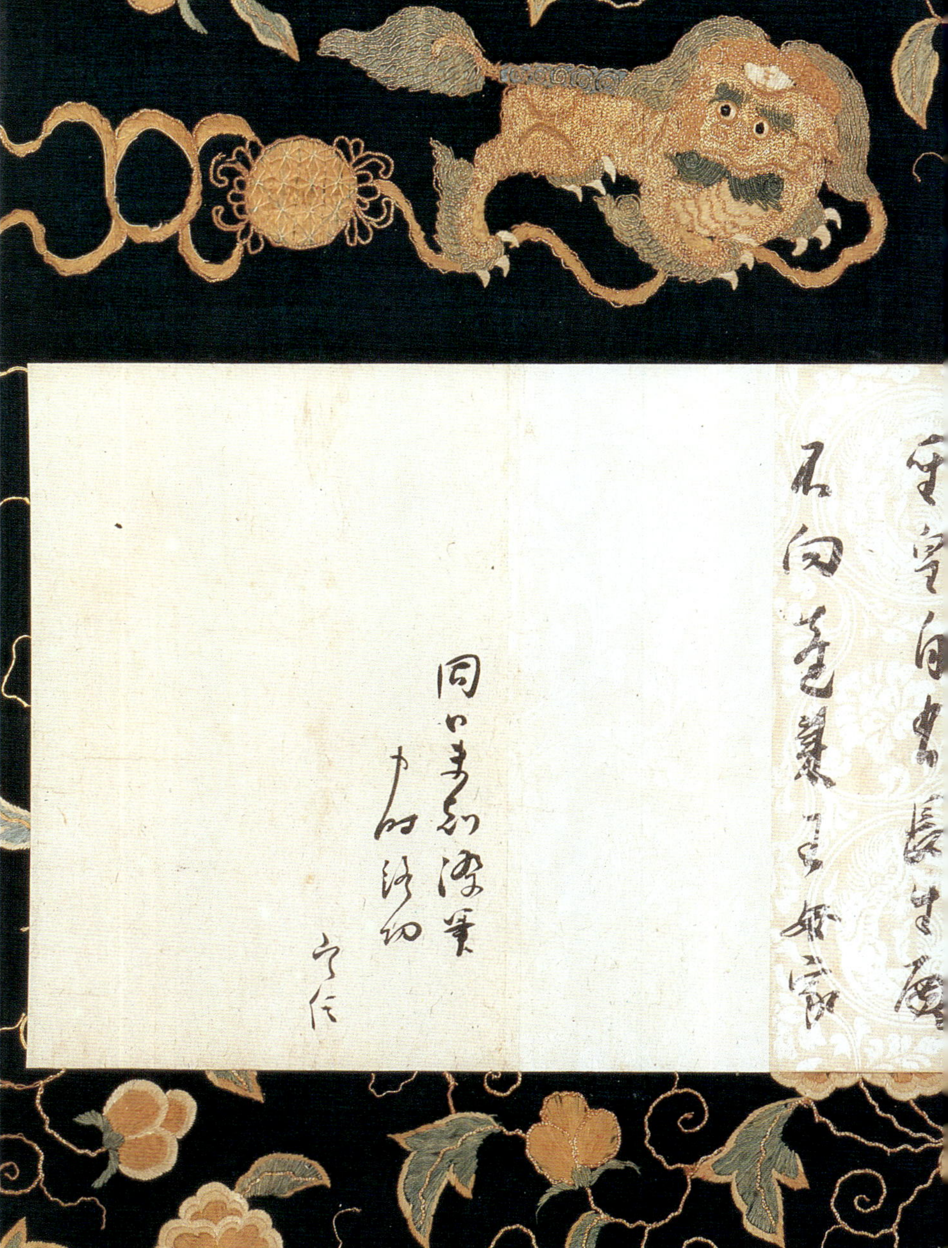

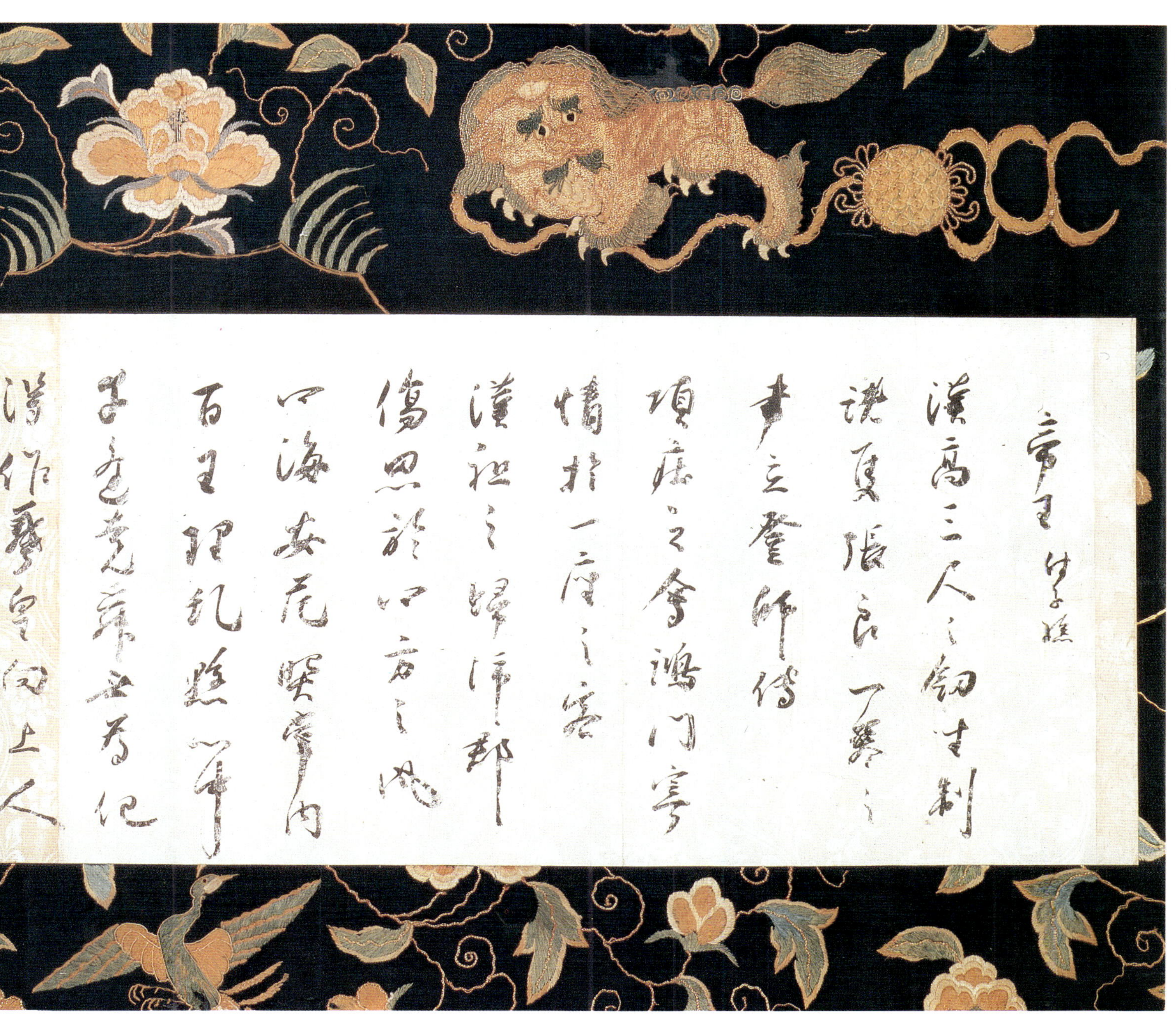

28

Fragment of the *Illustrated Tales of
the Three Jewels*
Known as a *Tōdai-ji gire*
三宝絵詞断簡（東大寺切）

Heian period, 12th century
Ink on mica printed paper
24.3cm × 15.2cm
Agency for Cultural Affairs

The Illustrated Tales of the Three Jewels
(*Sambō ekotoba*) is a collection of Buddhist
stories and accounts compiled by Minamoto
no Tamenori (?-1011) in the late 10th century.
Written largely in *kana,* it probably was
intended as a text on Buddhism ("the Three
Jewels" means Buddhism) for noblewomen,
giving as it does tales (Skt: jātaka) of the
Buddha's previous existences, biographies of
Japanese holymen, and descriptions of rites
and ceremonies.

This hanging scroll is a detached fragment
from the oldest extant transcription, once a
three-volume set of booklets. Now dispersed in
several collections, the fragments and sections
are known as *Tōdai-ji gire*, because the
booklet set was once owned by the Nara
temple. According to a colophon in the largely
intact segment of the second volume and part
of the third owned by the Sekido family,
registered as an Important Cultural Property,
this version was written out in 1120. The
"Illustrated" (*ekotoba*) in the title suggests
that the work from the beginning was meant
to have pictures, but none are known. The
Tōdai-ji gire contain many notations for
"painting" where illustrations would have
been inserted. This fragment consists of one
page (in other words a half sheet as each sheet
was folded in half and the open ends bound
with thread into the spine), from the third
volume and its account of a ceremony called
the *Shiga denpō-e.*

The calligraphy is traditionally attributed
to Minamoto no Toshiyori (or Shunrai, *ca*
1055-1129). The fluid, graceful writing, noted
for its clarity and beauty, epitomizes the
mature style of Heian aristocrats in combining
Chinese characters with *kana.* The elegantly
understated paper, known as *karakami,* has
been ruled in faint ink lines after a roundel-
motif was woodblock printed in mica over a
white base-coating.

は花ふじ経をはじめむとてその人のた
小乗経の律論疏ち〳〵めむそれ
うべね一万六千由町をうれおもてなるくら
なけむといつわそれはいひうまてニ
きそてはなうちれんうたれむ　　智
とろよいそくの〴〵まもての
度論
なうま持せは第一なわなぞをもてのゆ

29

Fragment from the *Collection of Tsurayuki*
Known as an *Ishiyama gire*
貫之集下断簡（石山切）

Heian period, 12th century
Ink on decorated paper
19.9cm × 15.8cm
Agency for Cultural Affairs

The Collection of Tsurayuki (*Tsurayuki-shū*) is an anthology of *waka* poems by Ki no Tsurayuki (?872-945) a foremost poet of his generation. Now mounted as a hanging scroll, this fragment was originally one page (a half sheet) of the second of two booklet volumes, which contained Chapters 6 to 10. This *Tsurayuki-shū* was in turn part of a large set brushed by various noted calligraphers of the *Collected Poems of Thirty-Six Poets* (*Sanjūrokunin kashū*) handed down at what is now the Kyoto temple of Nishi-Hongan-ji. In 1929 the *Tsurayuki-shū* second volume, together with the *Collection of Lady Ise* (*Ise-shū*), were divided up and sold, and are now preserved in many collections. The appellation "Fragments of the Ishiyama Version" or "*Ishiyama gire*" comes from the fact that in 1549 the emperor Gonara gave the *Collected Poems of Thirty-Six Poets Set* to the priest Shōnyo, tenth abbot of the great Jōdo sect temple, Hongan-ji, which at the time was located at Ishiyama (present-day Osaka). The temple later was burnt, and relocated to Kyoto as the two much diminished temples, Nishi-Hongan-ji and Higashi-Hongan-ji.

The decorated paper of the page was first dyed yellow then decorated with scattered flecks of gold and silver foil and stamped or painted in silver with birds, butterflies and floral sprays. Two poems, following the heading "Theme unknown" are written in three lines each (with a partial verse inserted in two lines at center). The last line at left is part of a headnote for the following poem. Flowing, rapid brushwork runs the characters together in boldly modulated shades of *sumi* ink. The energetic calligraphic style suggests the calligrapher of this scroll is Fujiwara no Sadanobu (1088-1158) known for the "Large Character Version" fragments of the *Anthology of Japanese and Chinese Poems for Recitation, Wakan rōei-shū* (see Cat. No.27).

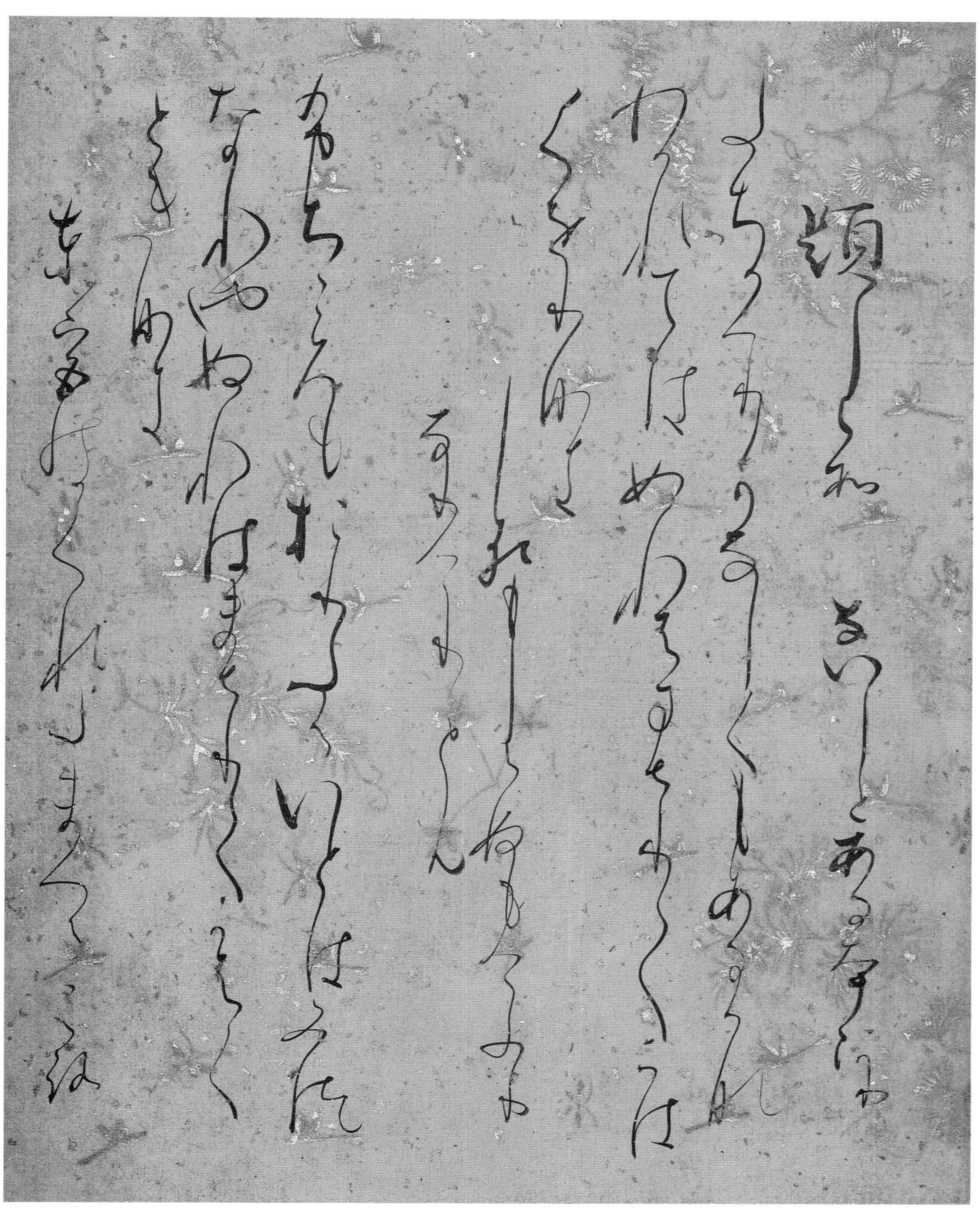

30

Imaginary Portrait of Fujiwara no
Takamitsu
One of a Series of "Thirty-six Immortal
Poets", known as the Satake Version
三十六歌仙切（高光）

Kamakura period, 13th century
Ink and colors on paper
35.8cm × 59.3cm
Itsuō Museum of Art, Osaka

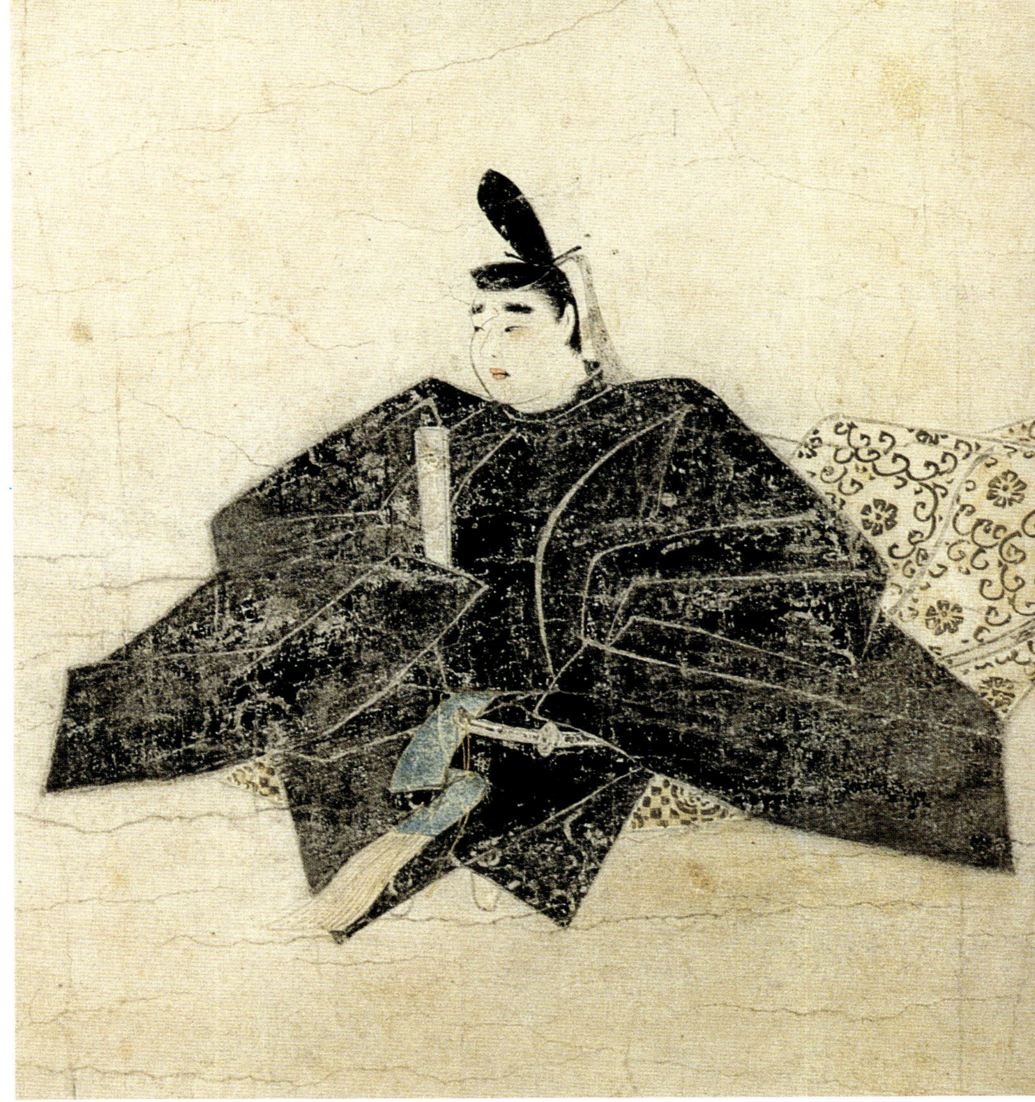

Perhaps at no other time or place was
poetry so integral a part of life as at the Japanese court of the Heian period. The ability to
compose verse was as essential for political
advancement as for writing love letters. No
honor was greater than to have one's poems
included in an imperial poetry anthology; and
at least one poet died from disappointment
when he was excluded. Members of the imperial house and high nobility regularly hosted
poetry competitions — a form of art that, over
the course of the Heian period, evolved from
sophisticated parlor games into an occasion for
serious literary criticism.

One of the most influential poets and cri-
tics of the Heian period was Fujiwara no Kintō
(966–1041), who rendered lasting judgement
on poets of the seventh through tenth centuries when he named thirty-six of them as
"Immortal Poets," or *kasen.* Kintō's selection
had an enormous impact on later generations,
and one result in the Kamakura period and
later was a vogue for *kasen-e,* or imaginary
portraits of the thirty-six immortal poets.

This portrait of Fujiwara no Takamitsu
(939–994) is from the earliest extant complete
series of imaginary portraits of Kintō's poets,
a handscroll formerly in the collection of the
Satake family, the hereditary daimyo of Akita.
The scroll is traditionally attributed to the
courtier-painter Fujiwara Nobuzane (1176?–
1276?), and well represents the life-like *nise-e*
style of portraiture in which he and his school
specialized.

Takamitsu is portrayed as a strikingly
handsome young man in formal court robes,
with a resplendent train of silvery floral
patterns on a pure white ground, comple-
mented by silver-and-white checkered
pantaloons. He wears a sword and a wide blue
sash, the insignia of a military appointment.
The inscription at the right of the painting
supplements this visual information with vital
statistics on Takamitsu's career and genealogy:
He is first identified as "Lesser Captain in the
Right Imperial Bodyguards," a prestigious
corps responsible for the personal safety of the
sovereign. Takamitsu was the "eighth son of
Minister of the Right [Fujiwara] Morosuke,
and his mother was Princess Gashi, the second

daughter of Engi [Era Emperor, Daigo]." In
961 he "took the tonsure, assuming the
Buddhist name Nyokaku. [Thereafter] he was
popularly known as the Lesser Captain of
Tōnomine," the mountainous area where he
lived in retreat. The inscription concludes with
a poem, ostensibly written by Takamitsu the
night before he became a monk: "In this world
where life is so hard, how enviable the moon,
clear and untroubled!" (Translation taken from
McCullough and McCullough, *A Tale of
Flowering Fortunes,* 1980).

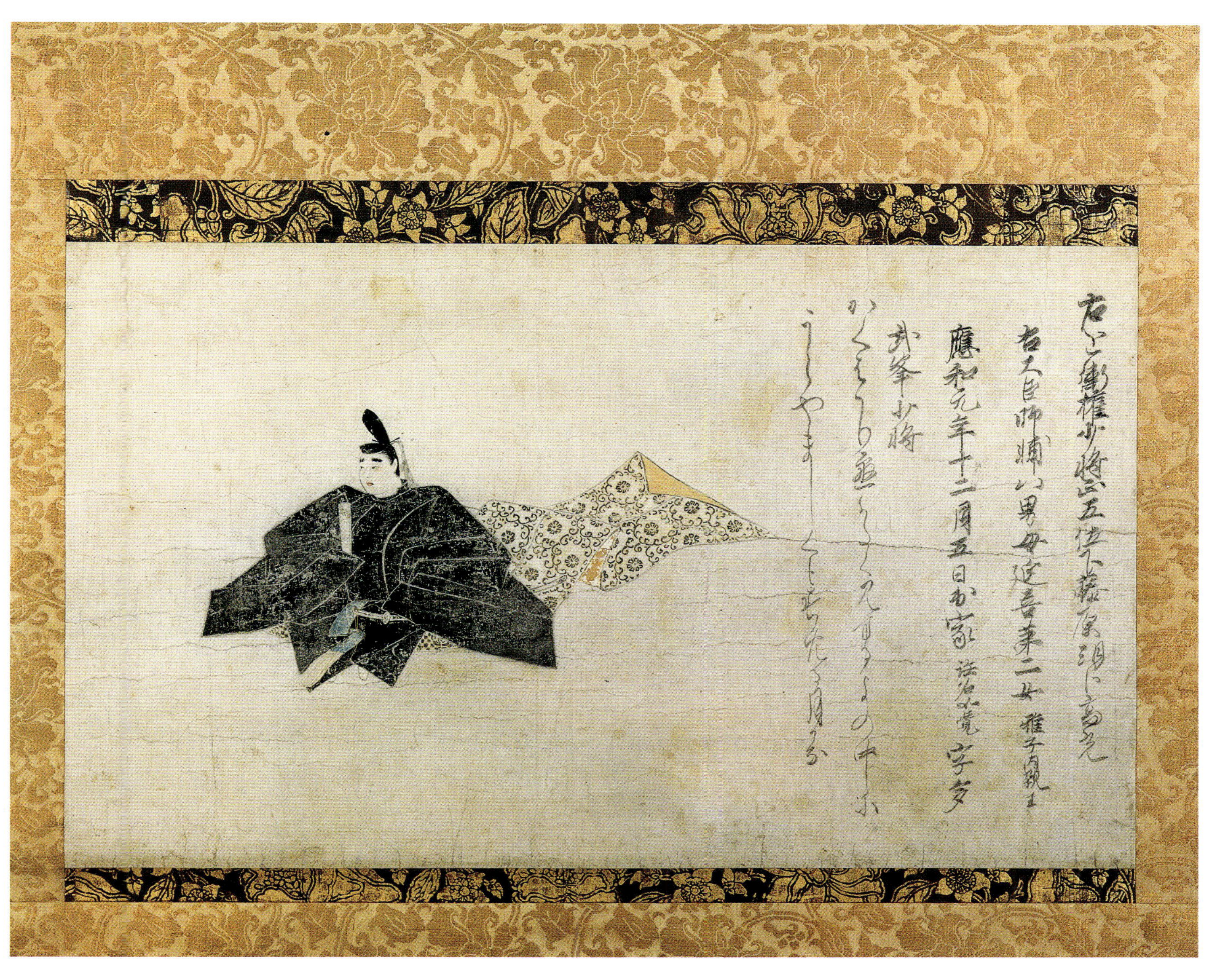

右近衛権少将正五位下藤原朝臣高光
右大臣師輔八男母延喜兼二女雅子内親王
武峯少将
應和元年十二月五日於家話石水覚字夕
かくばかりへがたくみゆる世の中に
うらやましくもすめる月かな

31

Bull and Groom
駿牛図断簡

Kamakura period, 13th century
Ink and light colors on paper
27.2cm × 42.7cm.
Fujita Art Museum, Osaka

Bullocks played an indispensable role in court life of the Heian and Kamakura periods, as the power for the nobles' favored form of transportation, the two-wheeled enclosed ox-cart. And like other appurtenances of the aristocratic life style, bullocks became the object of connoisseurship: by the mid-thirteenth century there was a highly developed discourse of oxen lore, as evidenced by the *Shungyū ekotoba,* the remaining text to a now-lost picture handscroll. The *Shungyū ekotoba* discusses such arcana as the origin and development of the ox-cart, the criteria of selection of superior bulls, and handling techniques used by famous grooms, concluding with panegyrics to famous bulls (*shungyū*) of past and present. A similar manuscript dated to 1305, entitled *Ten Pictures of Japanese Bulls,* (*Kokugyū jūzu*), describes its subjects in loving detail.

This painting of a bullock and its groom, now mounted as a hanging scroll, was once part of a handscroll of which seven other sections are known to survive, including two in American collections (the Seattle Art Museum and the Cleveland Museum of Art). Judging from an intact copy in the Tokyo National Museum, the original scroll (which lacked any text) depicted ten bulls arranged in facing pairs, a compositional device commonly used to suggest a competition. Although the relationship of the painting scroll to the two texts mentioned above remains uncertain, clearly it is a product of the same milieu. The attribution to the late Kamakura period is confirmed by stylistic analysis, notably by comparison to the quiet but assured draftsmanship of the Kōan era *Legends of Kitano Tenjin Shrine* (*Kitano Tenjin engi*) scrolls. The artist has portrayed a series of sleek, powerfully-built beasts, and imbued them with distinct personalities through nuances of pose. With its outstretched snout, upturned horns, and jauntily arched tail, this animal is perhaps the most engaging of the group. The unique inclusion of a human figure here suggests that the pair may represent the bull Ka'in and his handsome trainer Yaōmaru, prominent during the 1240s.

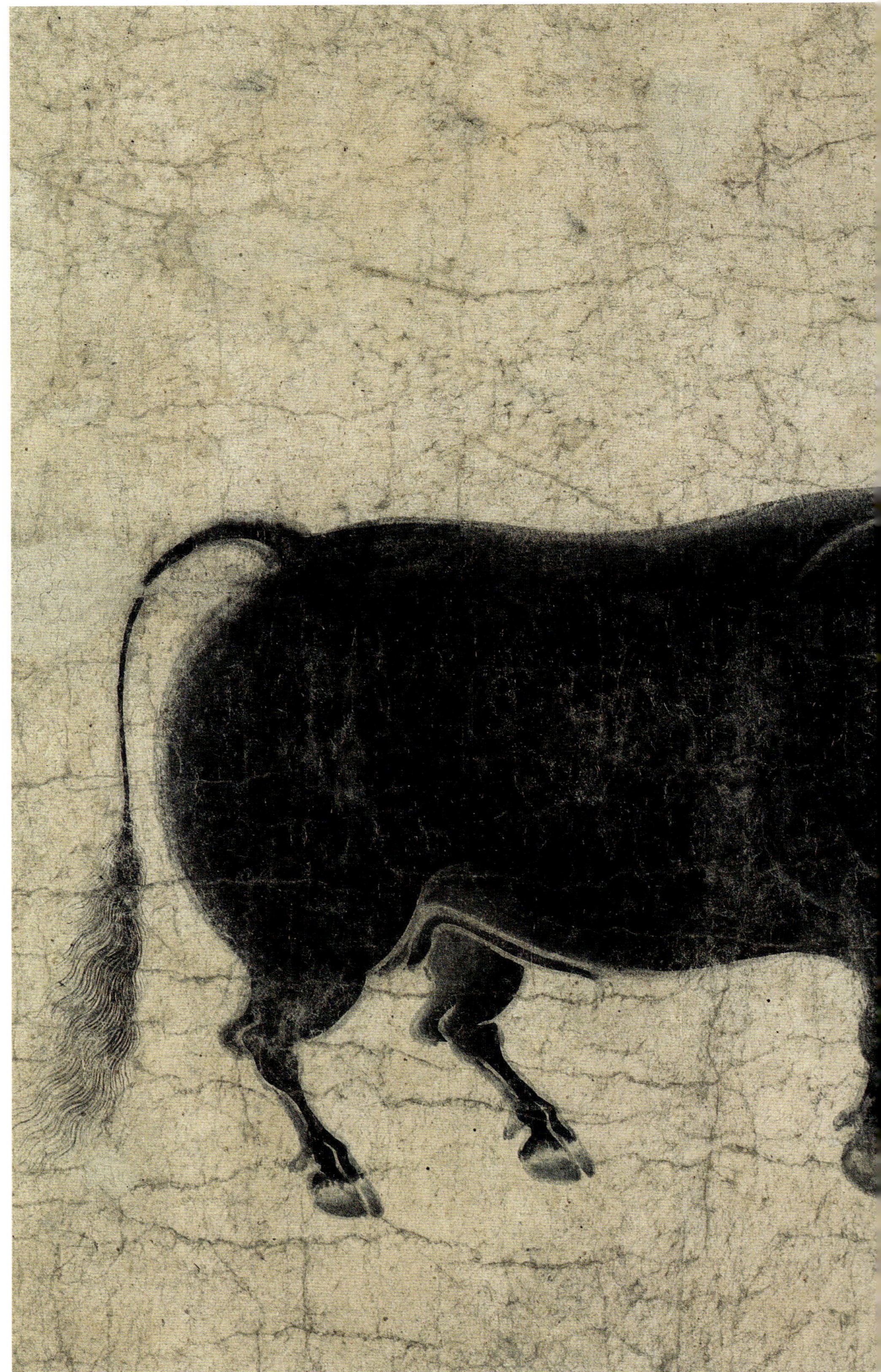

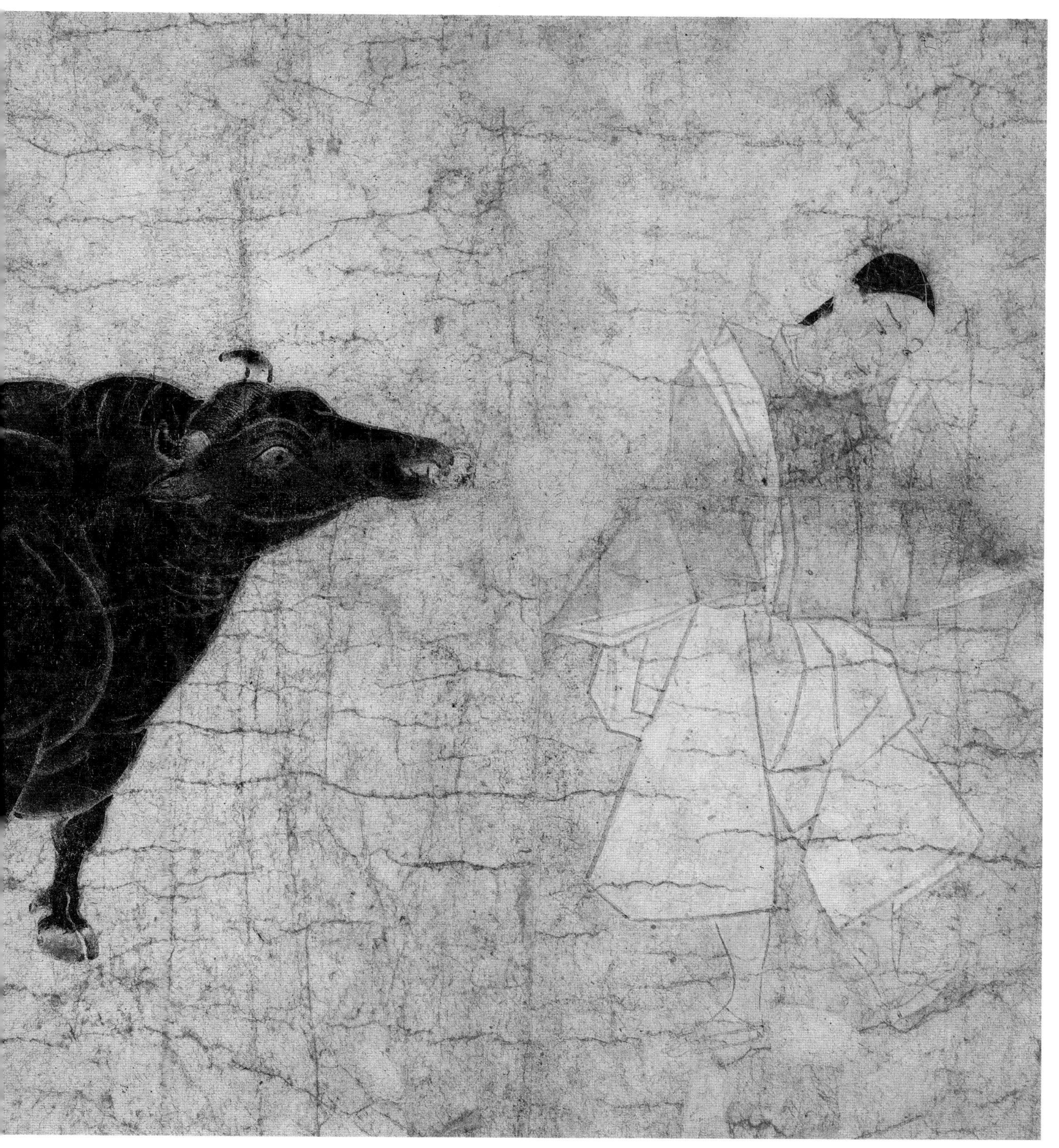

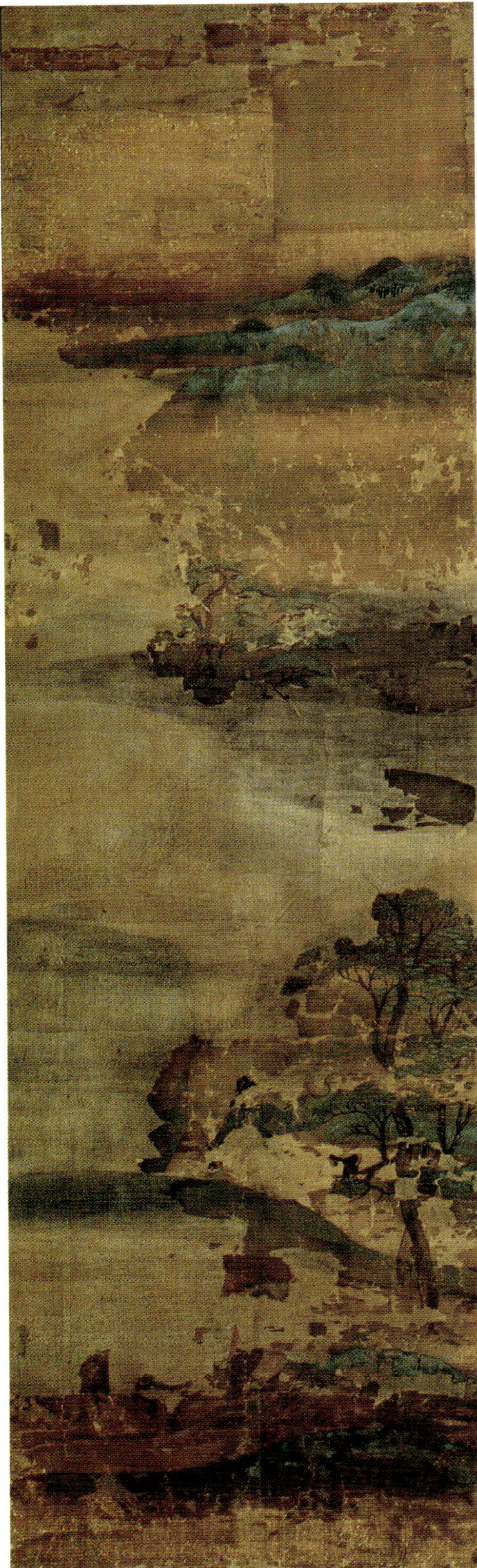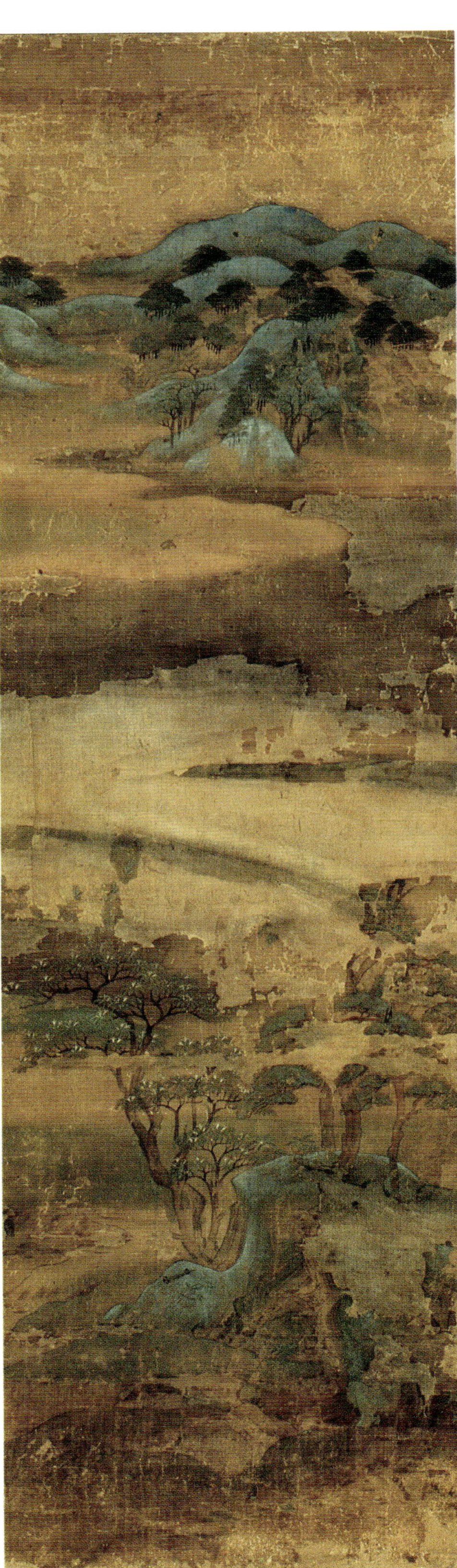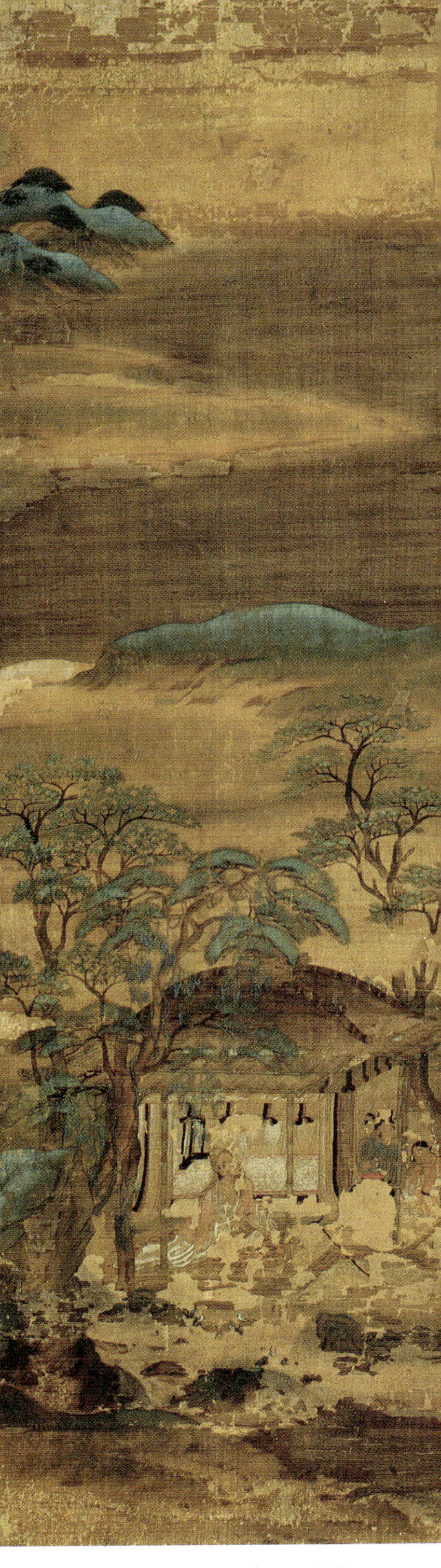

32 ⊙

Landscape Screen, known as a *"Senzui Byōbu"*
山水屏風
Heian period, 2nd half of 11th century
Ink and colors on silk; each panel
146.4cm × 42.7cm
Kyoto National Museum

This imagined Chinese landscape, by an unknown Japanese artist, is centered on a rustic villa set under pine trees entwined with spring wisteria, where a gentleman *literatus* or hermit sits with brush and paper composing poetry. A young nobleman in Chinese dress with retainers approaches to pay a call. According to one interpretation, the scene depicts the secluded abode of the Tang poet Bo Juyi (Jp: Hakurakuten; 772-846) whose lyrical poems, replete with natural metaphors, were much favored by Heian aristocrats attempting to master Chinese poetics.

The mounting is in the earlier style which prevailed until the 14th century where paintings on silk (not paper) were mounted on

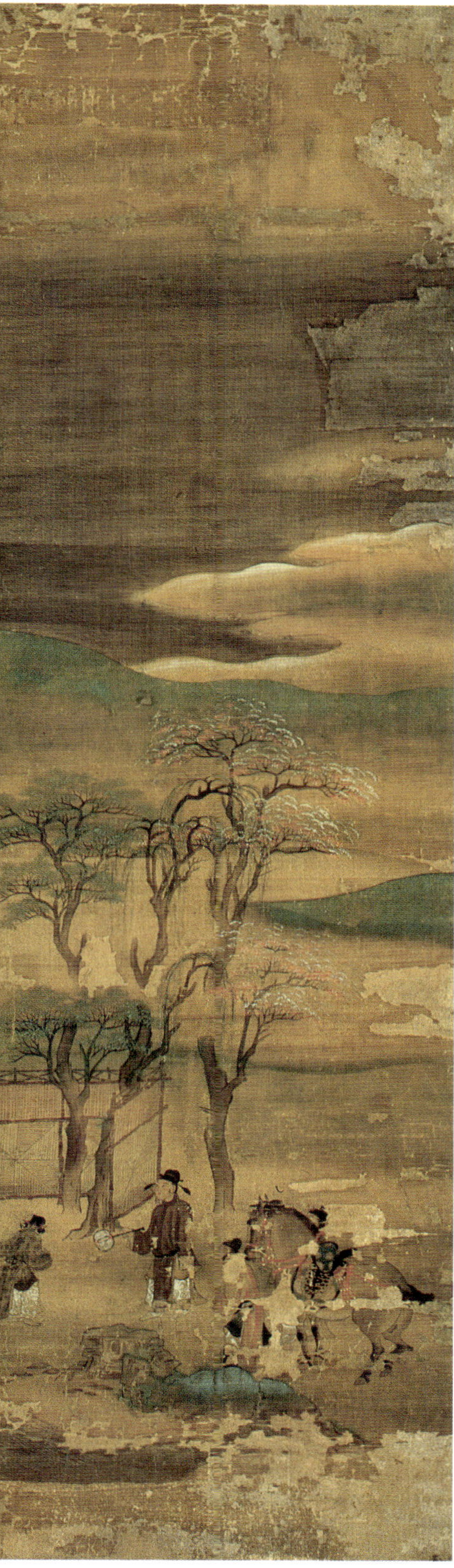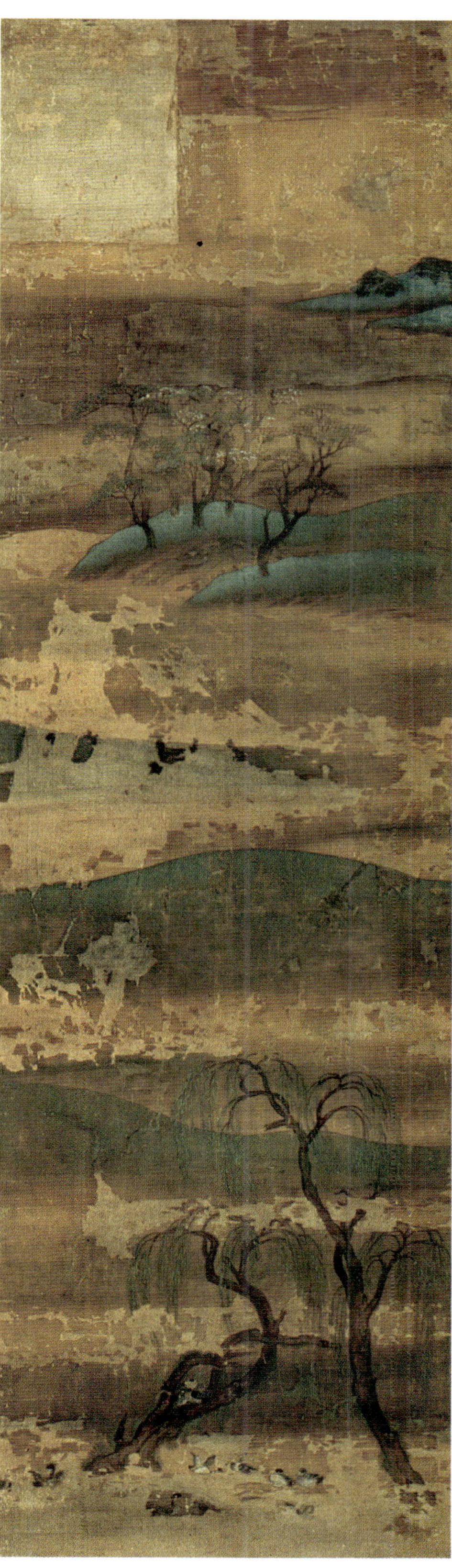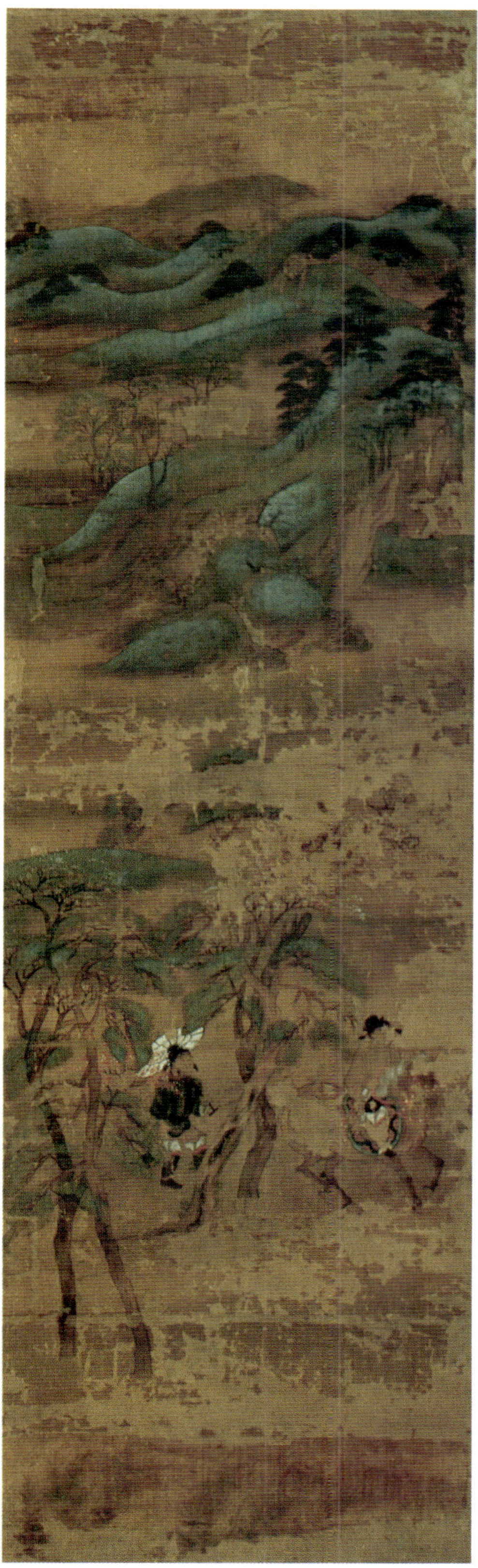

panels each set off by a framing band of silk brocade. Panels could be mounted singly or attached together with flexible hinges to create a folding screen (Jp: *byōbu*).

According to records, at least from the 8th century exotic Chinese subjects and scenes (known as *kara-e*) on screens were used to decorate and partition rooms at the Imperial Palace and in the mansions of the nobility. Secular paintings with Japanese themes and scenery became increasingly popular in the 10th century and were known in distinction to *kara-e* as *yamato-e* (or "Japanese painting" after the name Yamato, the plain around Nara considered the heart of the Japanese nation under the imperial family). Stylistically, both *kara-e* and *yamato-e* derived from the same brightly pigmented and richly detailed color-painting tradition of Tang (7-9th c) China. However, because no aristocratic domestic buildings from the Heian period have survived, nearly all the large-format secular paintings and furnishings have perished. In fact, this is the only screen with Chinese scenes known to be extant from the period.

This early type of landscape screen came to be called, generically, *senzui byōbu* (or "landscape folding screens") — a variant on the term *sansui* ("landscape"). From the late 12th century such landscape screens were employed as backdrops at ordination rites (*kanjō*) in the esoteric Buddhist sects for priests of high birth. Screens with Japanese scenes (*yamato-e*) also came to be categorized as *senzui byōbu*. By the 14th century the display of *senzui byōbu* (landscape screens) had become a fixed requirement at ordination rites and esoteric temples treasured their screens accordingly. Thus this originally secular screen probably owes its continued existence to being carefully handed down at the great Kyoto Shingon temple of Tō-ji.

The screen provides the clearest evidence of the Heian tradition of "Chinese" *kara-e*. However the color harmonies and more flowing outlines show an increasingly Japanized stylistic expression associated with developments in *yamato-e*. Some scholars have also pointed to the softened peaks or undulating shore-line as more representative of the landscape around the Kyoto capital than majestic Chinese scenery. A good comparison can be made with the *yamato-e* landscapes that form the backgrounds for Buddhist paradise scenes on the inside walls and doors of the Phoenix Hall (Byōdō-in, Uji), dated *ca* 1053. This comparison helps to place the screen no later than the second half of the 11th century.

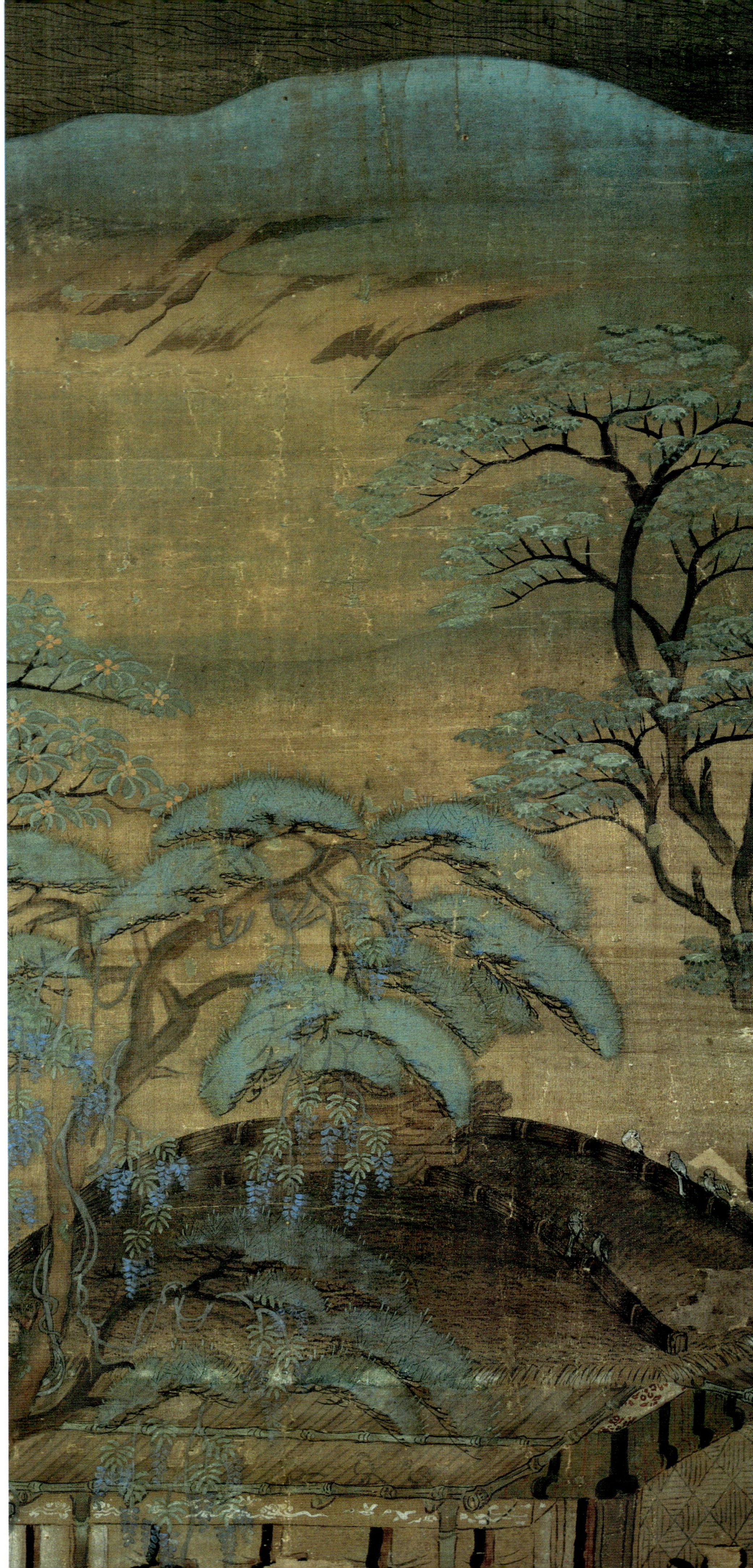

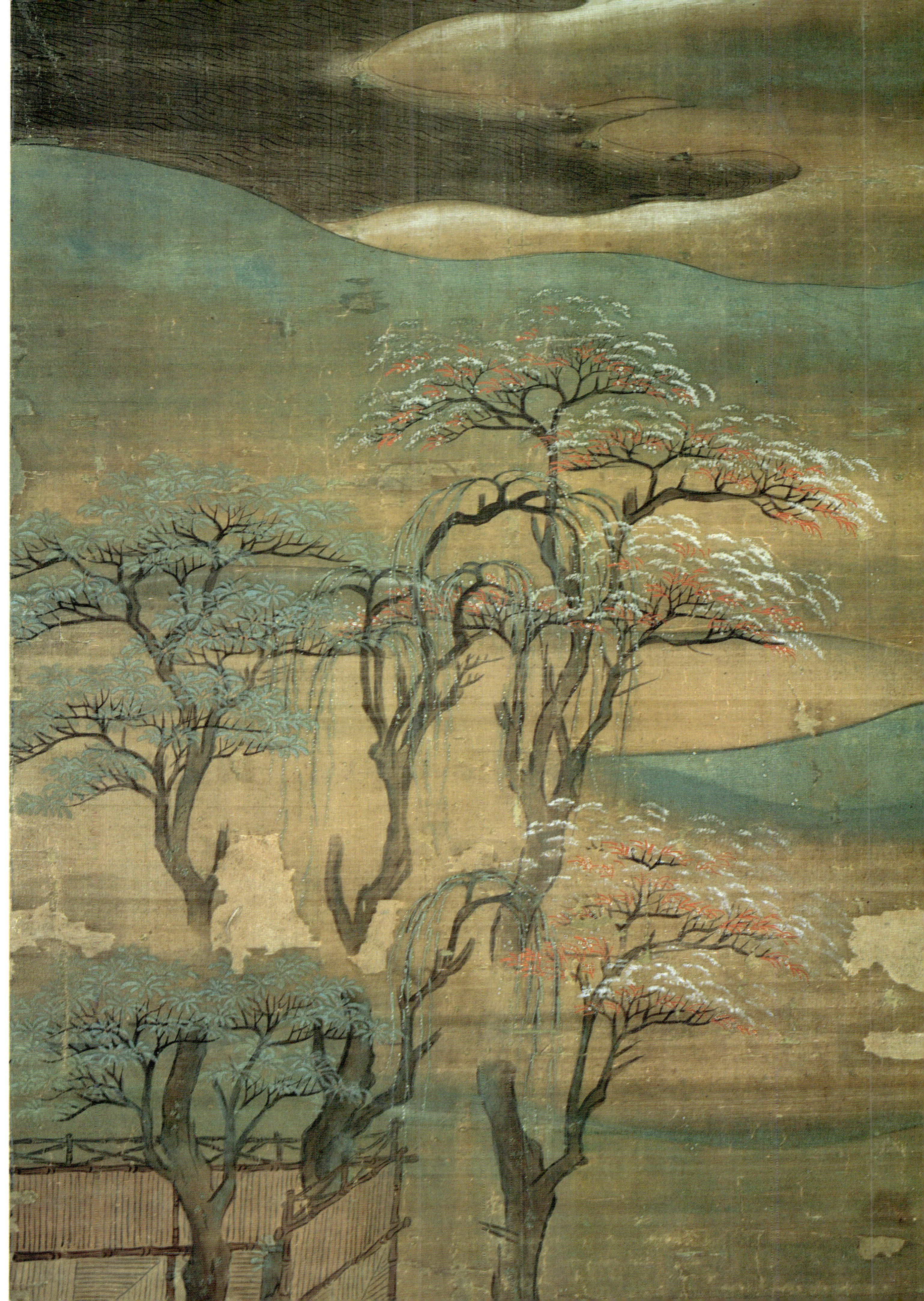

33 ◎

Bugaku Dancers
舞楽図

Kamakura period, 14th century
Ink and colors on silk
103.6cm × 136.4cm
Kitano Tenman-gū, Kyoto

This is the earliest known painting on the theme of *bugaku*, which are dance pieces performed from the late Nara or early Heian period (8th/9th century) at the Imperial court both by nobles and guilds of professional dancers and musicians. *Bugaku* over the centuries came to influence performances outside the palace and variants were often danced at shrine or temple festivals. Much *bugaku* is performed in masks. Many of them have exotic or fear-some aspects reflecting diverse origins (like the music) from as far away as Central Asia or India transmitted to Japan through China and Korea. The costumes, richly embroidered and woven silk, are either predominately red or blue-green. This reflects the two major types of music for *bugaku* (recorded since the mid-Heian period) into the musical style of Tang China (red) or that introduced from the ancient Korean kingdoms (blue-green). The colors also are based on the division of Heian nobles into ranks on either the Left or Right of the Imperial presence so that courtiers were required to wear either red or blue-green robes at court. The cut of *bugaku* costumes is in the fashion of civil or military aristocratic dress during the Heian period. Also included in *bugaku* are dances for children and a group of ritual dances and music called *(mi) kagura* performed at the court to propitiate Shinto gods.

These two paintings were originally affixed to both sides of a single-panel free-standing screen, but have been remounted into the present framed panels. One panel depicts young boys performing an auspicious dance for longevity, *Ennen no mai*, under the cherry blossoms. They dance to the accompaniment of cymbals and drums, with low-ranking Buddhist monks known as *yusō*, who excelled in performing and martial arts, watching and joining in. The *kagura* dance performed on the second panel appears to be set at the shrine of Kitano Tenman-gū. Here musicians play clappers, a type of zither (*koto*) and other instruments, while the dancers follow the leader of the troupe to perform. In these paintings, although damaged and retouched, the rendering of the dancers is detailed and rich in variety. The compositions with different massings of figures avoid a single focus or stylization and draw the viewer's eye from group to group.

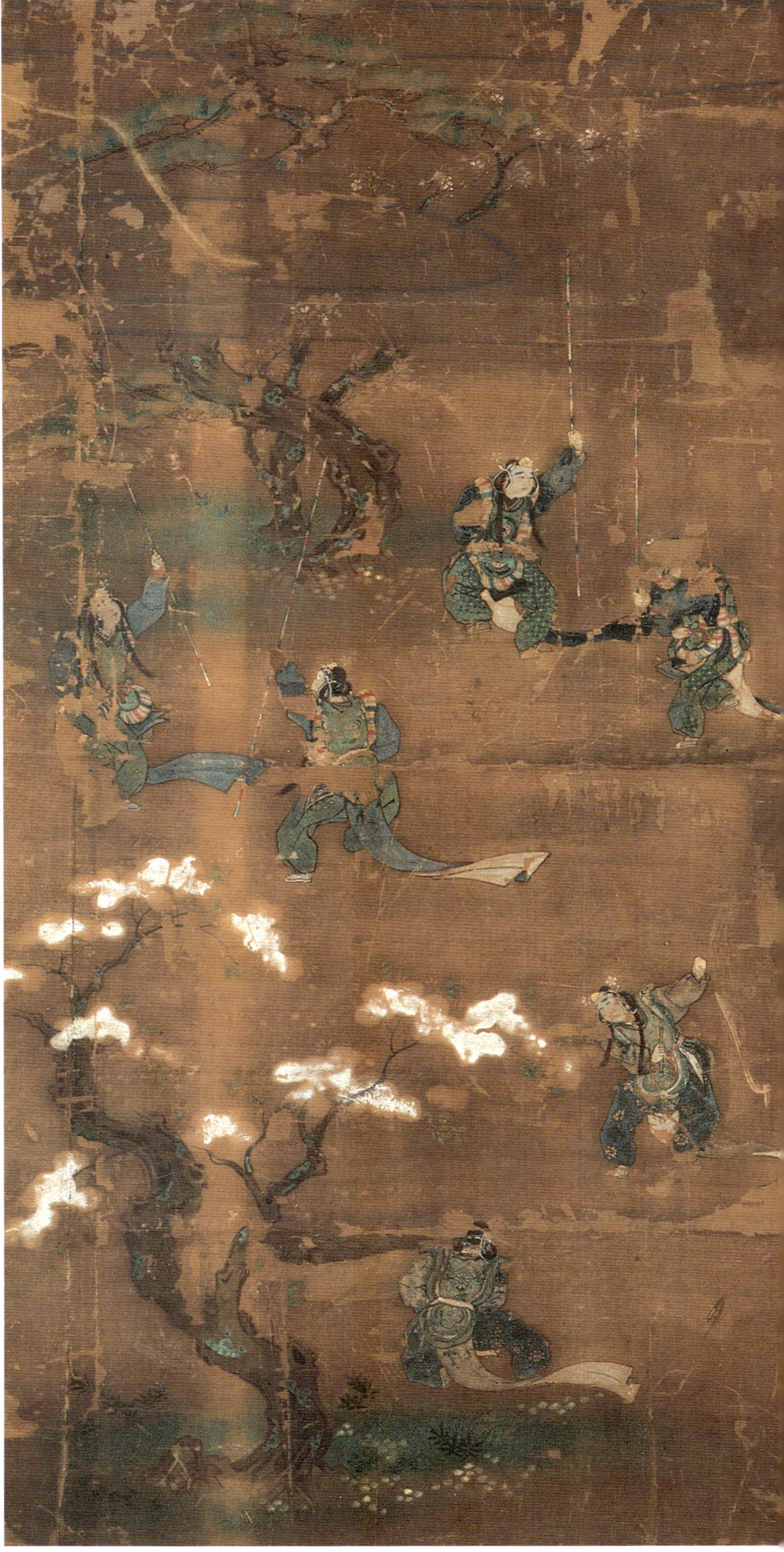

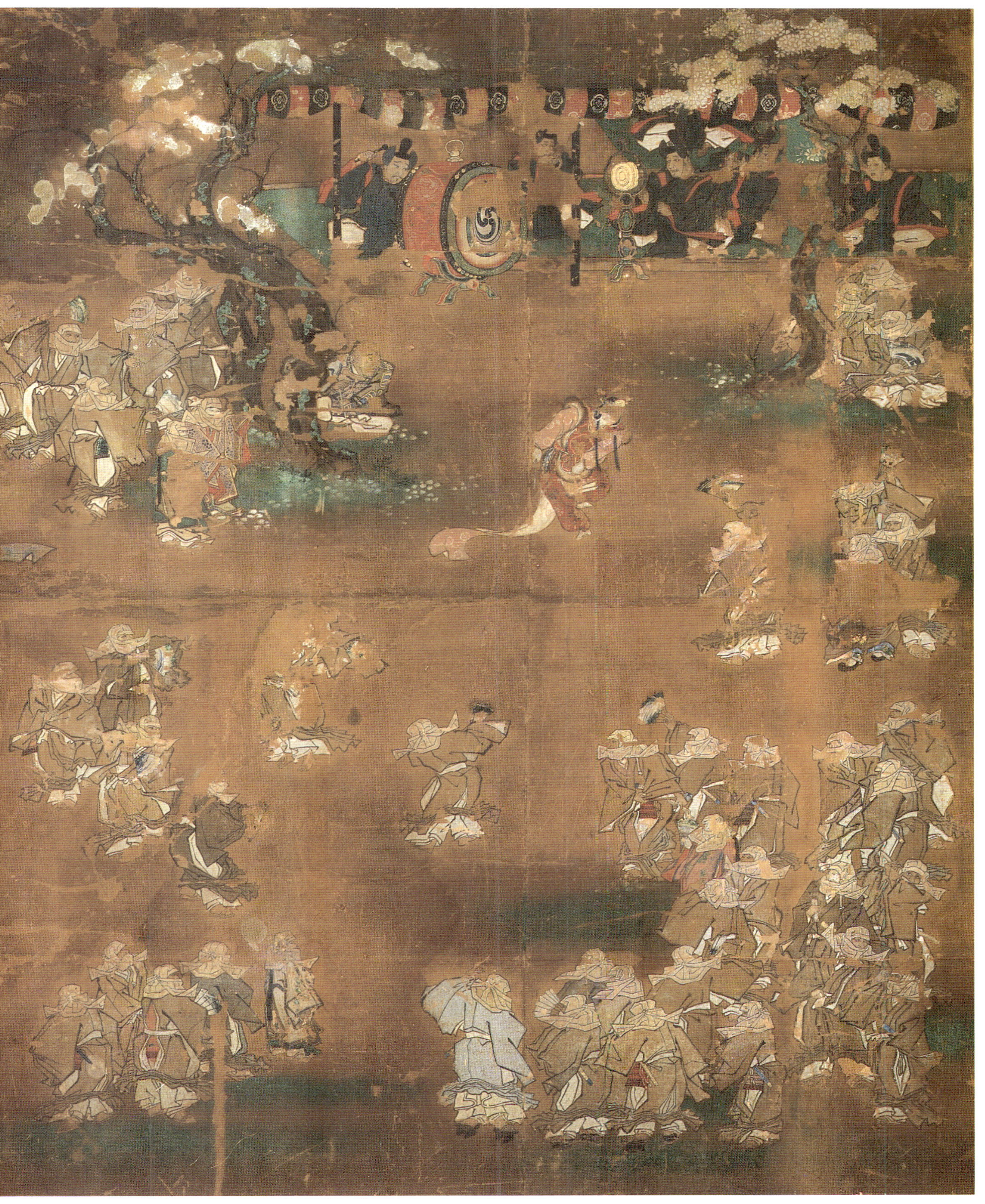

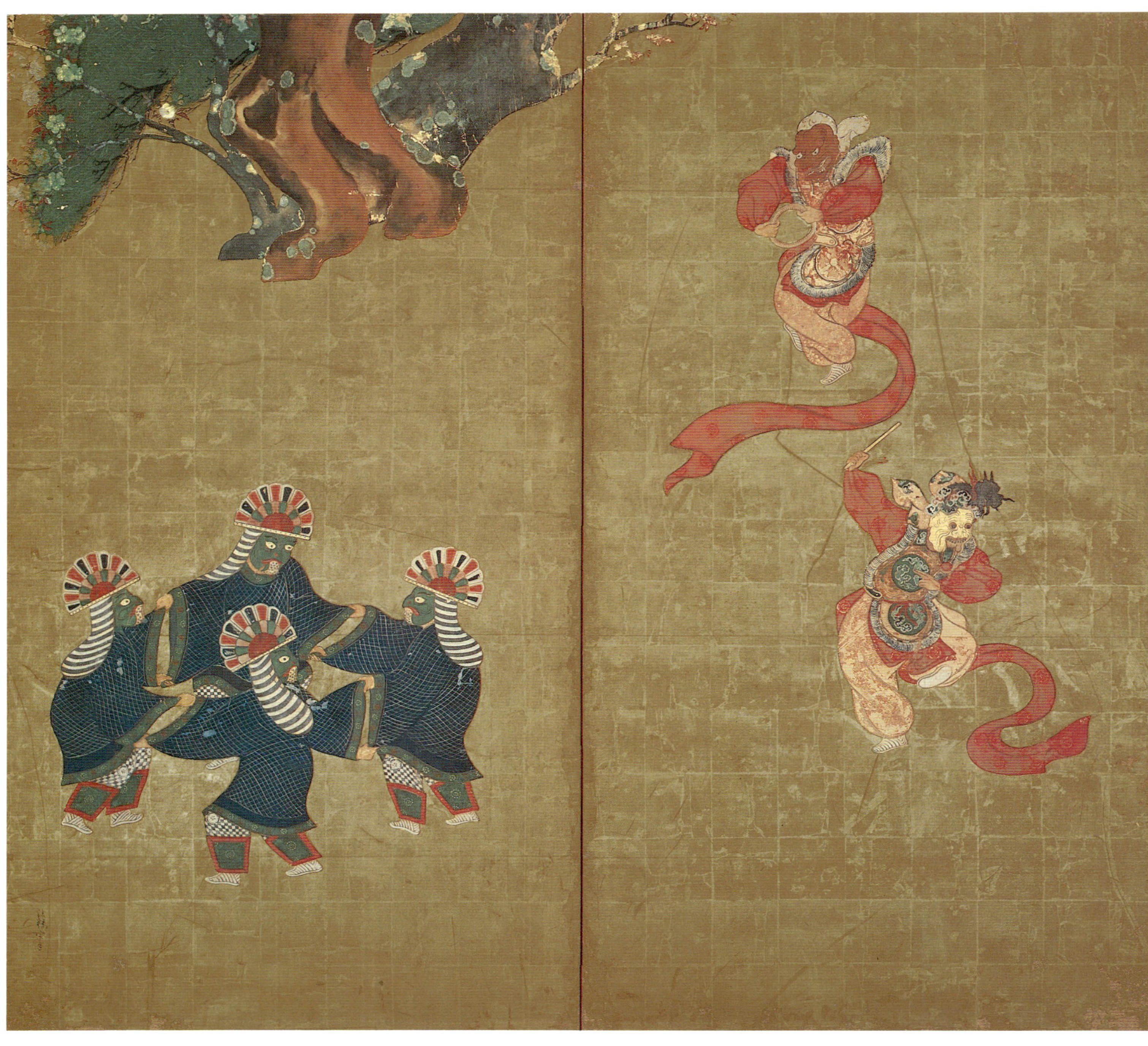

34 ◎

Bugaku Dancers
By Tawaraya Sōtatsu
舞楽図屏風

Edo period, 17th century
Pair of two-fold screens; ink, colors, and gold-leaf
on paper; each, 155.5cm × 170.0cm
Daigo-ji, Kyoto

Tawaraya Sōtatsu (?–1643?) is known for
the way he picked up themes and motifs from
the *yamato-e* tradition of scroll and genre
paintings dating back to the Heian period,
enlarged individual elements, and arranged
the figures against largely empty backgrounds,
here vibrant squares of gold-leaf. These screens
show *bugaku* dancers in a depiction that
follows in the lineage of genre painting beginning with Cat. No.33. Not many paintings on
this theme are known. Sōtatsu has alternated
dancers in red with those in blue-green, after
one *kagura* dancing figure, reflecting the division of *bugaku* discussed under Cat. No.33. He
also has captured the essence of *bugaku* which
tends either to be solo pieces of striking strong
movements or moderate dances performed by
a group. The musicians are indicated by the
decorated drums and curtain at lower right,
balanced by the pine and cherry tree at upper
left.

The several dances can be identified. From
the right: the *kagura* dance, *Saisōrō*,
performed as an old man, clad in white; two
dancers in long trailing dark-blue costumes
perform *Nasori*; the *Genjōraku* solo dance of
an exotic "Persian" in a vermillion mask,
holding a ring symbolizing a snake; the
"Dragon Prince" (*Ryō-ō*) another forceful
dance performed in a dragon mask; and finally
"*Konron hassen*", a moderate ring-dance of
four performers in blue.

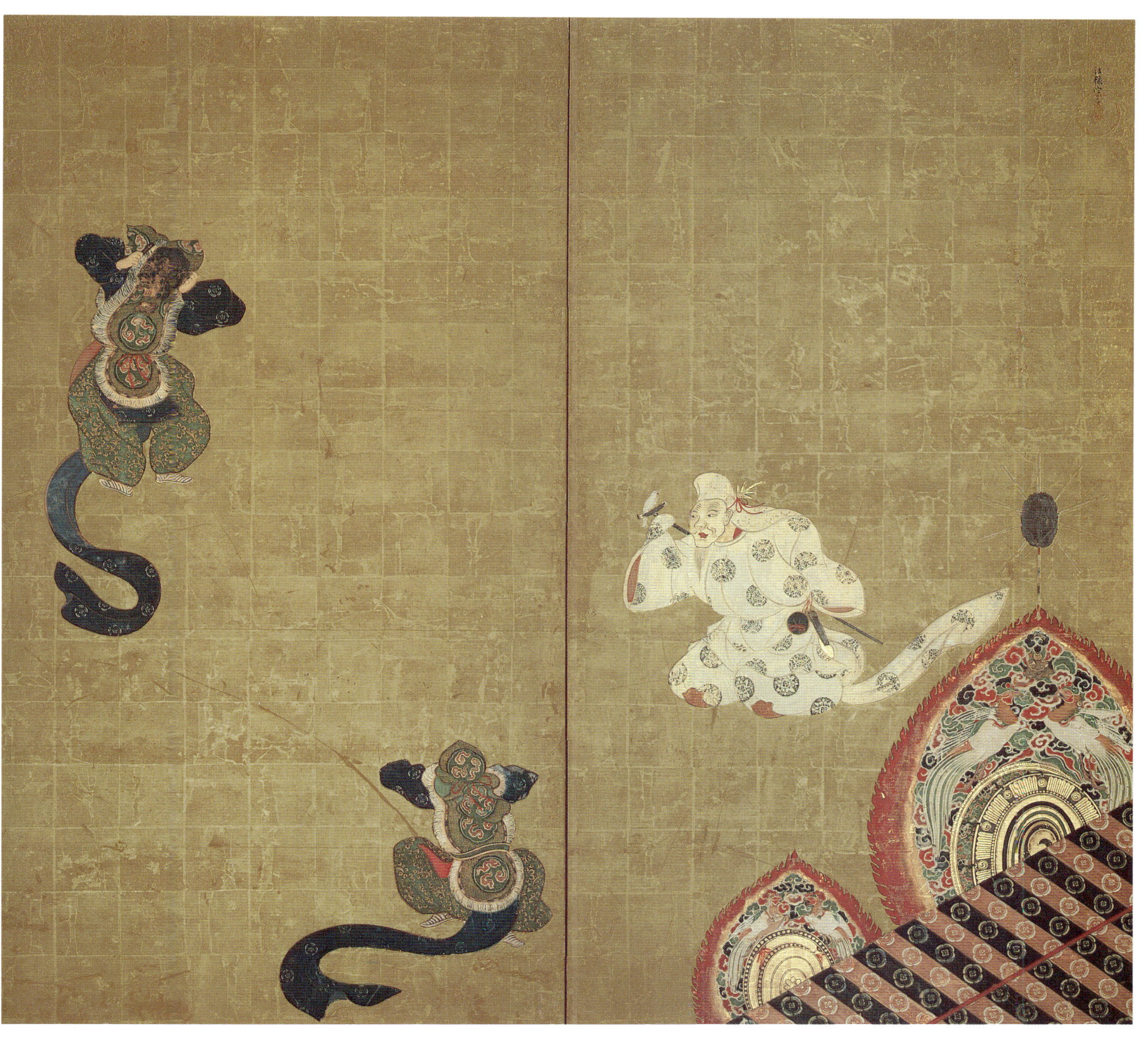

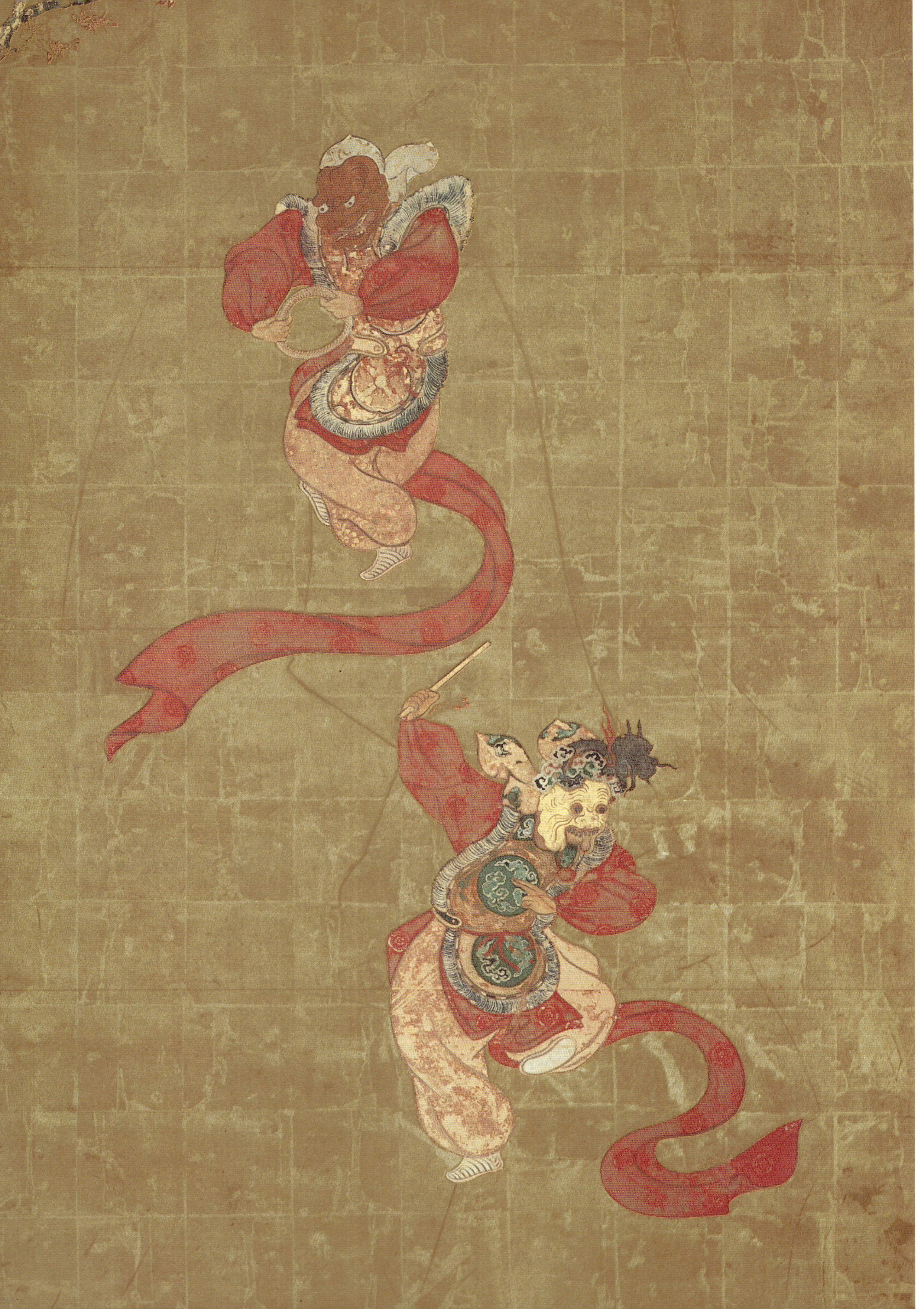

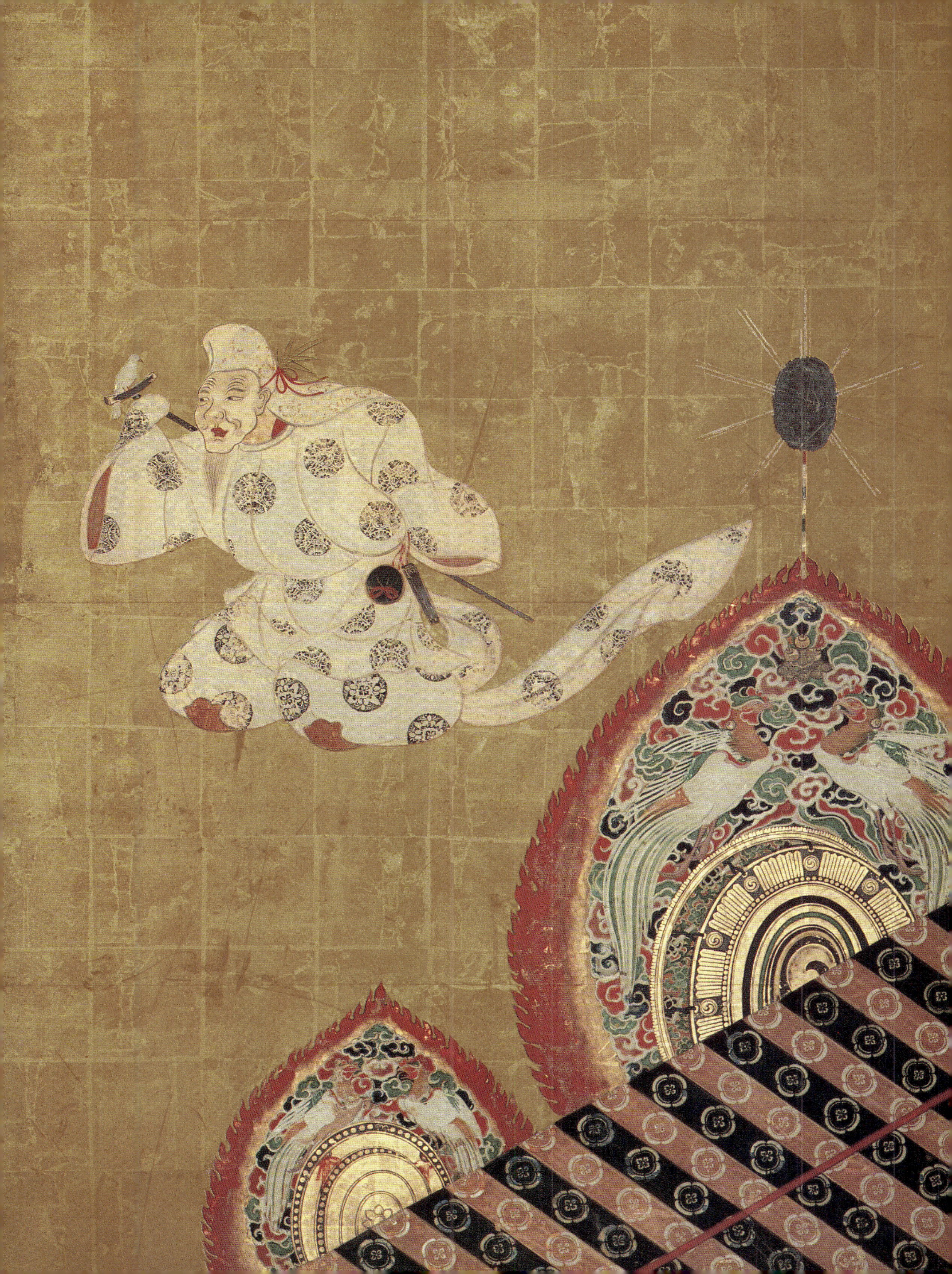

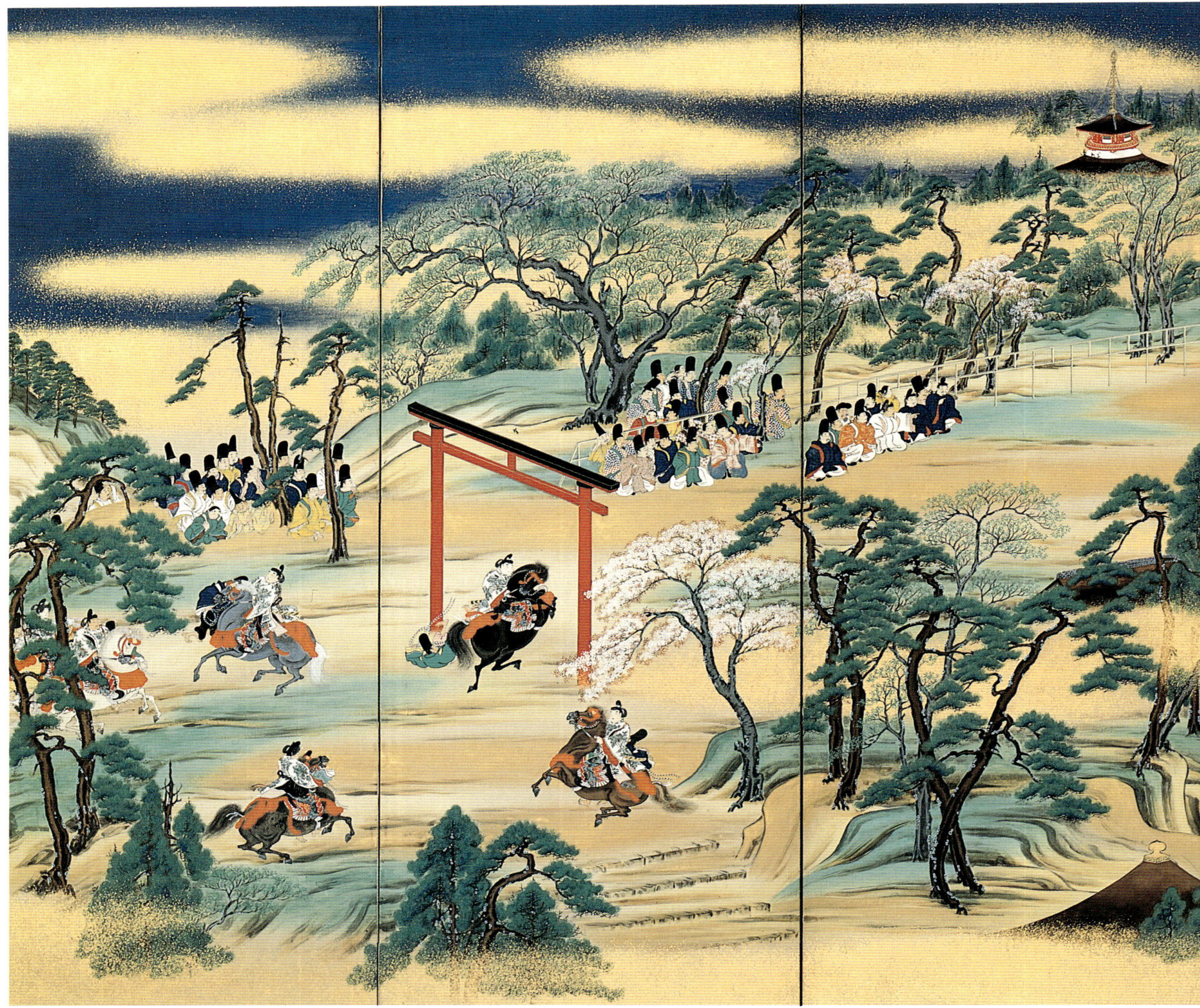

35-1

35

Festival at Iwashimizu Hachiman
Shrine
Annual Equestrian Archery at the Palace
By Reizei Tamechika
石清水臨時祭・年中行事騎馬図屏風

Edo period, ca 1860
Pair of six-fold screens; ink and colors on paper
Each 155.0cm × 362.2cm
Hakutsuru Art Museum, Hyyogo

The right screen depicts a festival at the
Shinto shrine, Iwashimizu Hachiman (see Cat.
No.20), near Kyoto, which took place on the
Day of the Horse in the Third month according
to the old lunar calendar. The main event was a
procession of ten horses through the gate up to
the main shrine. Cherry blossoms indicate the
spring season. The ceremonies at the shrine
repeat observances held, with interruptions
since the Heian period, at the Imperial Palace
on the day before, which traditionally included
an exorcism for the emperor and a parade of
horses.

The left screen presents a show of mounted
archers held on the Fifth day of the Fifth
month. The painting is a copy of the event at
the Ukon Riding grounds of the Imperial
Palace as depicted in the "Illustrated Handscroll of Annual Rites and Ceremonies" *Nenjū
gyōji ekotoba*. This famous set of originally 60
scrolls was painted in the *yamato-e* style
around 1158, but is now extant only in fragments and a partial, copied version made by
Sumiyoshi artists in the early 17th century.

Reizei Tamechika (1823–64) was a leading
artist in the revival of *yamato-e* themes and
techniques in the early 19th century. See Cat.
No.39. He is known for his diligent study and
copying of paintings especially handscrolls of
the 10th–14th centuries. Here Tamechika
re-interprets in a large-scale format, where the
panels run contiguously, many of the motifs
and stylistic devices of the earlier tradition.

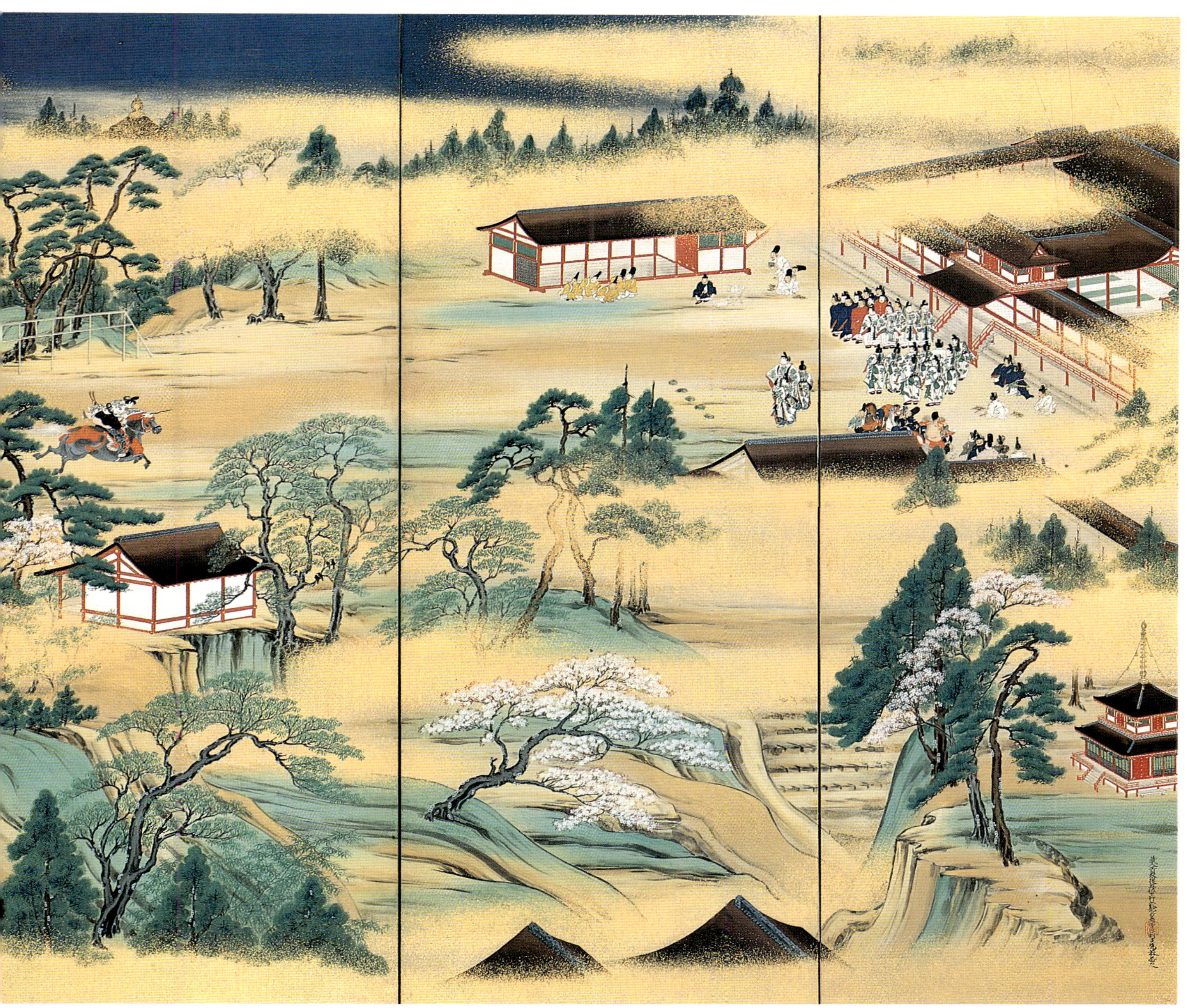

However important aspects, such as the color tonalities and impression of recession, are strikingly different from Heian period works.

From the artist's inscriptions at lower left and right corners we learn that he painted the screens between his thirty-fourth and thirty-eighth year. Other records indicate that Tamechika at thirty-two married Ayaginu, daughter in the family of hereditary priests at the Buddhist temple affiliated with Iwashimizu Hachiman. It seems likely that the artist had an opportunity to watch the Horse Procession festival, which had been revived in 1813.

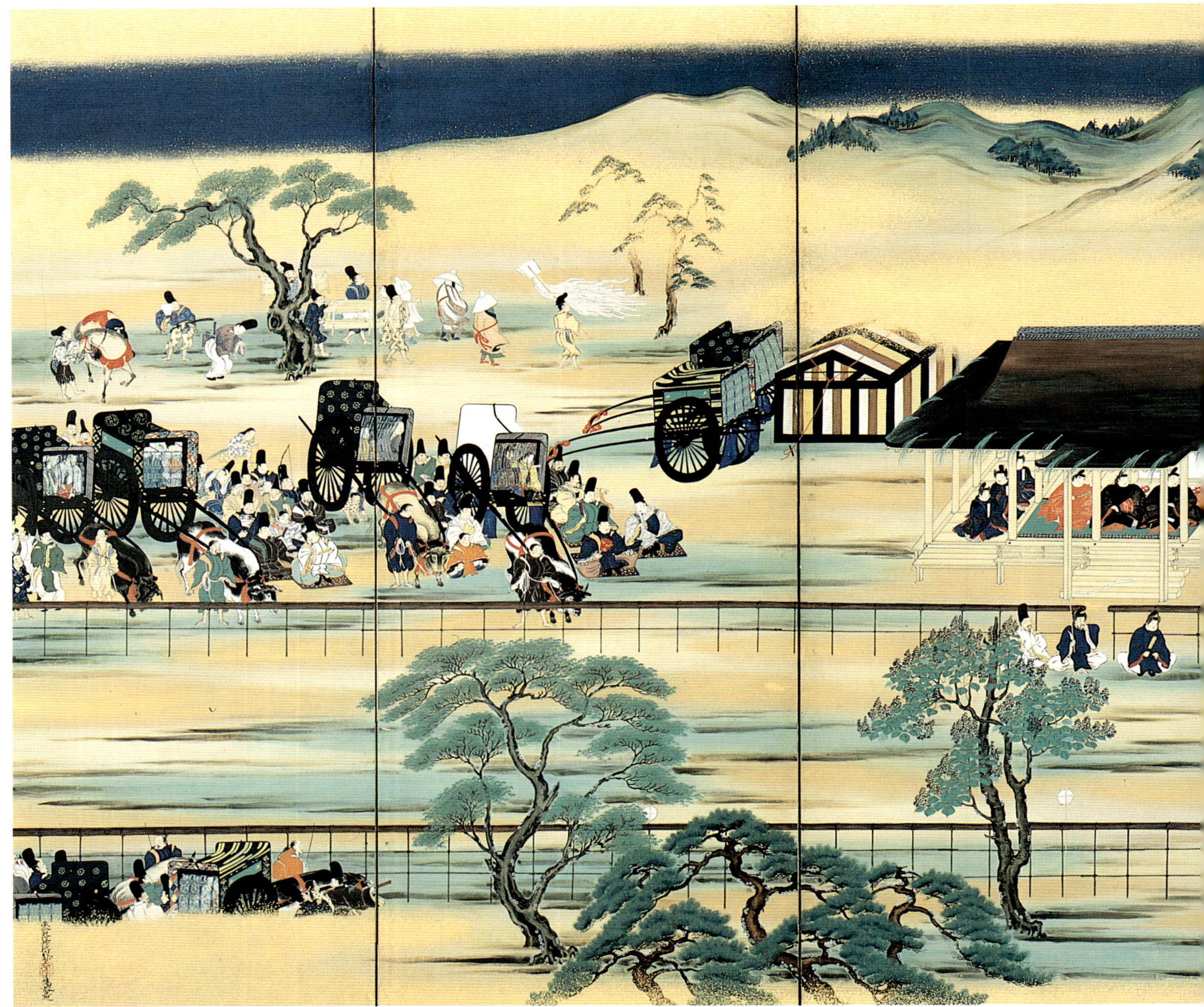

35-2

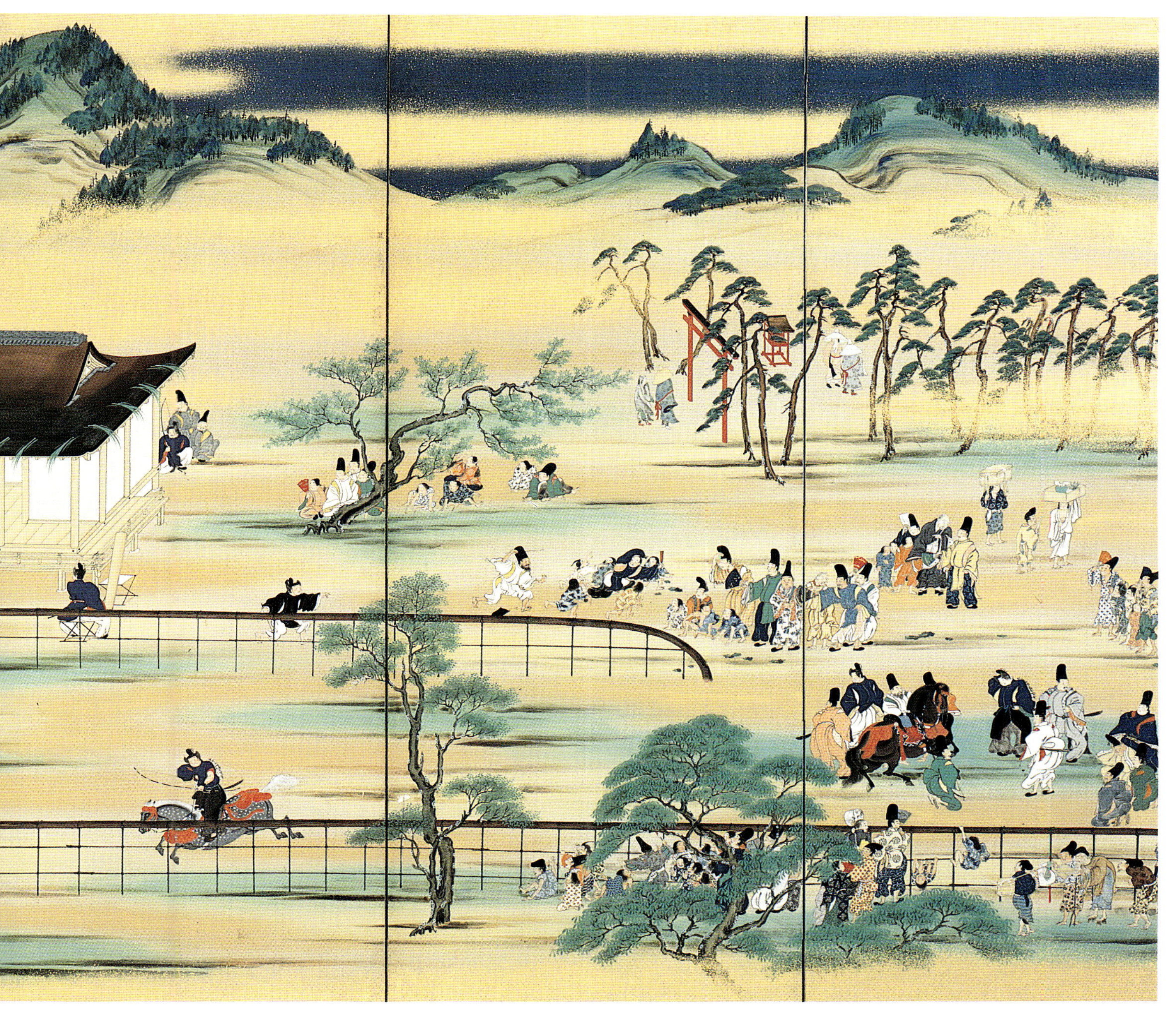

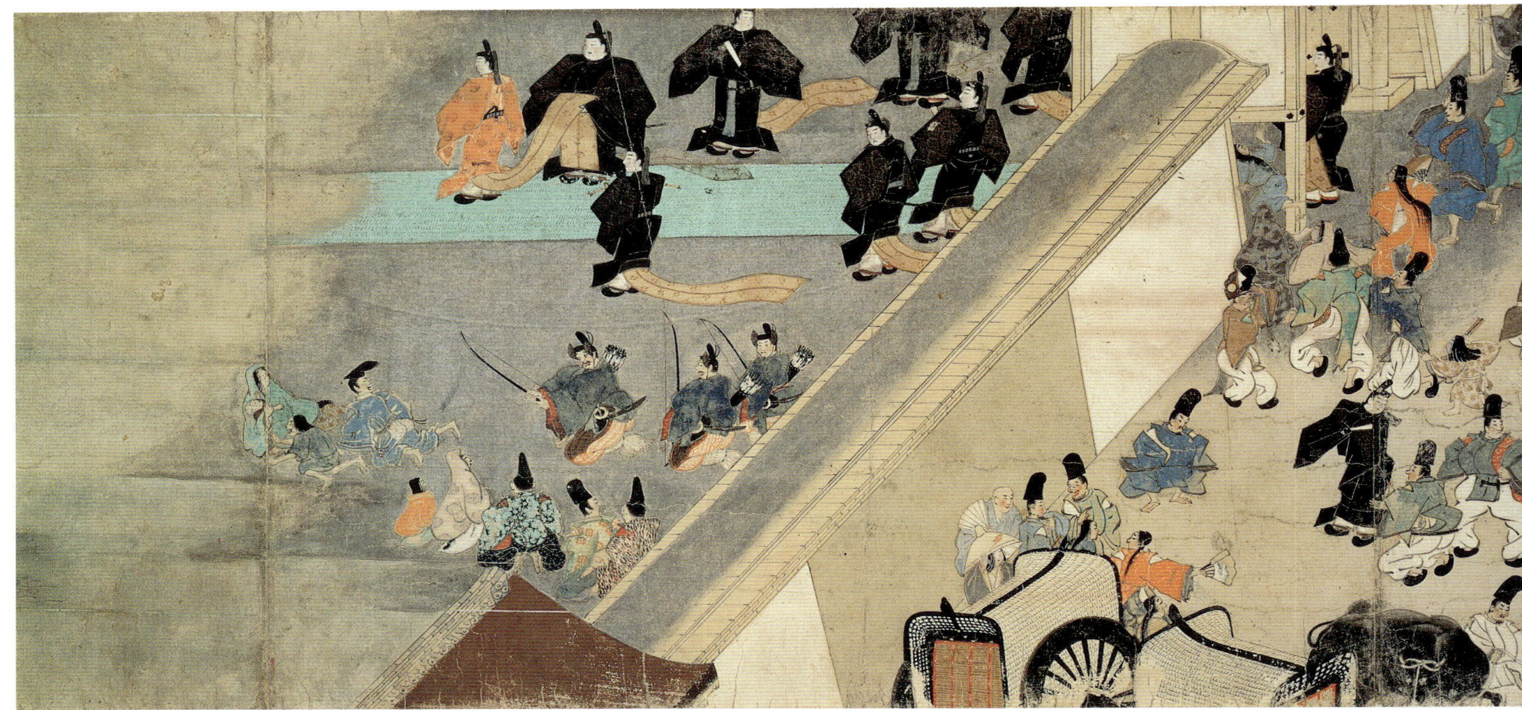

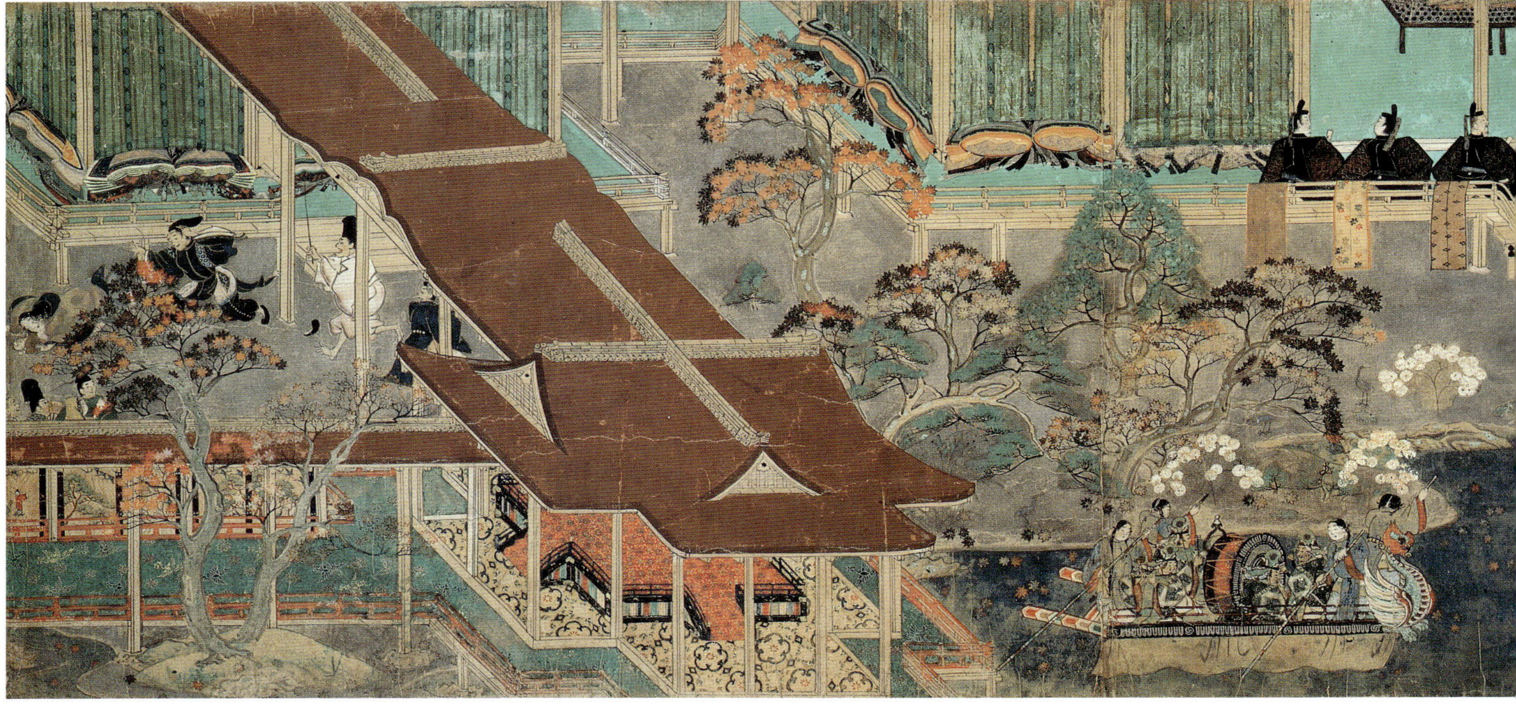

36 ◎

Illustration of "An Imperial Visit to the Horse Races" Chapter
駒競行幸絵詞

Kamakura period, early 14th century
Ink and colors on paper
34.2cm × 383.0cm
Izumi City Kubosō Memorial Museum, Osaka

This handscroll illustrates scenes from the chapter, "An Imperial Visit to the Horse Races" (*Koma kurabe gyōkō*), in *A TALE OF FLOWERING FORTUNES* or *Eiga monogatari*. It is a long, 40 chapter, anecdotal history, probably written at least in part by a court lady around 1040, that describes the golden age of the Heian aristocracy. It centers on the court and the great regent, Fujiwara no Michinaga, who brought his family to its apex of power and fortune early in the 11th century.

The paintings are now extant in two partial scrolls, neither of which has scenes of the horse races that give the work its title. The first handscroll (not on exhibit), owned by the Seikadō Library, depicts Akiko, the Empress Dowager (and Michinaga's daughter), on a visit to the Kaya-no-in mansion of Michinaga's son, Yorimichi, on the 14th of the Ninth month in 1024. The second, on exhibition, consists of one section of text and one illustration of the visit to the same mansion made five days later (on the 19th) by Akiko's son, Emperor Goichinojō, the Empress (another of Michinaga's daughters) and the Crown Prince.

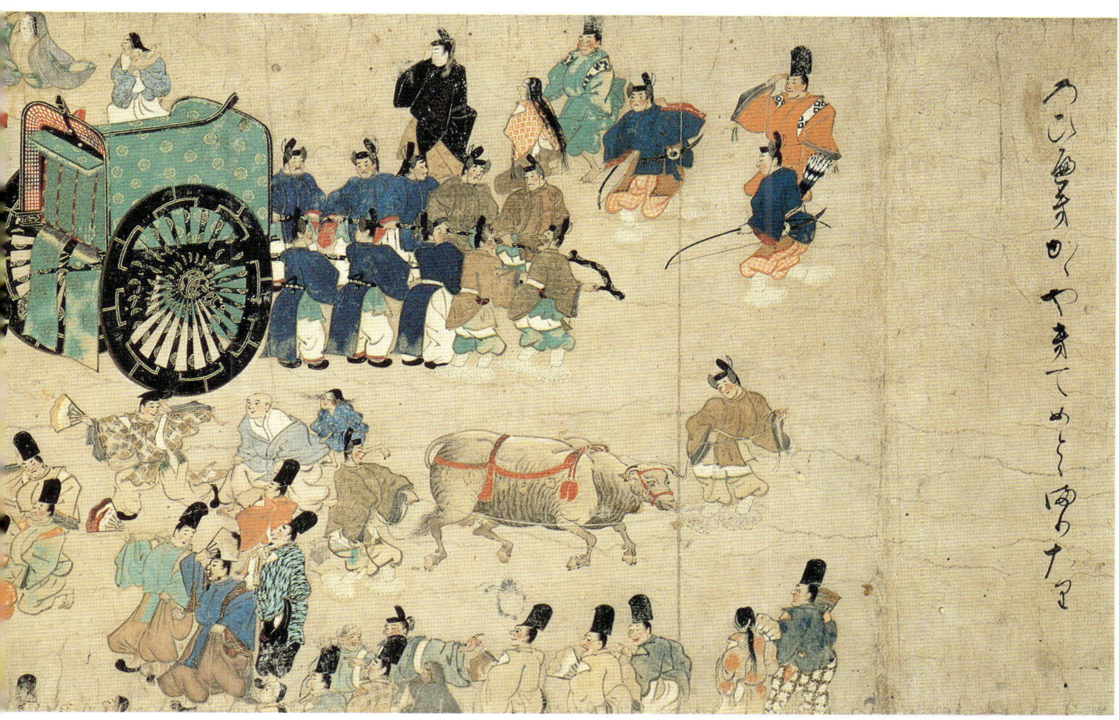

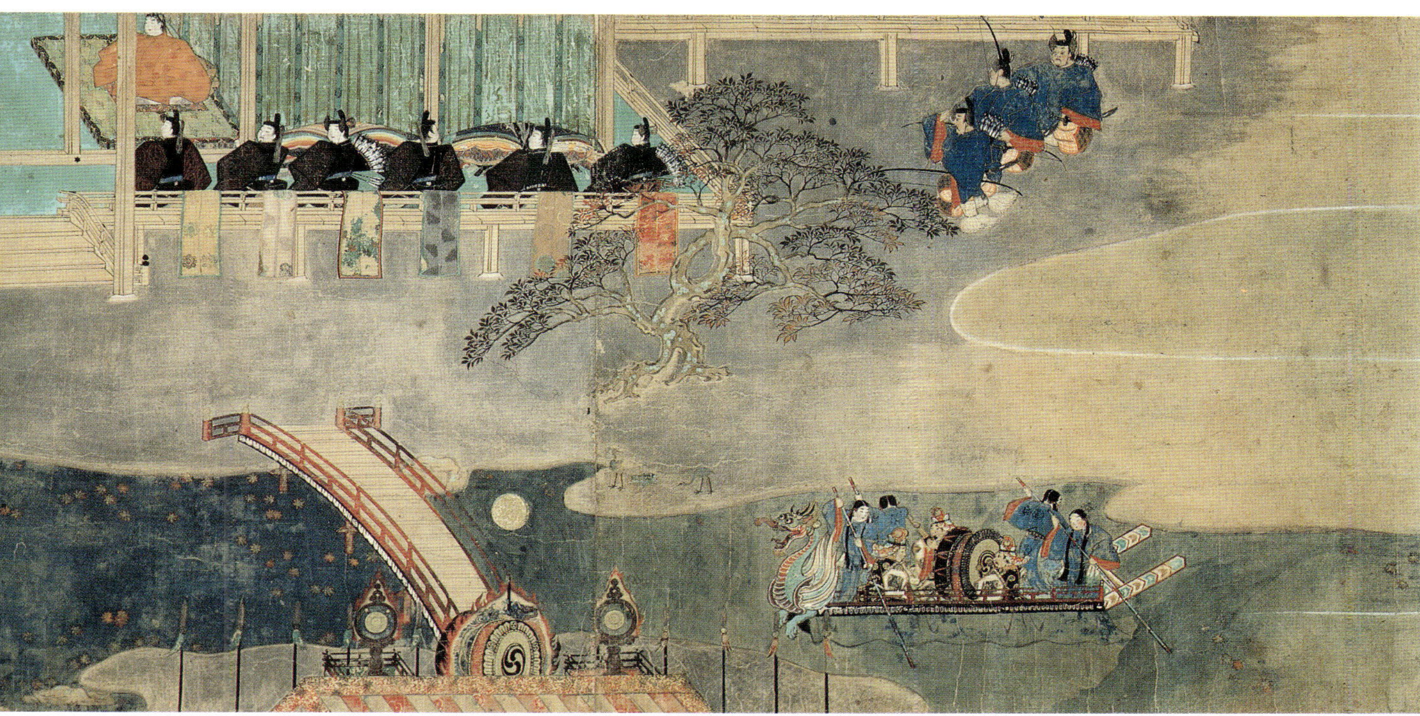

The opening scene shows the arrival of the Crown Prince who has entered the gateway with his entourage, leaving his ox-cart. Next the Emperor, his consort, the prince, noblemen, and noblewomen behind the curtains of the *shinden*-style main wing of the mansion, enjoy music from boats in the garden. The bright opaque pigments, carefully drawn and outlined figures, traditional compositional layouts (i.e. angled gateway leading in, frontally positioned mansion with pond), are typical of the conservative, increasingly stylized expression of *yamato-e* of late Kamakura handscroll paintings. Scholars associate the style with followers in the atelier of the early 14th century court painter, Takashina Takakane.

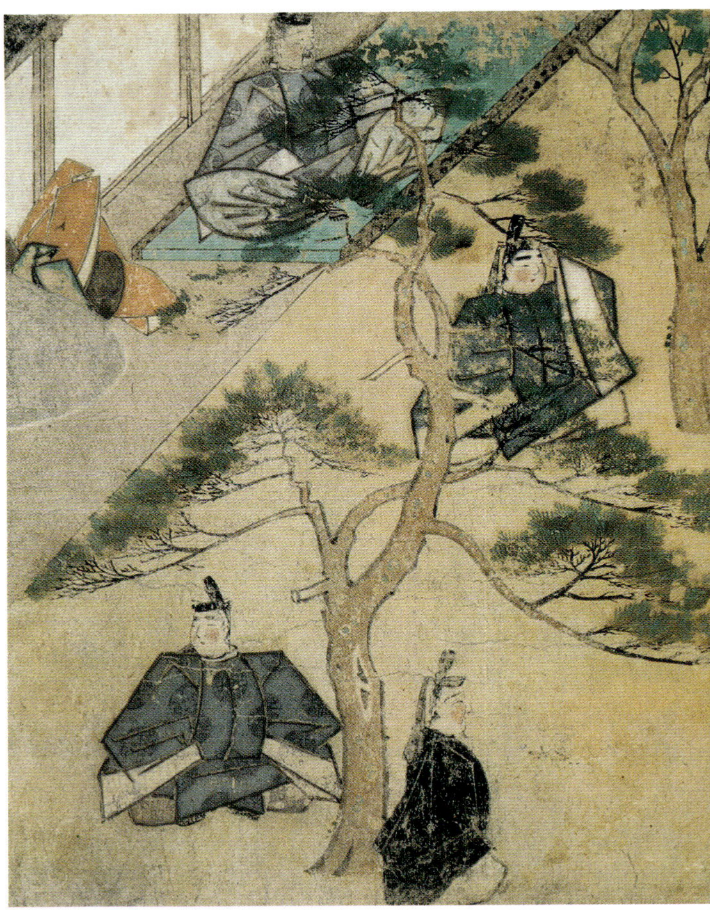

37 ◎

Illustrated Handscroll of the "Pliant
Bamboo Romance"
なよ竹物語絵巻

Kamakura period, 14th century
Ink and colors on paper
30.6cm × 1340.5cm
Kotohira Shrine, Kagawa

This illustrated narrative handscroll, or
emaki, presents the "Pliant Bamboo
Romance", *Nayotake monogatari,* also known
as the "Tale of Naruto Chūjō". There are nine
illustrations, with all (except the opening
painting which has lost its text passage)
preceded by a section of narrative. The story
tells how the retired emperor Gosaga became
enamored of the beautiful wife, whom he
happened to encounter in the audience of a
game of *kemari* kickball held one spring, of the
Third Minister of the Imperial Bodyguards.
To the emperor's attendant who brings
Gosaga's first love letter, however, the lady
replies, before fleeing, by quoting an old poem
about the transitoriness of love, which by
implication compares herself to a young and
pliant bamboo (*nayotake*). The title is taken
from this poem, because, in the end, the lady
bends to the status and charms of the Emperor
who succeeds in winning her. The romance
(with minor variants on the text passages here)
is found in the *Collection of Well-known Tales
of Past and Present,* (*Kokon chomon-jū*),
compiled in 1254.

The paintings of the handscroll show
characteristics in common with the "Miracles
of the Gods of Kasuga" (*Kasuga Gongen
reiken-ki-e,* 1309) and other works of the court
atelier of Takashina Takakane. However, they
show a growing tendency to depict relatively
large human figures, stylized in the rendering
of faces and decoratively flattened in forms,
placed in somewhat repetitive architectural
settings. The patternized compositions help to
date the work to the late 14th century.

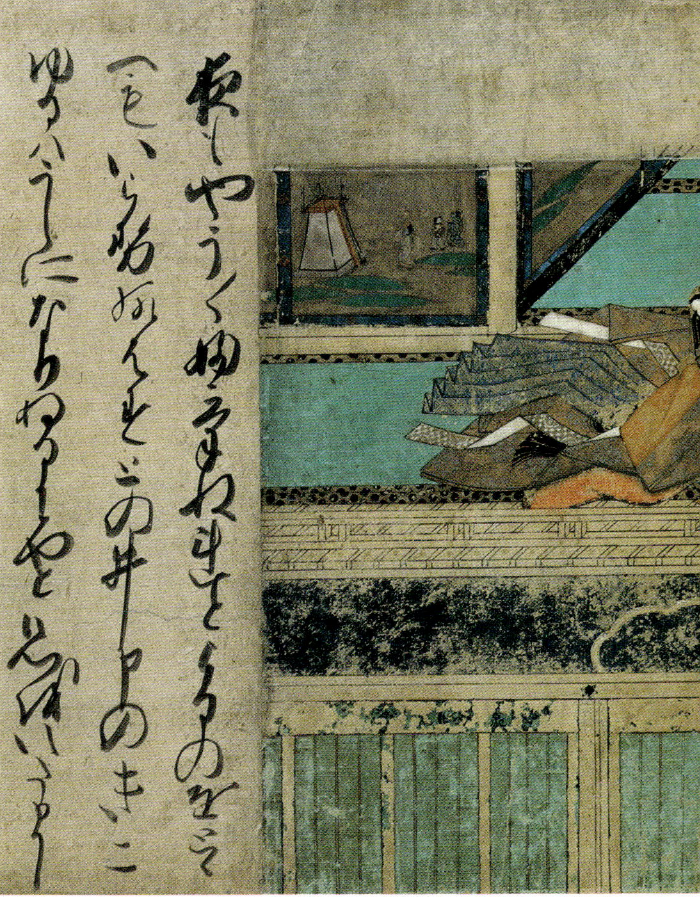

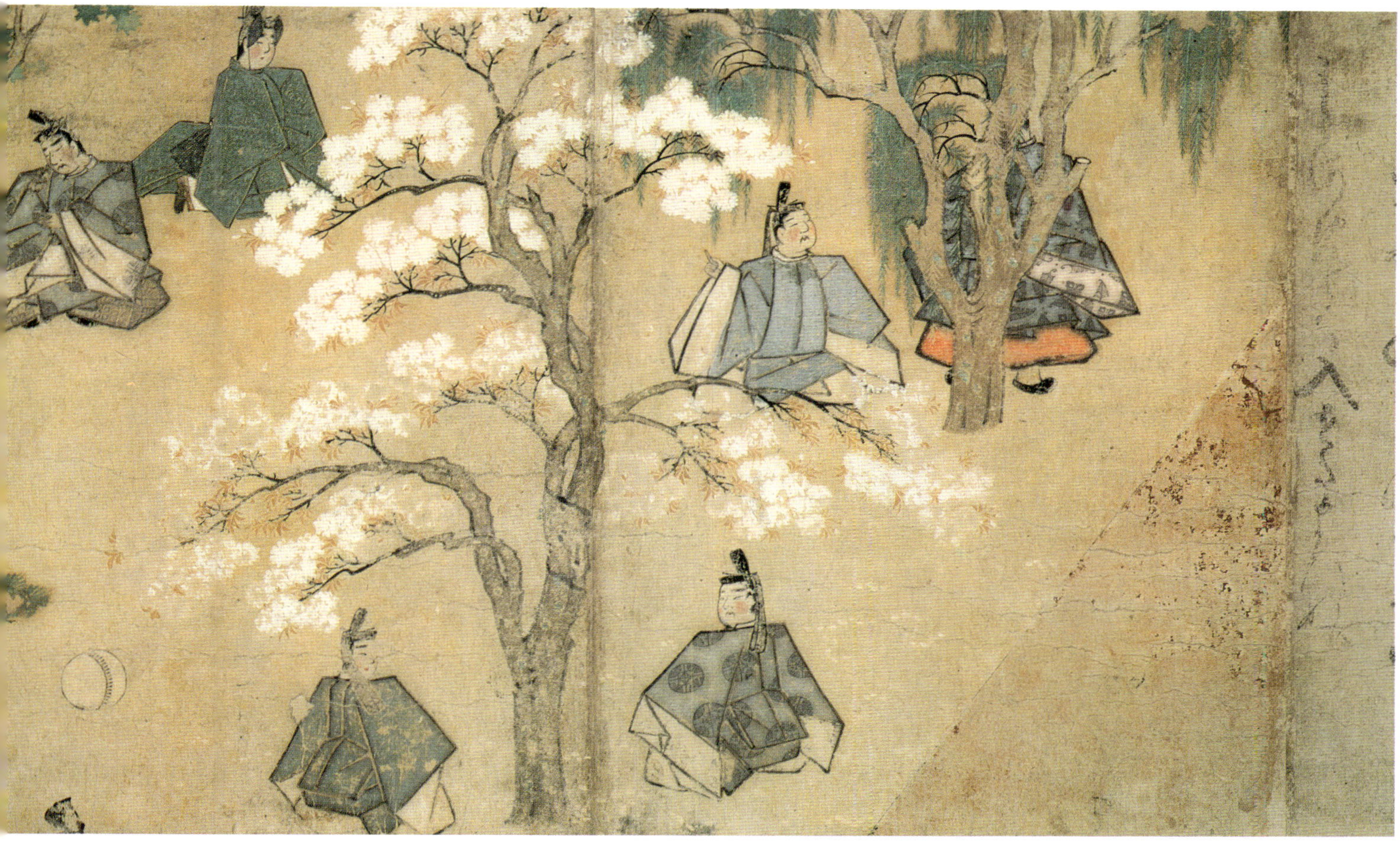

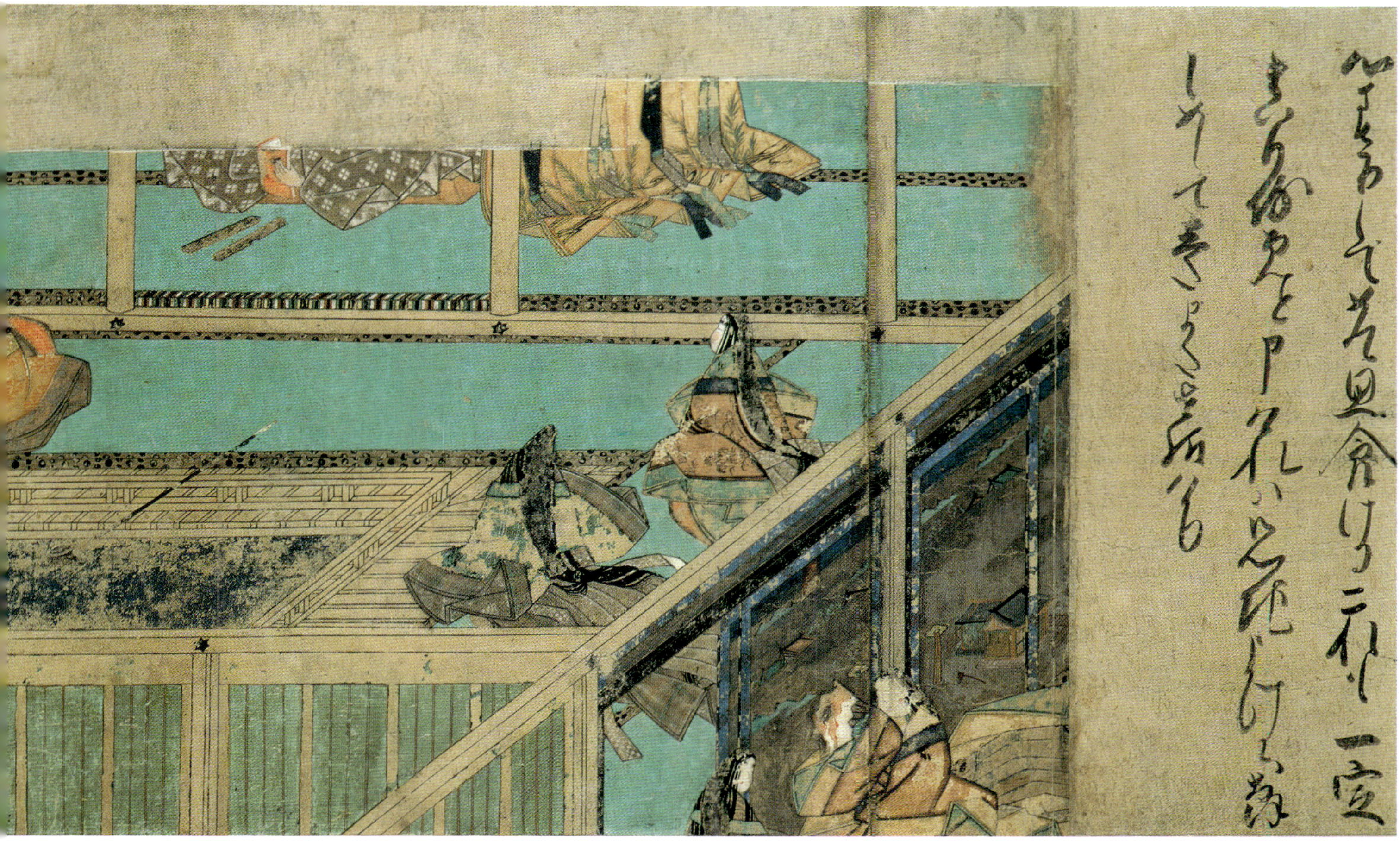

38 ◎

Handscroll of Lord Takafusa's Confessions of Love
隆房卿艶詞絵巻

Kamakura period, 13th century
Paper, ink with touches of red
25.5cm × 685.0cm
Nat. Museum of History and Ethnology, Chiba

This handscroll, known in Japanese as *Takafusa-kyō tsuyakotoba emaki,* illustrates in 4 or 5 scenes a romantic story related to the lengthy verse "Dew [Amorous] Words" by Fujiwara no Takafusa in which he poured out his unrequited love for a beautiful court lady, Kogō. Takafusa was a courtier and poet at the end of the Heian period (12th century) and at the time already the son-in-law of the mighty regent Taira no Kiyomori. The scroll opens with the text of the long poem, called a *chōka,* written here in unbroken lines composed of alternating five and seven syllables terminating in a double line of seven, followed by three poems in reply.

Over the years several explanations for the scenes which follow have been proposed because there is no narrative story text. The first scene probably depicts Takafusa and Kogō admiring the cherry blossoms from a veranda. Next, Takafusa and Kogō (her lady attendants having retired semi-discreetly to a corner at far left) exchange words of love. The next scene is comparatively short with just the lady placed in the foreground and shows Kogō preparing to confirm her love in writing. Then in a long scene we find Kogō instead has fallen to the invitation of Emperor Takakura (r.1168-80). Court ladies of the imperial harem are grouped around a table (a wrapped *koto* is placed against the wall) followed by an interior with two gentlemen and Kogō. Then follows the concluding landscape scene, marked at the center by the *torii* gate of Kitano Shrine and (to the left) Takafusa's carriage. This depicts his pilgrimage to assuage his sorrow.

The scroll features interior compositions divided by garden scenery (with one landscape) rendered in delicate linear painting done almost exclusively in *sumi* (carbon black in water with a binder of *nikawa* animal collagen glue). Although at first glance they may appear to be the ink underdrawings for heavily pigmented illustrations in the style and technique of, for example, *The Illustrated Diary of Murasaki Shikibu* (Cat. No.46), in fact these are technically polished, finished paintings. The ladies' long hair, the stiff hats (*eboshi*) of the gentlemen, furnishings, and some of the metal fittings and lattice work of the achitectural settings are done in glossy black accents that (with touches of red in the

depiction of lips) add a marvelous rhythm to the composition.

The abbreviated facial features and voluminous robes of the carefully isolated and immobile figures leave the viewer's imagination to fill in the emotional or erotic tension and resulting actions implied by the poetic text. Half-hidden among the trees in the garden scenes are syllable characters, clues taken from the poem to be deciphered to give further delight to the cognoscenti among the early viewers. The addition of these syllables (*ashi-de*) highlights the sophisticated interdependence of poetry and visual depiction that sustains this piece and was a hallmark of the courtly aesthetic.

While the number of works in this elegant linear ink style, known as *hakubyō-ga* (literally "white-drawing"), never approached colored paintings, there are several extant handscroll paintings done with ink dating from in or after the 13th century. Some evidence has been uncovered that *hakubyō-ga* may have been favored by talented amateurs among aristocratic ladies who were cultivated in painting along with poetry and calligraphy, but may not have had the inclination to work with extensive pigments. In any event, scholars consider this work among the best of the type, ranking it with the 13th century extant illustrations for the "Ukifune" chapters of THE TALE OF GENJI (Tokugawa Reimeikai Fd. and the Yamato Bunkakan collections), and probably produced by a professional atelier connected to the court.

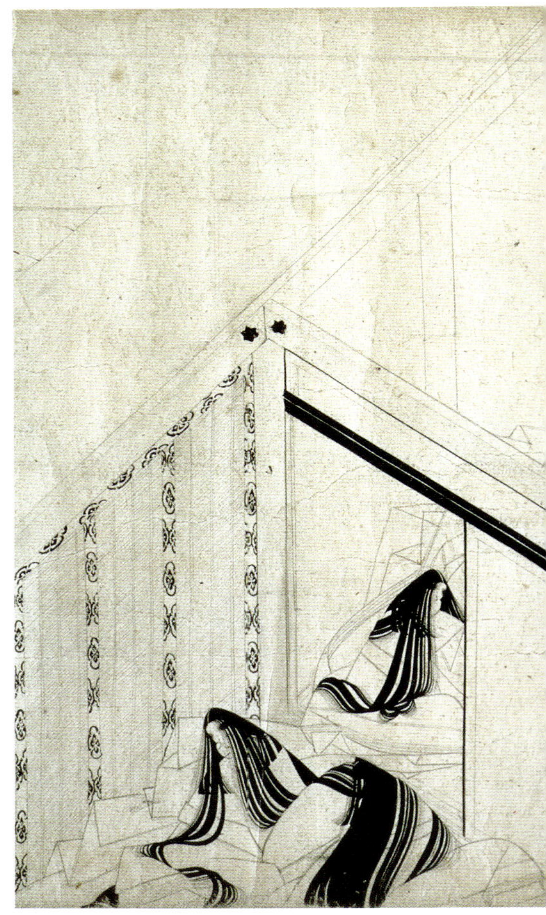

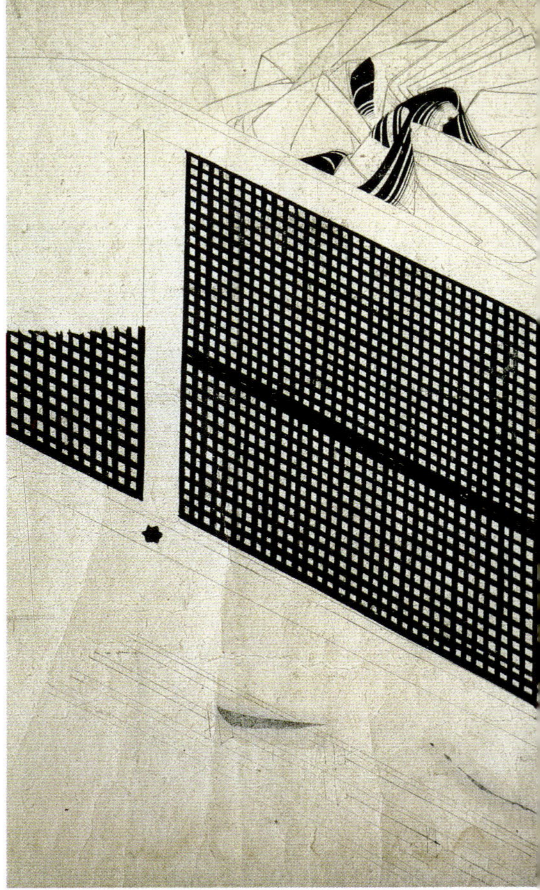

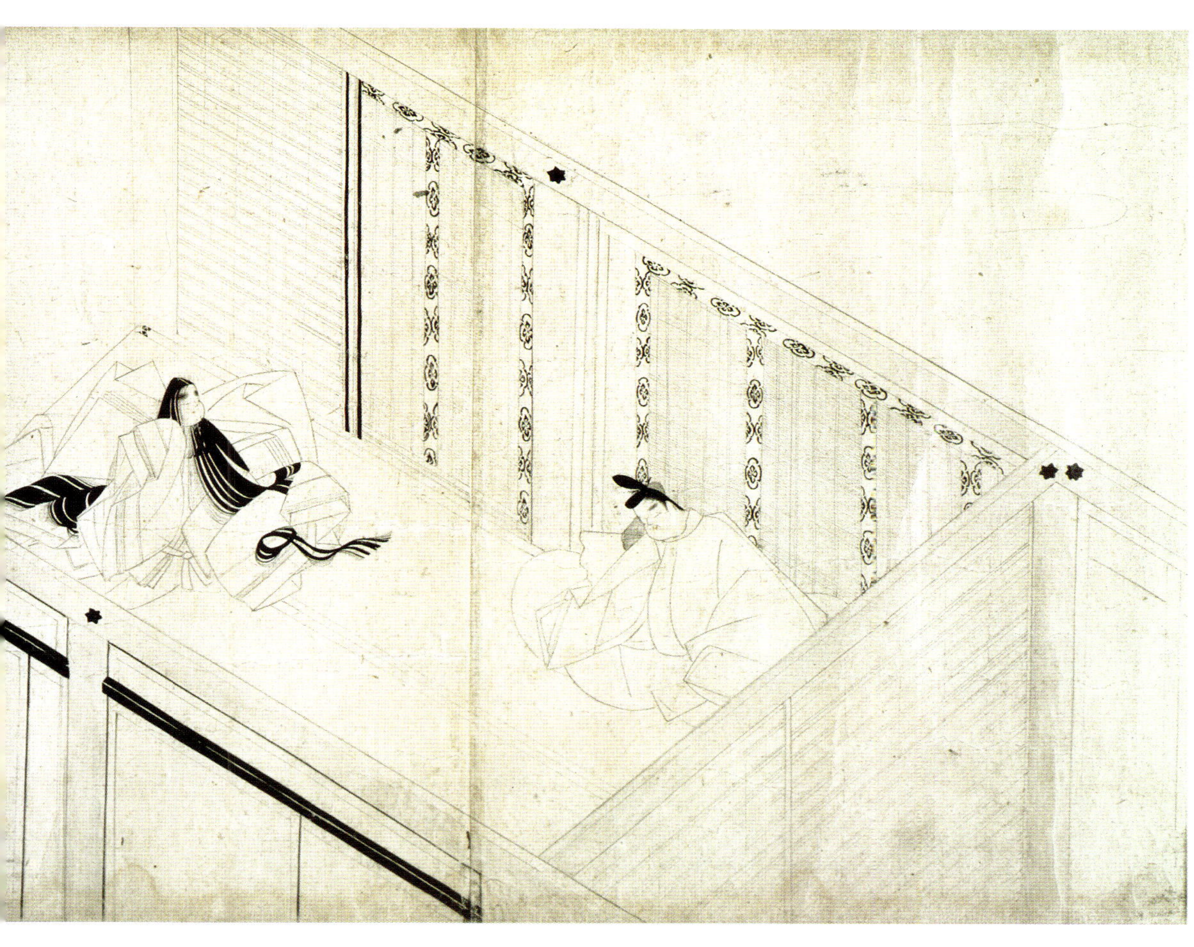

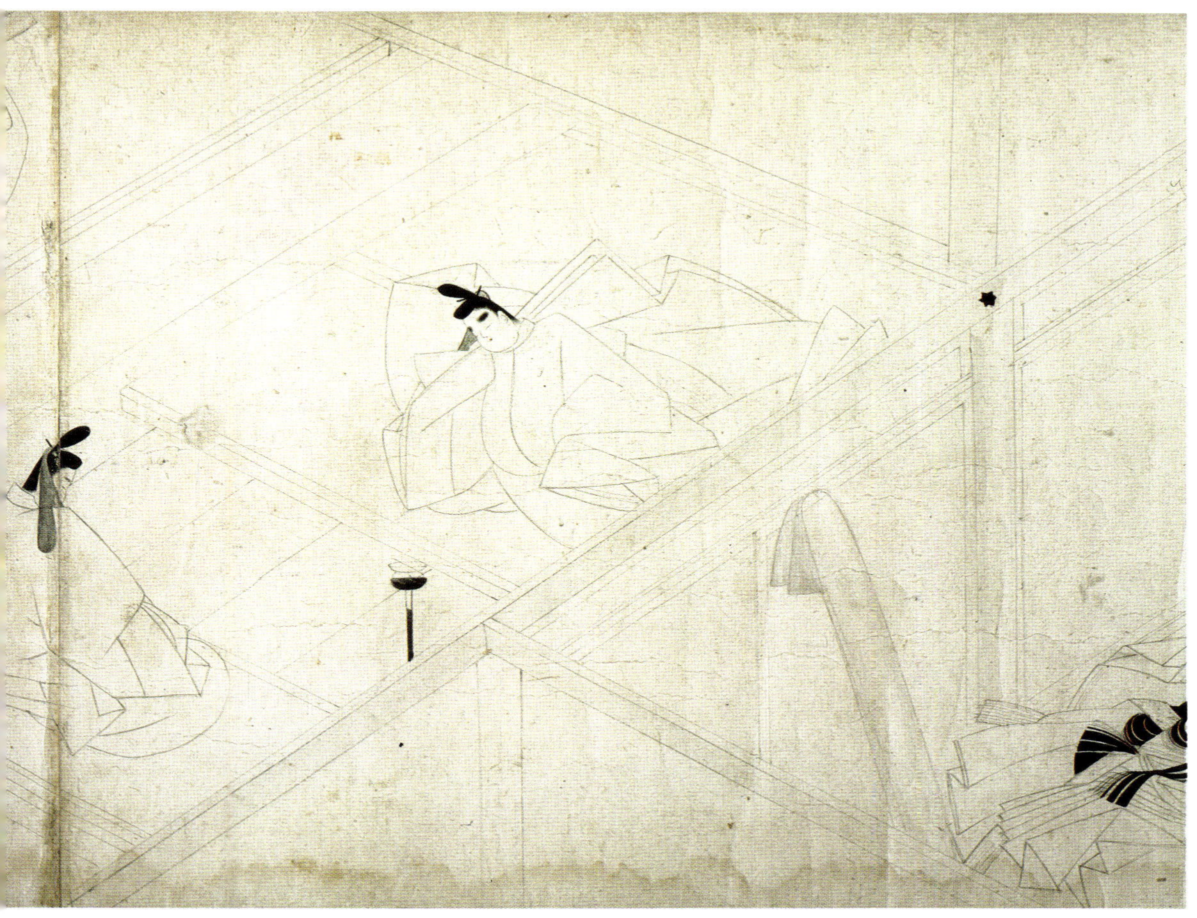

39

Merriments in Spring and Autumn
By Reizei Tamechika
春秋行楽図

Edo period, late 1850's
Pair of hanging scrolls; ink and colors on silk
Each, 202.2cm × 42.1cm
MOA Museum of Art (Sekai Kyūseikyō Foundation), Shizuoka

These paintings nostalgically depict scenes of aristocratic amusements set sometime in the distant past, based on Tamechika's extensive experience studying and copying old handscrolls in the *yamato-e* style. The painting on the right shows nobles gathered on the veranda for music. While ladies look on, they play the lute (*biwa*), flute, clappers and *sho* reedpipes. The abbreviated architectural setting captures the essence of Heian aristocratic dwellings, where flimsy shutters and screens could be removed to open the interior to the garden with its pond or flowing water. The left painting depicts young noblemen out in the hills gathering mushrooms.

Tamechika has carefully observed the importance of the changing seasons, each marked by conventional motifs (cherry blossoms for spring and mist and mushrooms for autumn) established in the Heian period and handed down both in the poetic canon and visual depictions.

Reizei Tamechika (1823–64), whose technical skill was evident at an early age, was adopted into the Kyoto branch of the Kanō school of painters. A monarchist in the troubled times at the end of the Edo period, he was influenced by the more politically active Ukita Ikkei and others to attempt a revival of *yamato-e*. In stylistic terms he injected, with mixed results, a measure of realism into the miniaturist, brightly colored and largely enervated *yamato-e* style of the Tosa school painters (despite his Kanō school affiliations), who were still known as the official painters to the court. Tamechika was assassinated in 1864 by lordless samurai who it is said were suspicious of his visits to the Sakai family. His visits had been innocent of political purpose, but rather to copy the 12th century Heian masterpiece in their collection, handscrolls of "The Courtier Ban Dainagon".

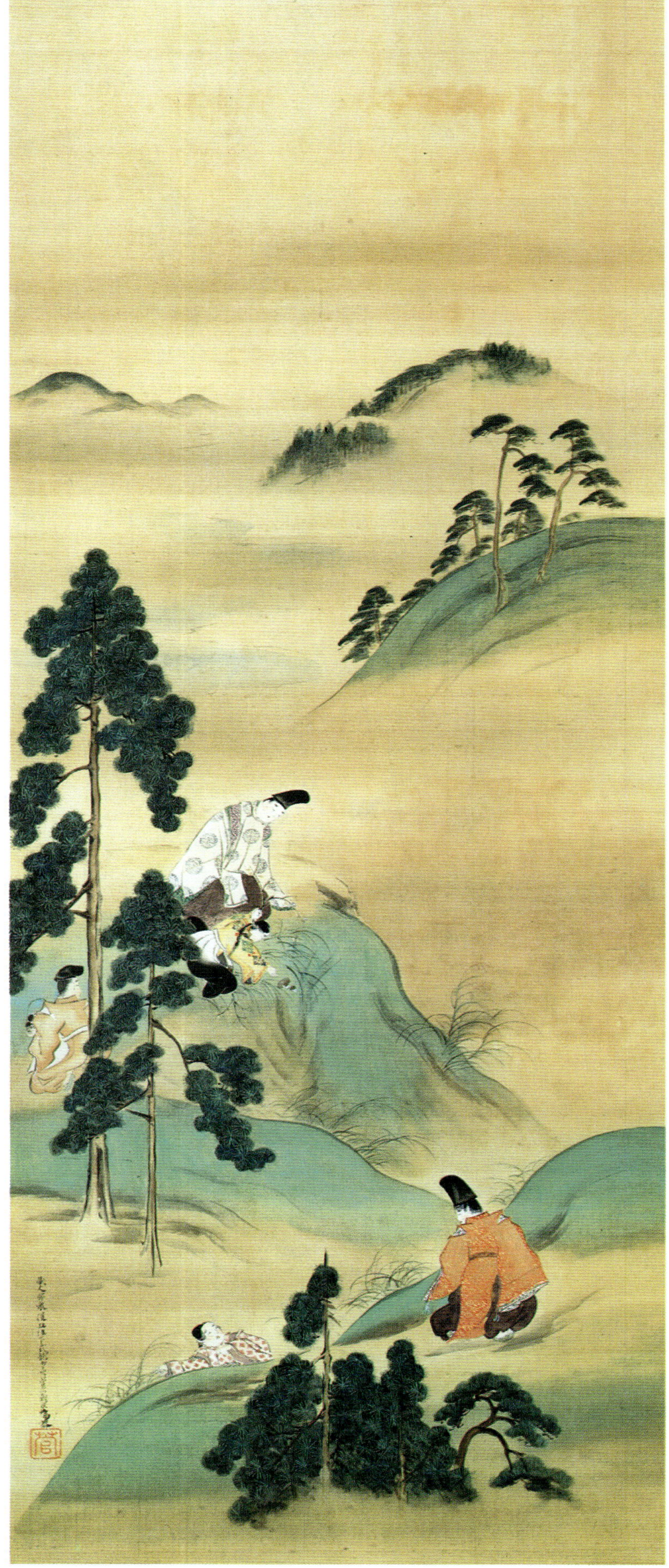

39-2

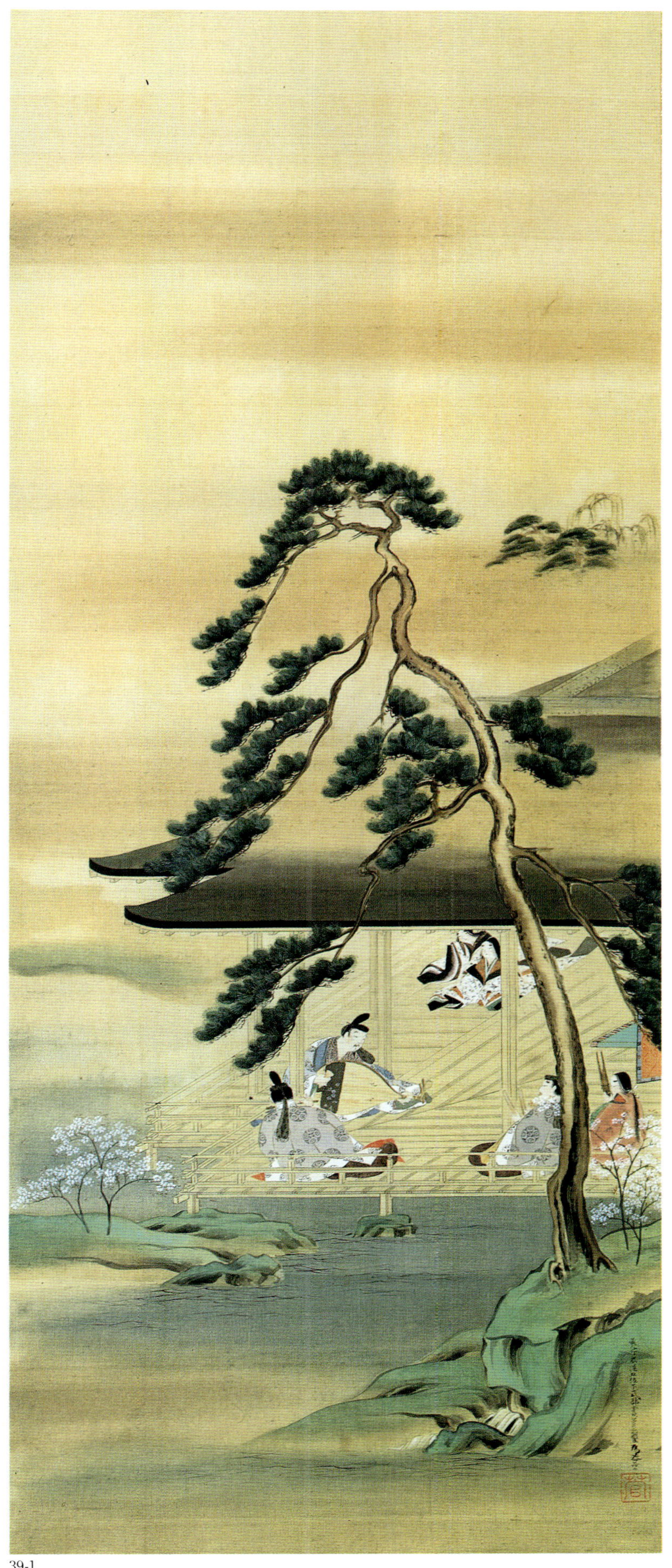

39-1

40

The Mirror Seller
By Reizei Tamechika
鏡売図

Edo period, 1850–55 (dated in inscription)
Ink and colors on silk
100.6cm × 48.7cm
Tokyo National Museum

The painting illustrates a story, written out
in the two colored rectangles at the top, from
the *Konjaku monogatari* ("Tales From Times
Now Past"), Vol.42 no.48, a large compendium
of edifying and religious tales assembled early
in the 12th century.

One rainy day in the Fifth month a woman
visited the nobleman Ōe no Sadamoto
(?–1034) with bronze mirrors for sale. He
noticed a paper attached to one, inscribed with
a Japanese-style (*waka*) poem about the transitoriness of life. Moved, his faith in Buddhism
deepened, prompting him eventually to take
the tonsure. The *Konjaku monogatari*
continues in another quasi-historical tale to
relate the recognition that Sadamoto received
for his religiosity in China where he went as
a pilgrim and eventually died.

This depiction by Tamechika (1823–64),
see Nos.35, 39, sets the figures of the nobleman, an attendant, and the woman in the main
section and corridor of a simplified Heian-
Kamakura aristocratic wooden dwelling, with
a cypress (*hinoki*) shingled roof. The raised
lattices and open walls put no barrier between
the interior and the garden. This not only epitomizes an important feature of traditional
domestic architecture, but allows the viewer to
see into the personal space of the figures.
Perhaps because so much of aristocratic life,
especially of the noblewomen, took place
indoors, artists depicting nobles, beginning in
the Heian period, relied on the artistic convention of open buildings, which extended
at times even to removing the roofs. And, as
with most secular painting in the courtly or
yamato-e tradition, there always is included
some depiction of nature — not wild and
awesome, but usually circumscribed and tame,
such as a seasonal symbol of a few flowers or
blossoming tree branch.

The central concept of the aristocratic
aesthetic embodied in this painting is that an
aspect of nature, whether in the single
metaphor of the standard, short Japanese-style
(*waka*) poem or a moment captured in a
painted scene, reflects the inner psychological
state of the individual. While no Heian painting is known that shows quite so clearly the
dripping rain off the eaves, the rain-bent plants
in the garden are a standard Heian poetic and
visual reference to melancholy and world-

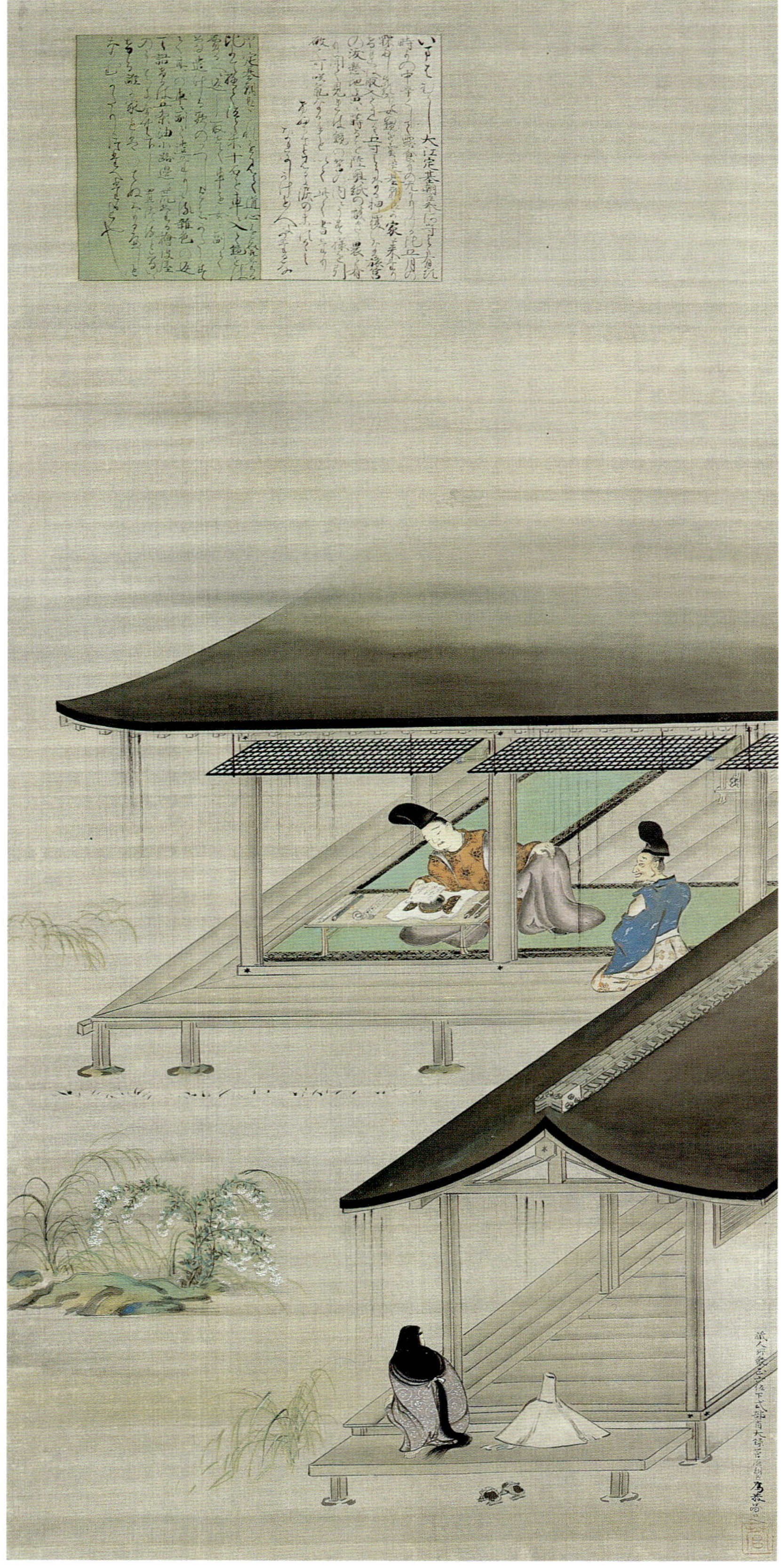

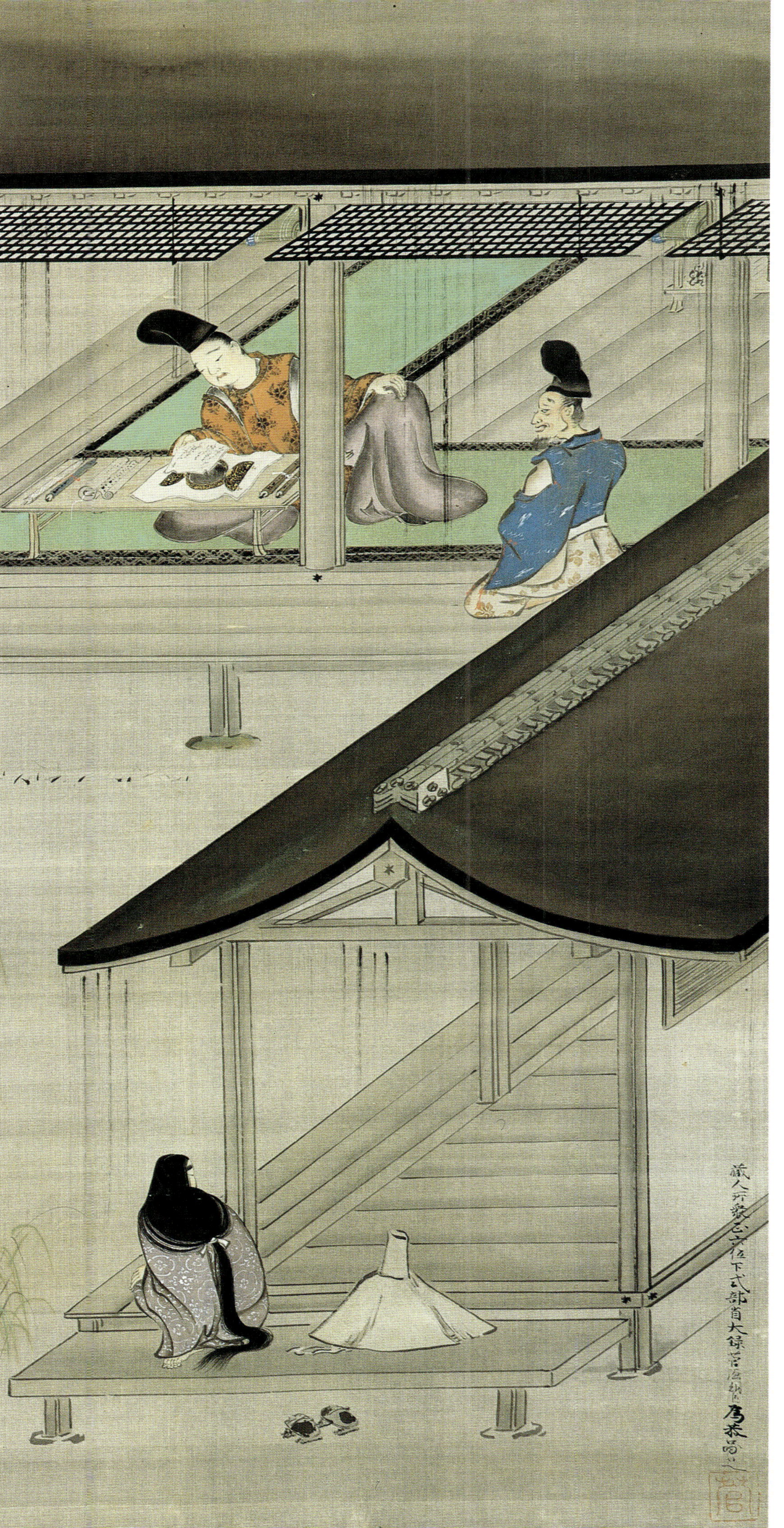

蔵人所衆忘六位下式部首大録官位加朝臣
為恭寫

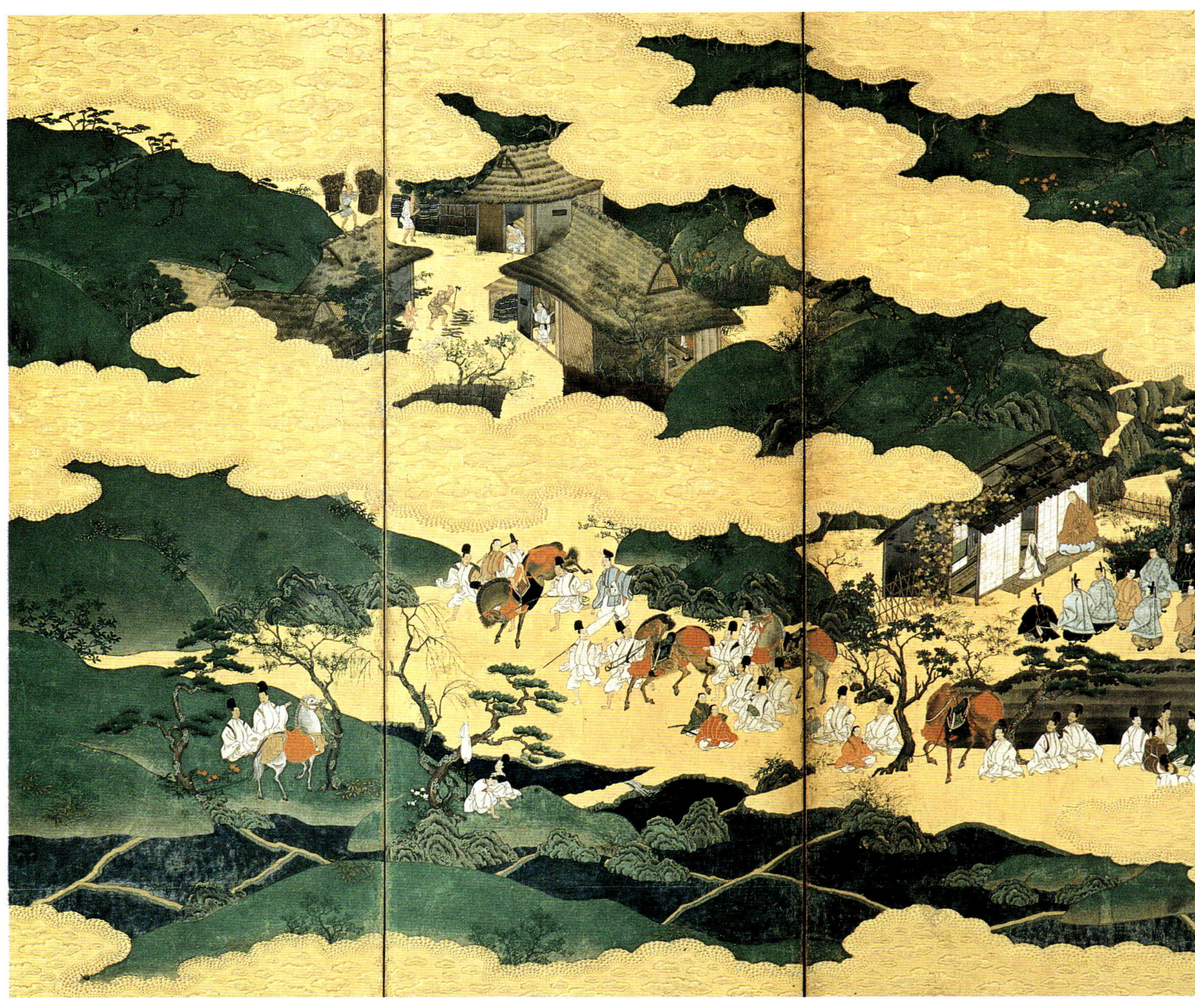

---

weariness.

Despite the overt Buddhism-tinged story basis, like so much of the art of the courtly tradition, the painting works on a simple emotional or immediately experiential level. It is not really necessary to know the tale. Beautiful designs, based on simplified elements of nature, while they can become so conventionalized as to be sentimental or even banal, are a strength of the tradition and an aspect that remains easily accessible to both Western and modern Japanese viewers.

41

Imperial Visit to Ōhara
大原行幸図屏風

Edo period, 17th century
Six-fold screen; colors and gold leaf on paper
150.0cm × 359.0cm
Fuji Art Museum, Tokyo

This screen illustrates the pathos-filled visit of the retired emperor Goshirakawa and his entourage to visit Kanreimon-in at the mountain nunnery of Jakkō-in in Ōhara, on the outskirts of Kyoto. Kanremon-in was the daughter of the mighty regent Taira no Kiyomori. He had installed his own family to replace the Fujiwaras in governing from behind the throne, and seen his daughter, consort to one of Goshirakawa's sons, produce the imperial heir. But in 1185 at the sea battle of Dannoura, the Minamoto warrior clan succeeded in defeating the Taira. This formally ended the Heian period because the Minamoto would move the seat of government to Kamakura. As the Taira forces were being completely destroyed, Kanreimon-in tried to drown

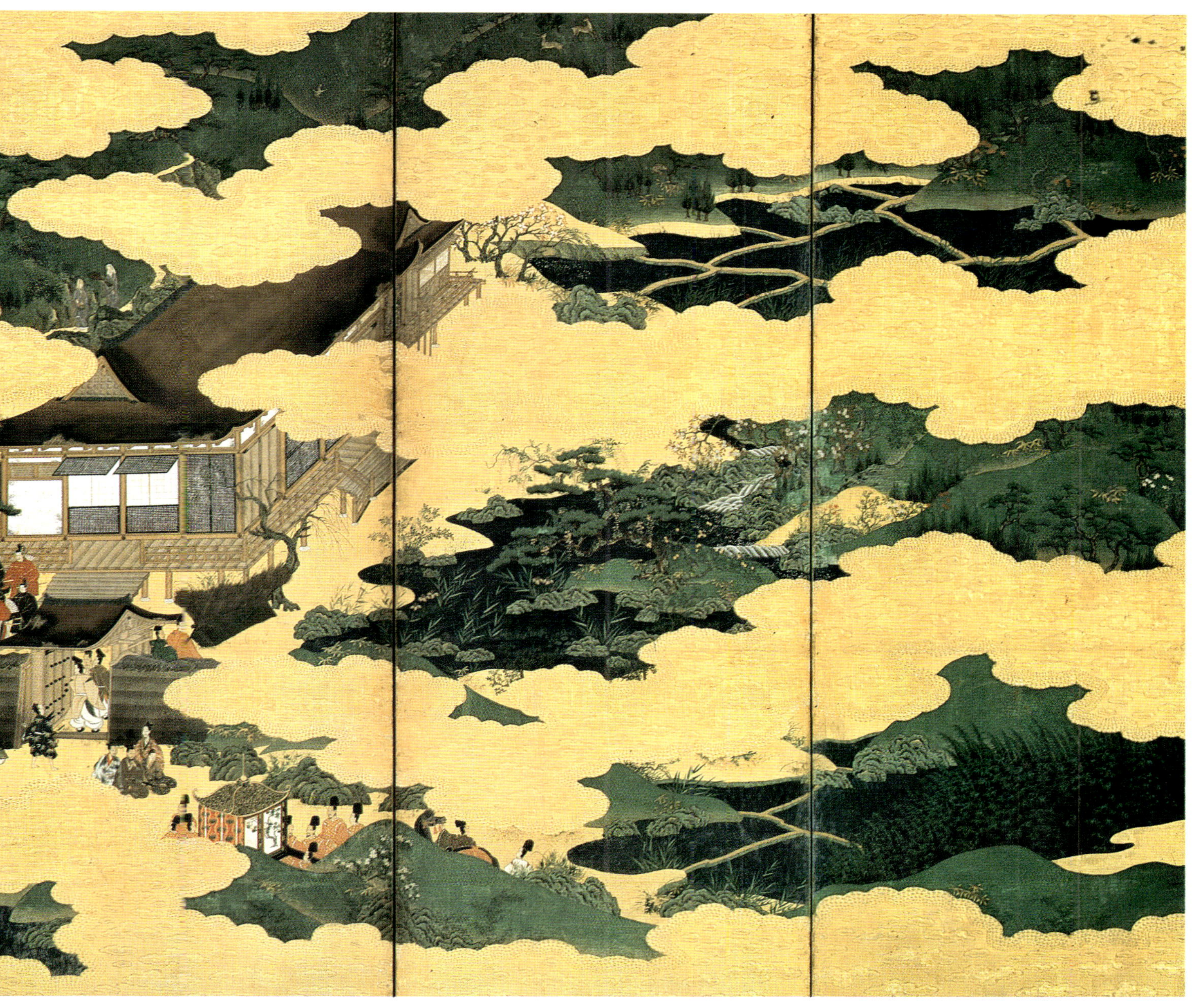

herself along with her mother and son, the child emperor Antoku (1178–85), but was rescued against her will to live, as a lone Taira survior, in impoverished seclusion at Ōhara.

In this depiction, her father-in-law Goshirakawa (shown standing on the veranda of the small building within the compound at left center) inquires after her, while two nuns, one of them Kanreimon-in, approach in amazement on the path at upper center.

The broad expanses of gold clouds (slightly patterned in relief) contrast with the rich greens of the landscape. The style of the human figures and brushwork in the rocks recall the slightly earlier *yamato-e* Tosa school style of the Momoyama period.

According to THE TALE OF THE HEIKE (*Heike monogatari*), the romantic history of the rise and fall of the Taira family compiled in the 13th century, on which the scene is based, Goshirakawa and Kanreimon-in pass this afternoon in 1186 reminiscing in tears about the glorious past and what might have been. The meeting is the still young and beautiful Kanreimon-in's only contact with the outside world until her death more than 20 years later.

Most paintings of THE TALE OF THE HEIKE, which were popular among warrior patrons in the 16th–18th centuries, depict battle scenes. Only this one non-military episode found a consistent audience. Perhaps its popularity lay in the portrayal of such poignant emotions. Later generations also appreciated the survival of aristocratic ideals and the imperial family (personified by wily Goshirakawa who survived his own intrigues against both the Taira and Minamoto) despite the vicissitudes of a succession of warrior families.

42 ○

Mirror, With Design of Cranes Carrying Pine Branches

松喰鶴鏡

Heian period, 12th century
Cast bronze: diameter 11.5cm
Agency for Cultural Affairs

The design on the reverse of this bronze mirror is of cranes with pine branches in their bills, circling the chrysanthemum-shaped standard center knob intended for a rope tassel. This crane design was a popular Japanized motif from the mid-Heian period (10th century) that shows the tendency to move away from the mythical and hieratic figures found on Chinese mirrors to feature more naturalistic motifs familiar to Japanese aristocratic patrons and artists. From the late 9th century when official contacts with China ceased, the Japanese arts of the Heian period increasingly show natural motifs usually rendered in linear, outlined forms.

Cast bronze mirrors like this, and Cat. Nos.17, 43-45, would have had the face polished smooth and plated with tin to give a good reflecting surface for cosmetic use. This mirror however, remains unplated, suggesting that soon after casting it received its incised engraving of a Thousand-Armed (Jp: Senjū) Kannon, by, in this case, a not very expert hand. The puncture holes also show that it was hung for Buddhist-Shinto worship (see Cat. No.17).

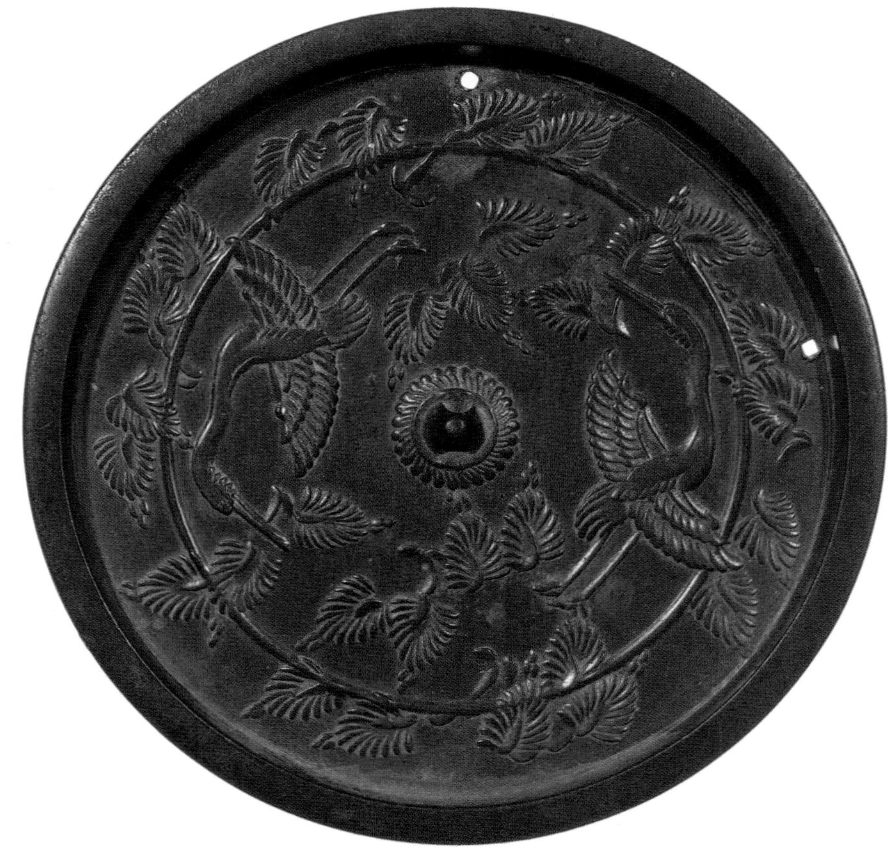

43

Mirror, With Design of a Pair of Birds
and Butterflies Amid Autumn Grasses
秋草双鳥鏡

Heian period, 12th century
Cast bronze; diameter 9.4cm
Agency for Cultural Affairs

This mirror and Cat. No.44 bear relief
designs on the reverse of a pair of sparrow-like
birds set amid autumn plants and grasses.
Added here are two butterflies, another motif
favored by Heian aristocrats. The designs are
not arranged in rigid symmetrical fashion, but
rather as naturalistic scenes where, especially
on this mirror the birds appear to be flying
though a palpable parting amid plants in a wild
meadow. The mirrors typify the naturalistic
designs and seasonal motifs of Heian aristocratic taste that crystallized in the 10th/11th
century.

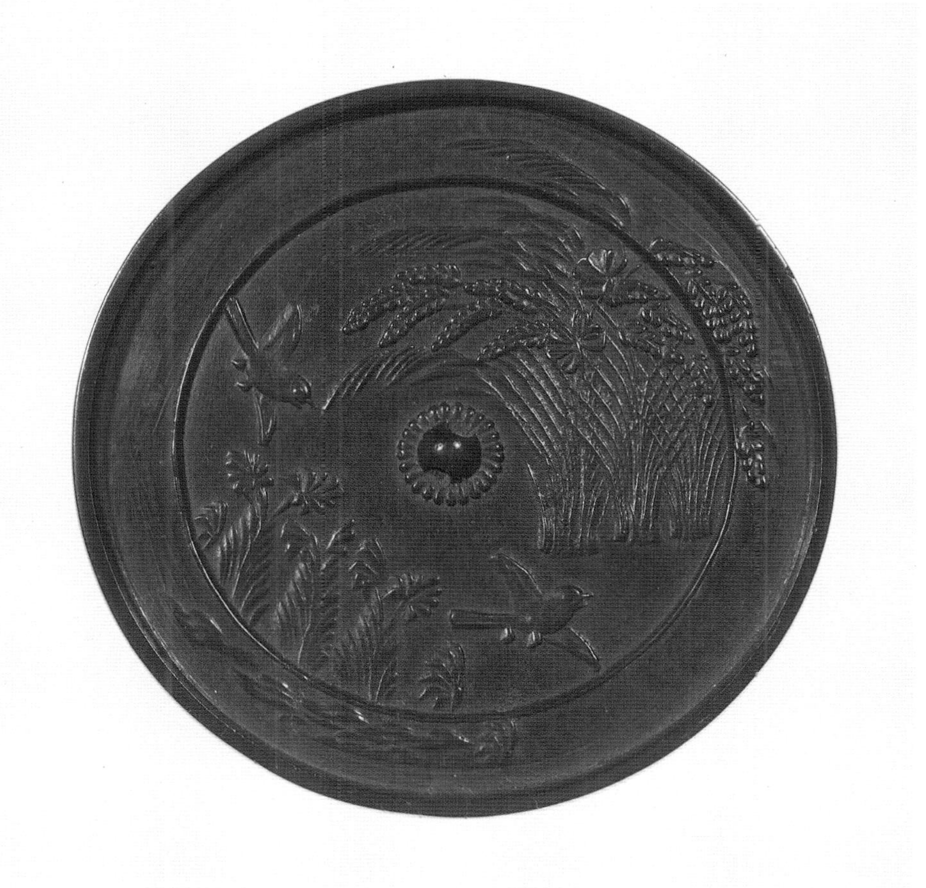

44

Mirror, With Design of a Pair of Birds Amid Autumn Grasses
秋草蝶鳥鏡

Heian period, 12th century
Cast bronze; diameter 11.5cm
Agency for Cultural Affairs

See explanation under Cat. No.43.

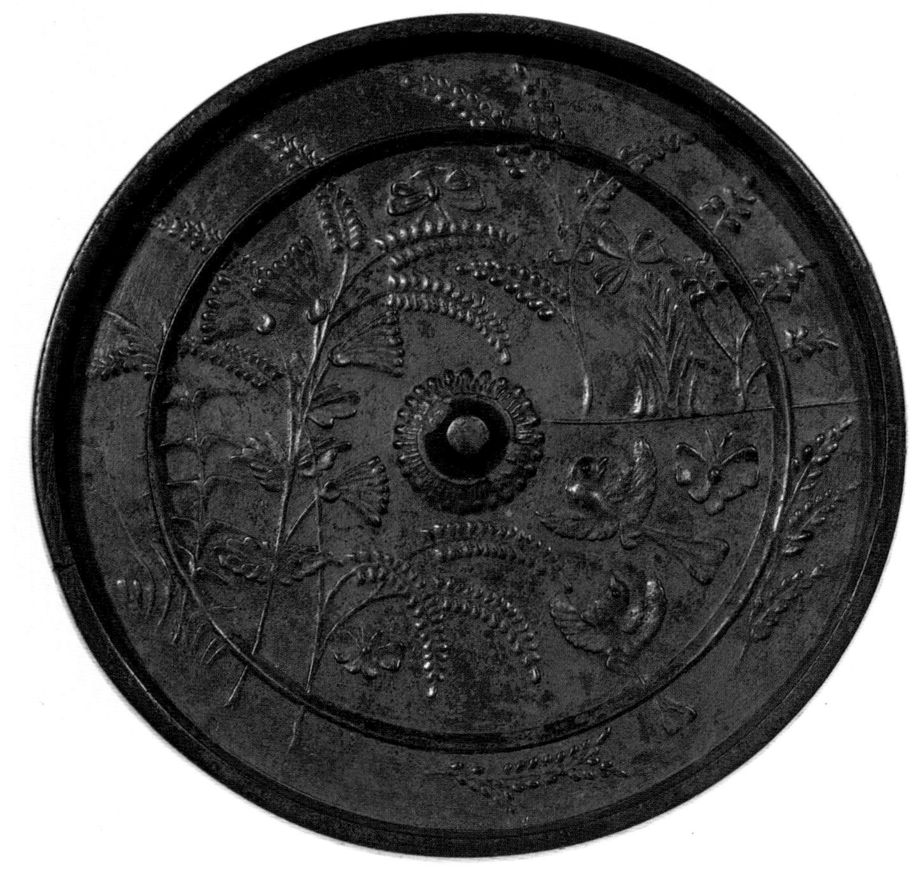

45

Mirror, With Design of Birds Amid Floating Wheels in a Stream
片輪車双鳥鏡

Heian period, 12th century
Cast bronze; diameter 10.3cm
Agency for Cultural Affairs

The mirror displays a pair of birds and partially submerged ox-cart wheels with a stylized stream motif in the outer border. This favorite motif of the 10th–14th centuries, called "partial wheels" (*katawa-guruma*), apparently was inspired by the prosaic sight of wooden cart-wheels kept half submerged in a stream or pond to prevent drying and cracking when not in use. In a similar way to mirrors No.42–44, a familiar Japanese scene from everyday life was incorporated into the design repertoire. The puncture hole shows that the mirror was probably suspended to use at a shrine, see Cat No.17.

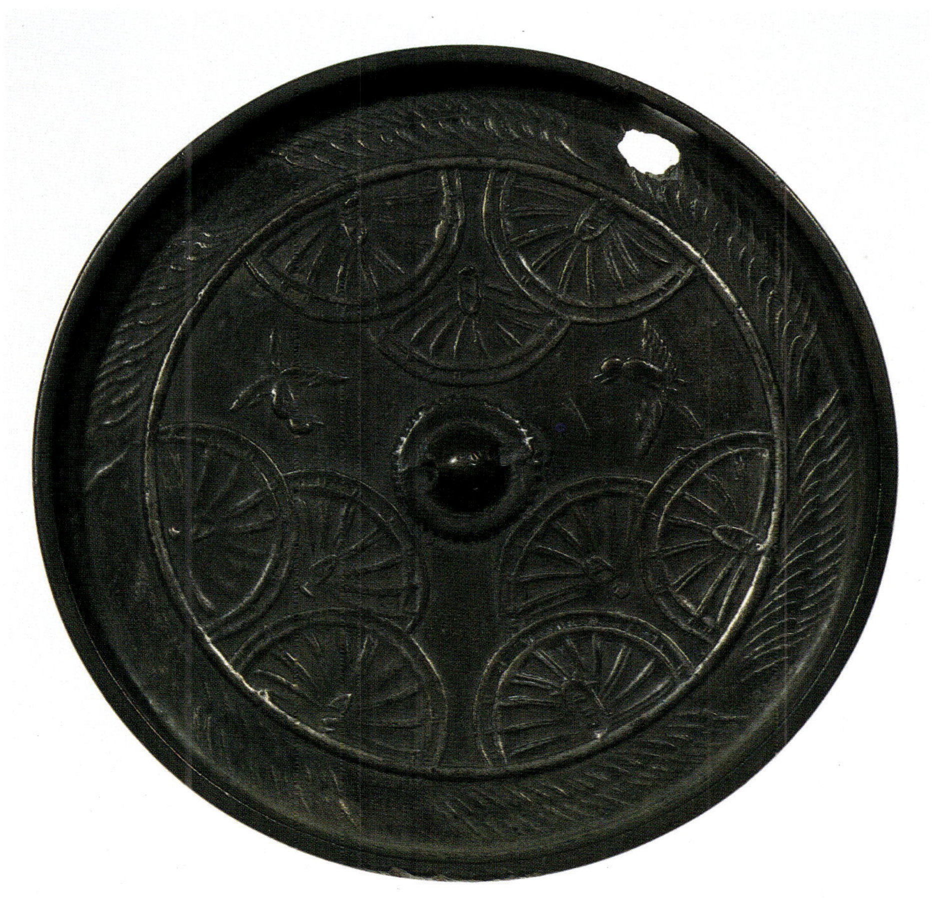

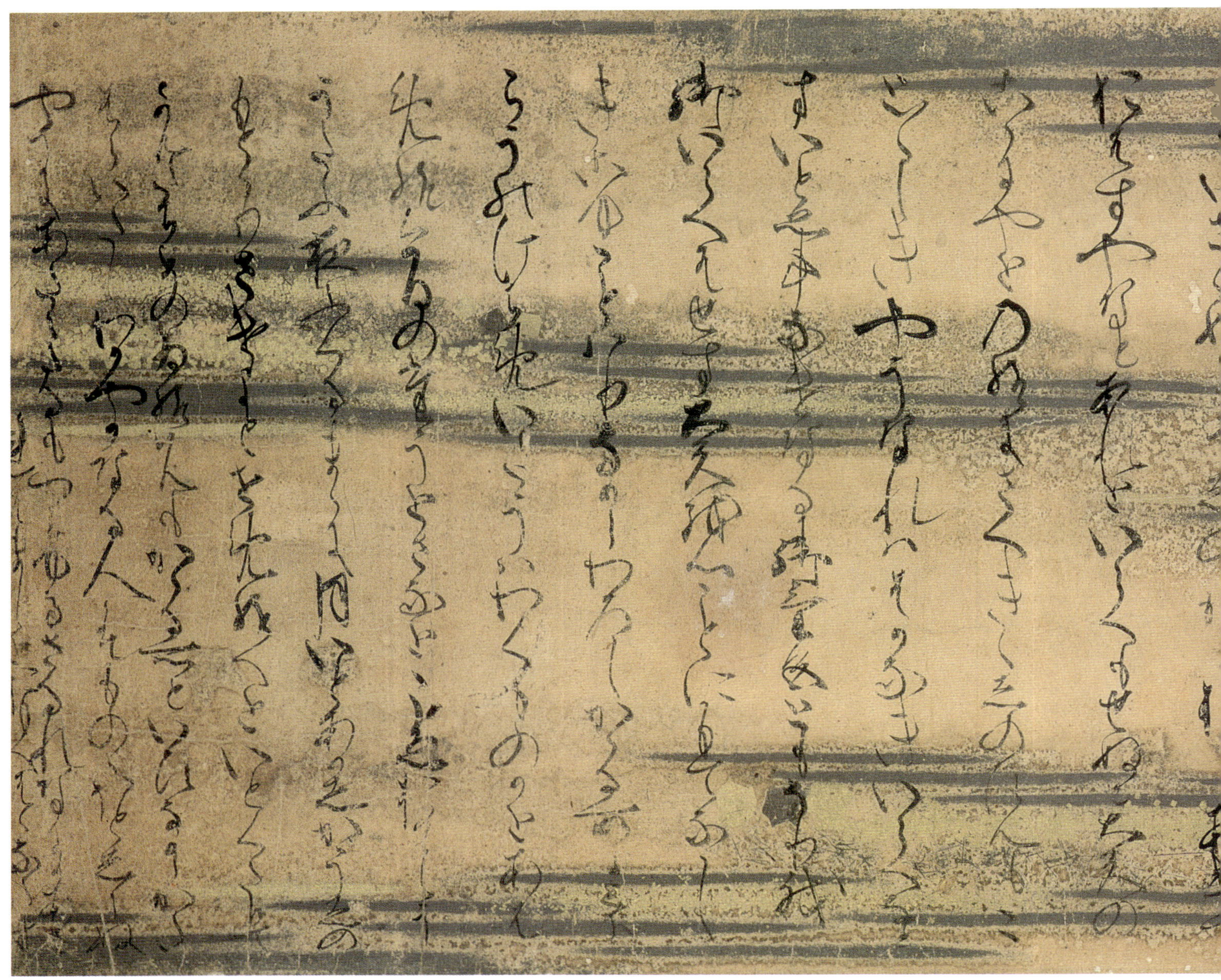

46-1

46 ⊙

Sections from *The Illustrated Diary of Murasaki Shikibu*
紫式部日記絵詞

Kamakura period, mid 13th century
Two sections of text and paintings; ink and
colors on paper, width 21.0cm
Gotoh Museum, Tokyo

These sections of text and their paintings
(now mounted separately for preservation)
depict two episodes from THE DIARY OF
MURASAKI SHIKIBU. Court lady Murasaki
Shikibu (dates uncertain; died *ca* 1015) is
renowned as the author of the great romantic
novel, THE TALE OF GENJI. The diary, or
more accurately, set of memoirs, along with a
volume of poetry is her only other work. It
consists of her reminiscences of a two year
period of court service to Empress Shōshi
(Akiko), daughter of Fujiwara no Michinaga,
which centers on the births of Princes Atsuhira
in 1008 and Atsunaga in 1009. These princes
(eventually becoming emperors) assured
Michinaga's, and his branch of the Fujiwara
family, ascendancy, giving him the real political power by governing as regent from behind
the throne. Murasaki Shikibu's account,
although biased towards her patron, accurately
reflects other records.

This mid-13th century illustrated version
of THE DIARY, which originally probably
consisted of 10 handscrolls, is the oldest transcription to survive. It is extant today only in
3 handscrolls and detached segments (including these two sections) of a fourth scroll scattered in various collections along with the
Gotoh Museum.

In order of the events, the first of the Gotoh
scenes (17th of the Tenth month, 1008) shows
two courtiers, returning through the palace

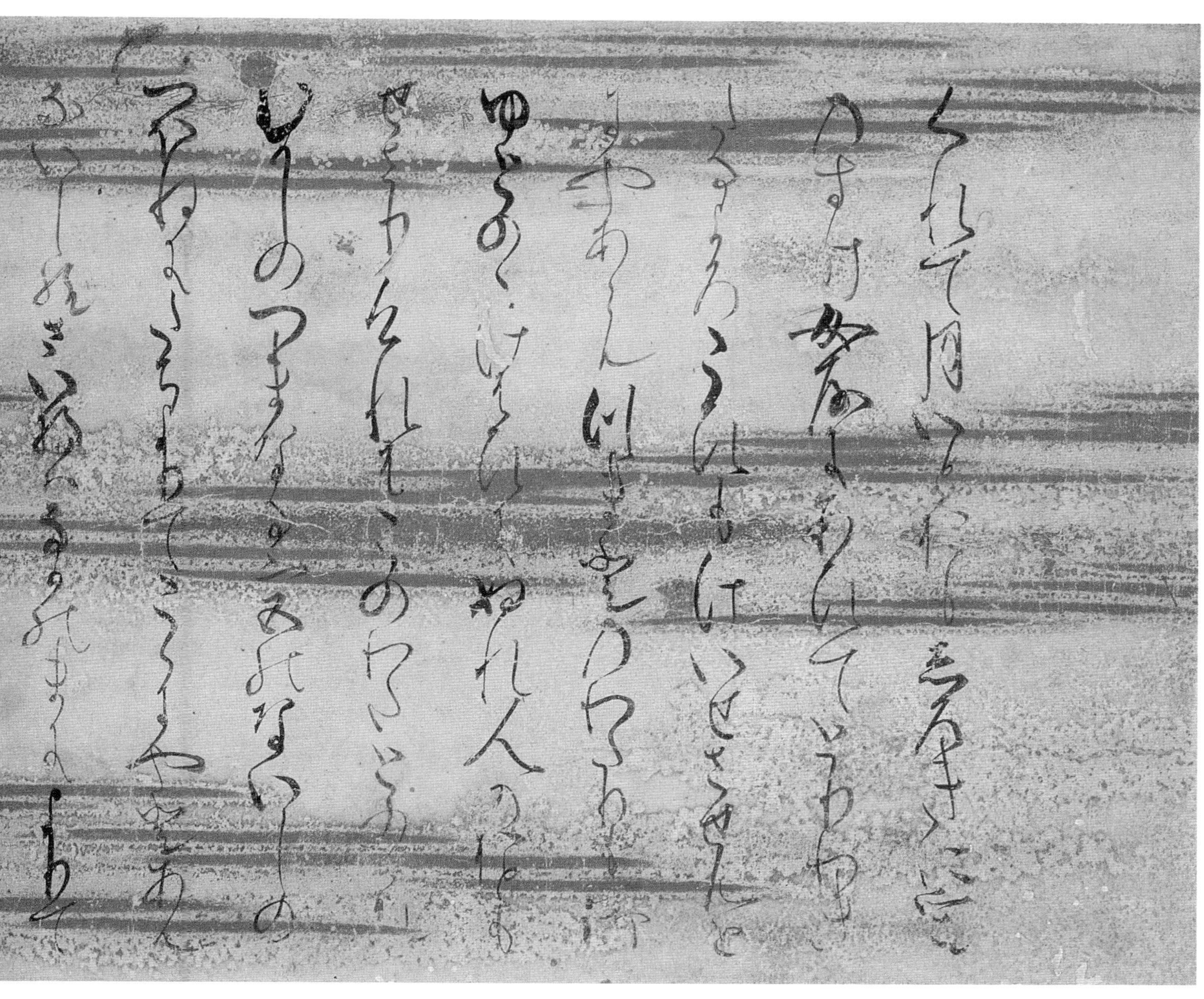

complex by moonlight after the birth of Prince Astuhira, stopping for a little dalliance at Murasaki's rooms. The figure holding ajar the lattice-shutter may represent Murasaki Shikibu or perhaps an attendant while the lady stands behind. The plump faces of the nobles are rendered in the abbreviated mask-like artistic conventions (slit eyes, small red mouths) established since the end of the Heian period for the portrayal of the nobility. It is said that this permitted the early viewers, who intimately knew the stories and poems involved, to more readily identify themselves with the characters. As in most painting in the *yamato-e* tradition, the emotions of the scene are conveyed in the aesthetic effects of color and pattern rather than realistic facial depictions. The off-center placement heightens a sense of (pleasurable) danger as the bold, flattened forms of the courtiers' costumed figures loom large over the ladies. Yet Murasaki Shikibu, just like the delicate dew-drenched plants in the moonlit garden, manages to hold her own, as if reinforced by the strong linearity of the lattice-shutters.

The second painting (1st of the Eleventh month, 1008) depicts part of the ceremonies, including an offering of food dishes supervised by the ladies of the household, for Prince Atsuhira, held in his mother's arms, on the 50th day after his birth. Murasaki Shikibu is thought to be shown observing the scene from lower right. The bold lines of the interior (revealed by the artistic convention of removing the roof) frame the baby prince in whom so many hopes reside. Although some of the opaque pigments (i.e. green of the *tatami* mat flooring) have flaked off, many of the exquisite and detailed patterns, for example on the robes, remain.

Because the paintings were done more than 200 years after Murasaki Shikibu lived, and

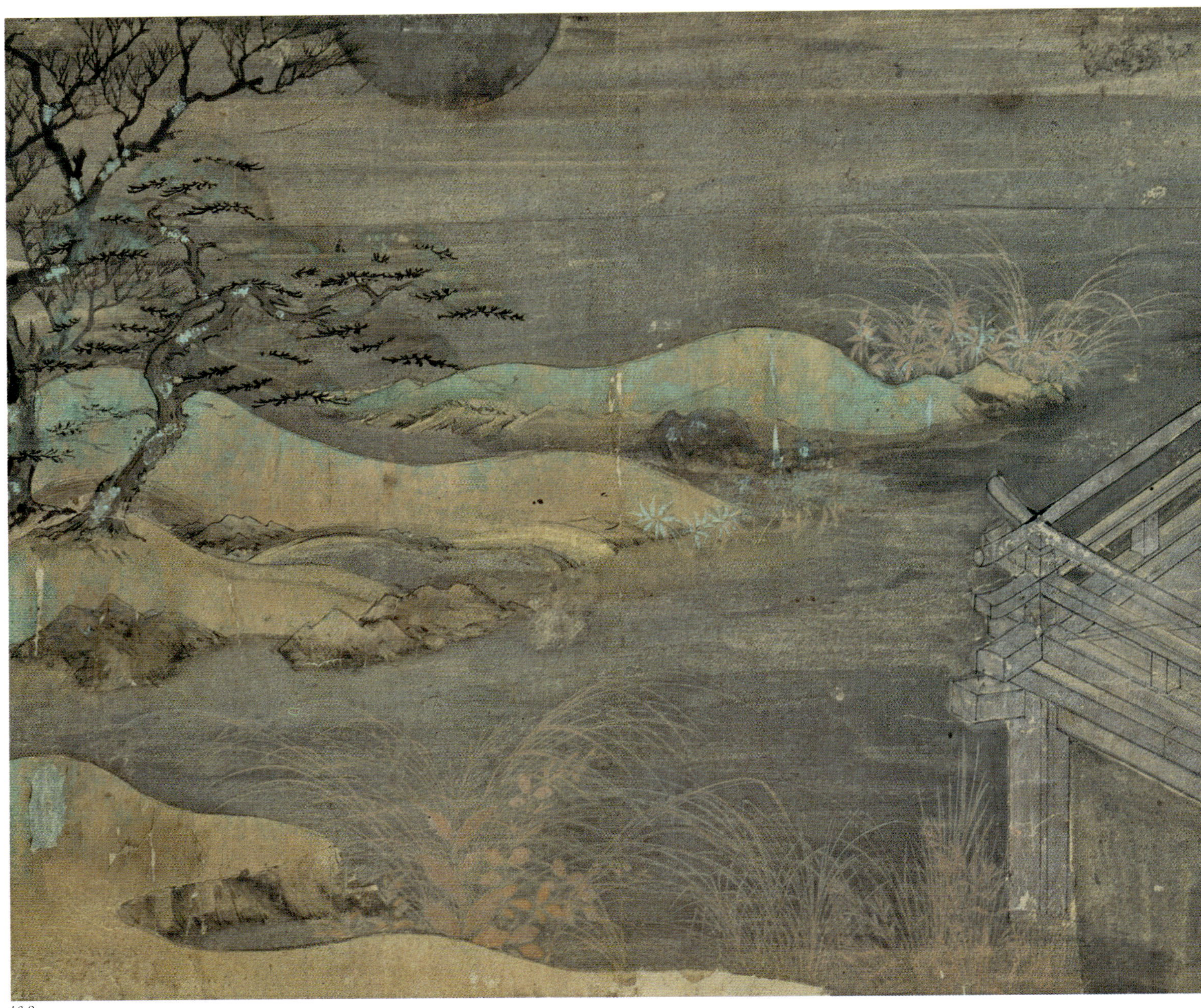

46-2

depict aristocratic life in the 13th century, some details, such as minor aspects of the fashions depicted, had changed since her time. But aristocratic taste and customs tended to be extemely conservative, and so the paintings convey well the ambiance of Heian aristocratic life. The noble patron(s) who commissioned the work nostalgically looked back to the golden age of the aristocracy just at a time (mid-13th century) when the fortunes of the remaining Kyoto nobles seemed about to rally.

The paintings are considered to be the product of a single atelier connected to the court. Compared to the famous mid-12th century *Illustrated Handscrolls of The Tale of Genji,* the compositions are more patternized and decorative, which reflects a major trend in *yamato-e* handscroll painting associated with the court ateliers during the 12th–14th centuries. The text passages were brushed in ink on paper decorated with cloud patterns achieved by sprinkling pieces of gold and silver foil interspersed with larger flakes. The calligraphic hand, although not yet conclusively identified, is thought to be one individual working around the 1240's.

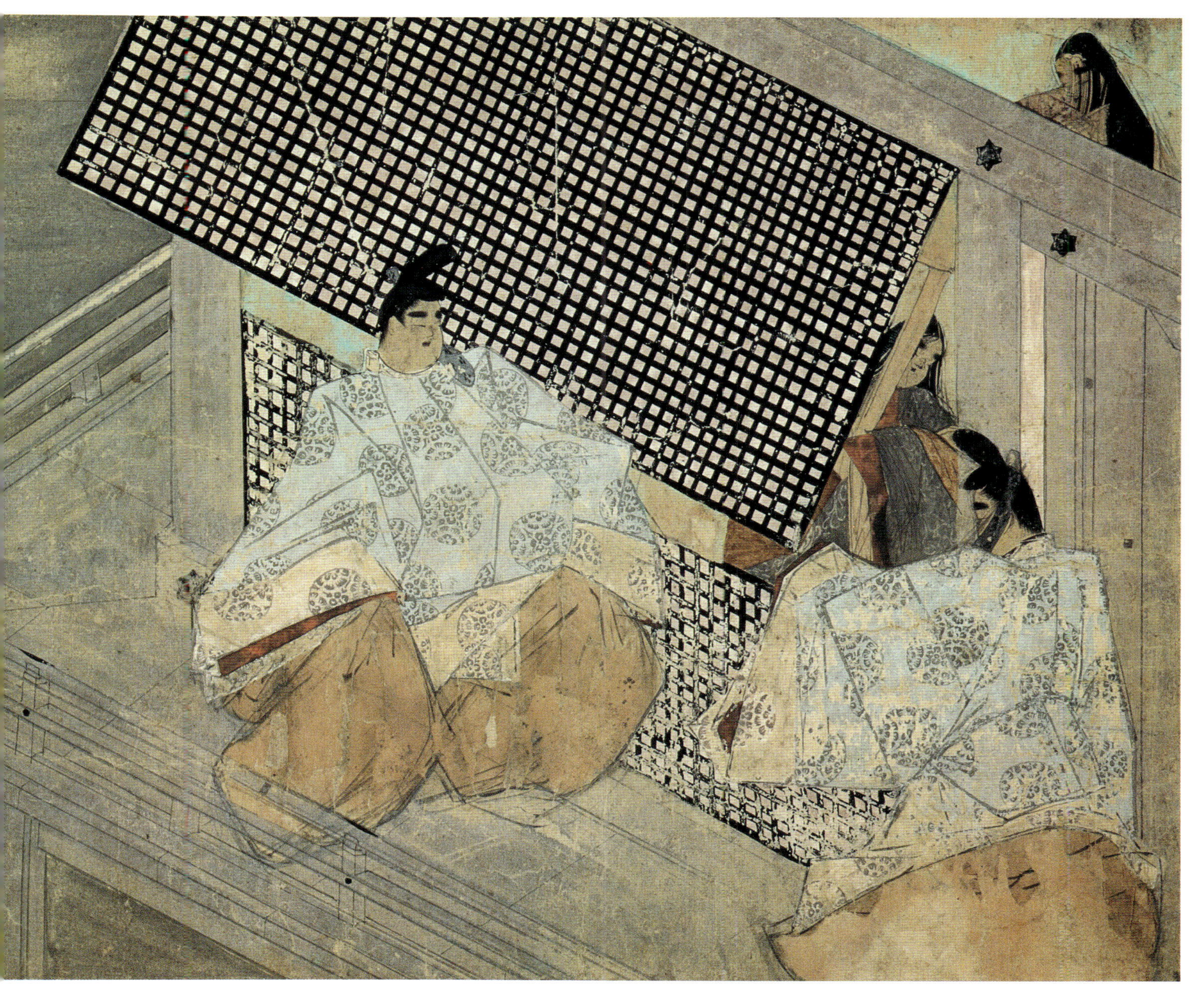

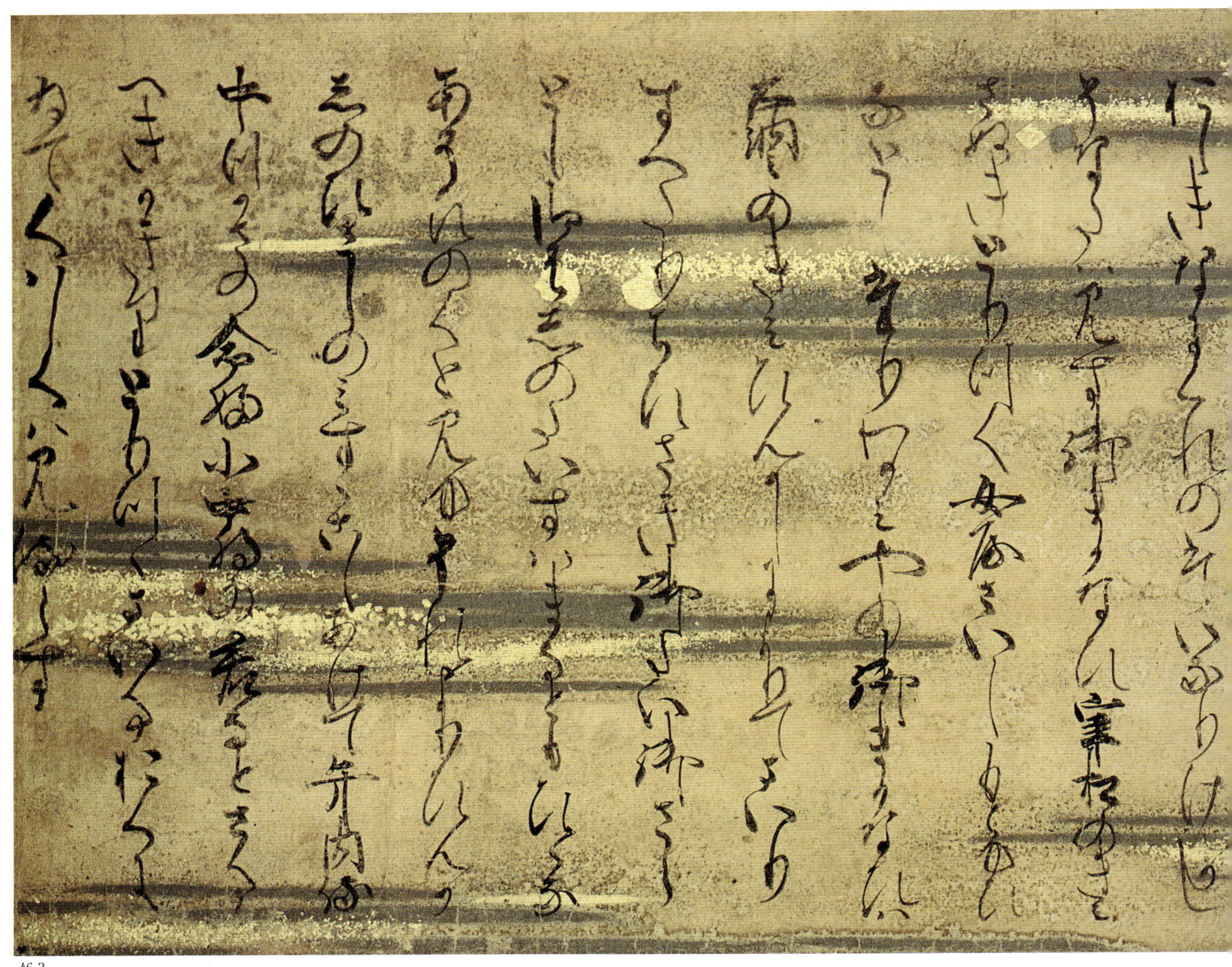

46-3,

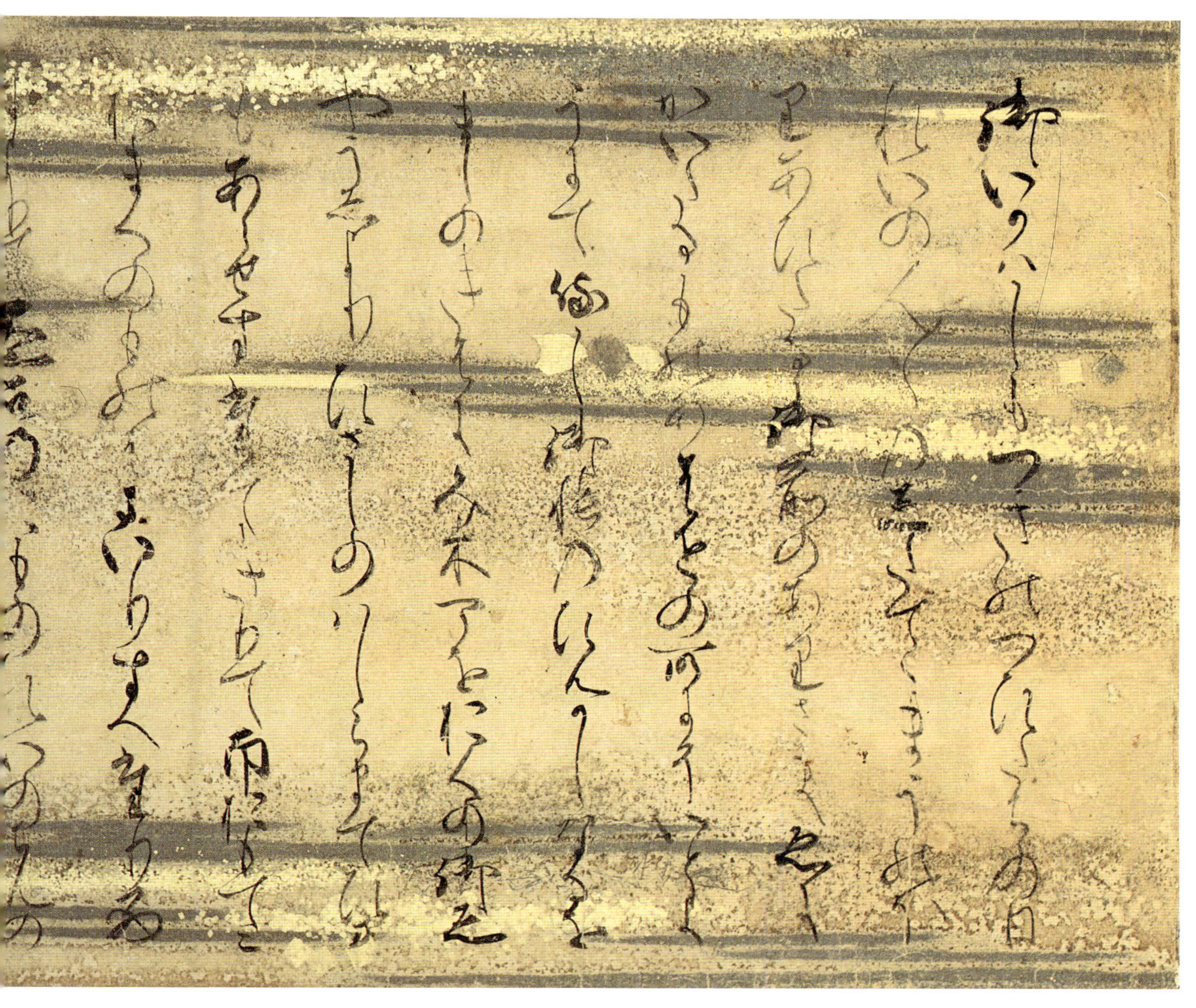

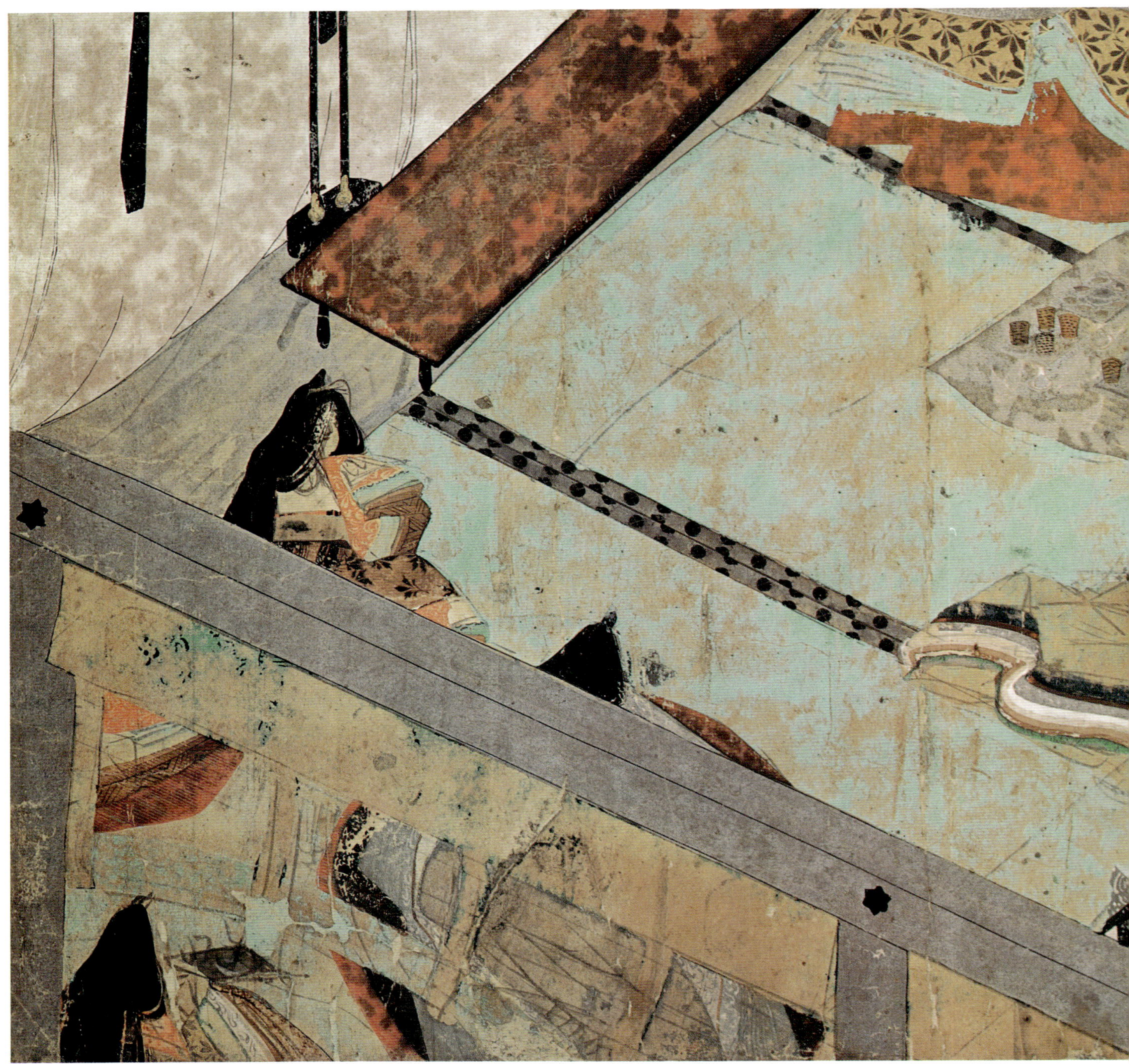

46-4

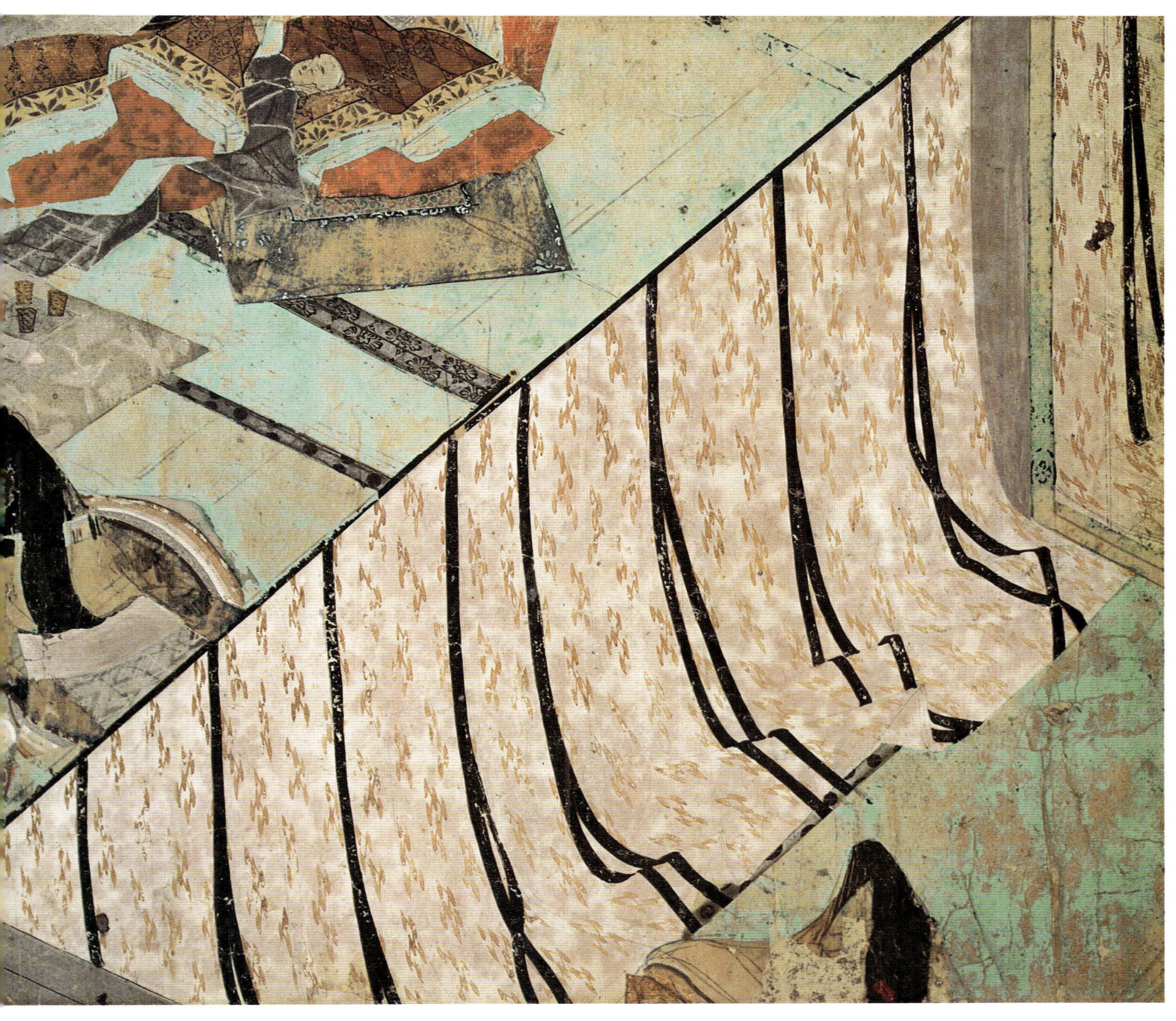

47

Fifty-Four Scenes from THE TALE OF
GENJI
By Tosa Mitsuyoshi
源氏物語図

Edo period, 17th century
Album; colors and gold-leaf on paper
Each 25.7cm × 22.5cm
Kyoto National Museum

Tosa Mitsuyoshi (1539-1613) used bright,
opaque (mainly mineral) colors and employed
extensive gold pigment, dust and gold-leaf,
especially in the cloud patterns which divide
and frame each scene, to create compositions
extravagant in their pattern combinations.
The Tosa school, which became identified as
the painters of the court atelier in the 14th
century, was largely unconcerned with the
pyschological realism or emotional introspec-
tion found in late Heian or Kamakura *yamato-e*
handscrolls on which the Tosa style was based.
Mitsuyoshi was free to exploit to the hilt the
rich effects of color and fine-line detailing,
such as in the beautiful patterns of the costumes.

THE TALE OF GENJI is a long romance,
now in fifty-four chapters, written in all pro-
bability by the noblewoman, Murasaki Shikibu
(see Cat. No.46) in the first quarter of the 11th
century. It describes private aristocratic life of
the period by centering on the personal events
and emotional developments of the hero,
Genji, the many ladies in his life, and in later
chapters, his progeny. THE TALE OF GENJI
is available in English translation by Arthur
Waley, or more recently Edward Seidensticker
(1976).

In the Mitsuyoshi work the choice of scenes
from each of the fifty-four chapters and of basic
compositions down to seasonal motifs and
certain props was largely decided by tradition.
Indeed Mitsuyoshi, who suceeded to the
headship of the Tosa school when Tosa
Mitsumoto was killed in battle in 1569, did
much to establish firmly the conventions and
style for Tosa depictions of THE TALE OF
GENJI. His influence has irrevocably linked
the Tosa school with these miniaturist, colorful representations.

A working knowledge of the episodes and
poems that mark the high points of THE TALE
OF GENJI was expected of any cultivated
aristocrat, or any warrior and his lady. Extensive narrative text passages from the novel
were unnecessary (and probably unreadable)
for Mitsuyoshi's audience. And while the years
of civil wars that racked the 16th century
before the re-unification of the nation and final
imposition of peace under the Tokugawa
shoguns (from 1603) meant many rough
warriors had little time for literary or artistic
pursuits — certainly the educated ideal was
maintained. Short texts with one or two poems
accompany each painting in these albums.

Recently the paintings were repaired and
remounted for preservation into four albums
from what had been two. At the time, ink seal
marks of Mitsuyoshi's artistic name (and
eventually religious name after taking the
tonsure) Kyūyoku, were found on the back
support of all the paintings. Only about 20
extant paintings are attributable by style and
quality to Mitsuyoshi, and these scenes are
among the few that actually bear his name.

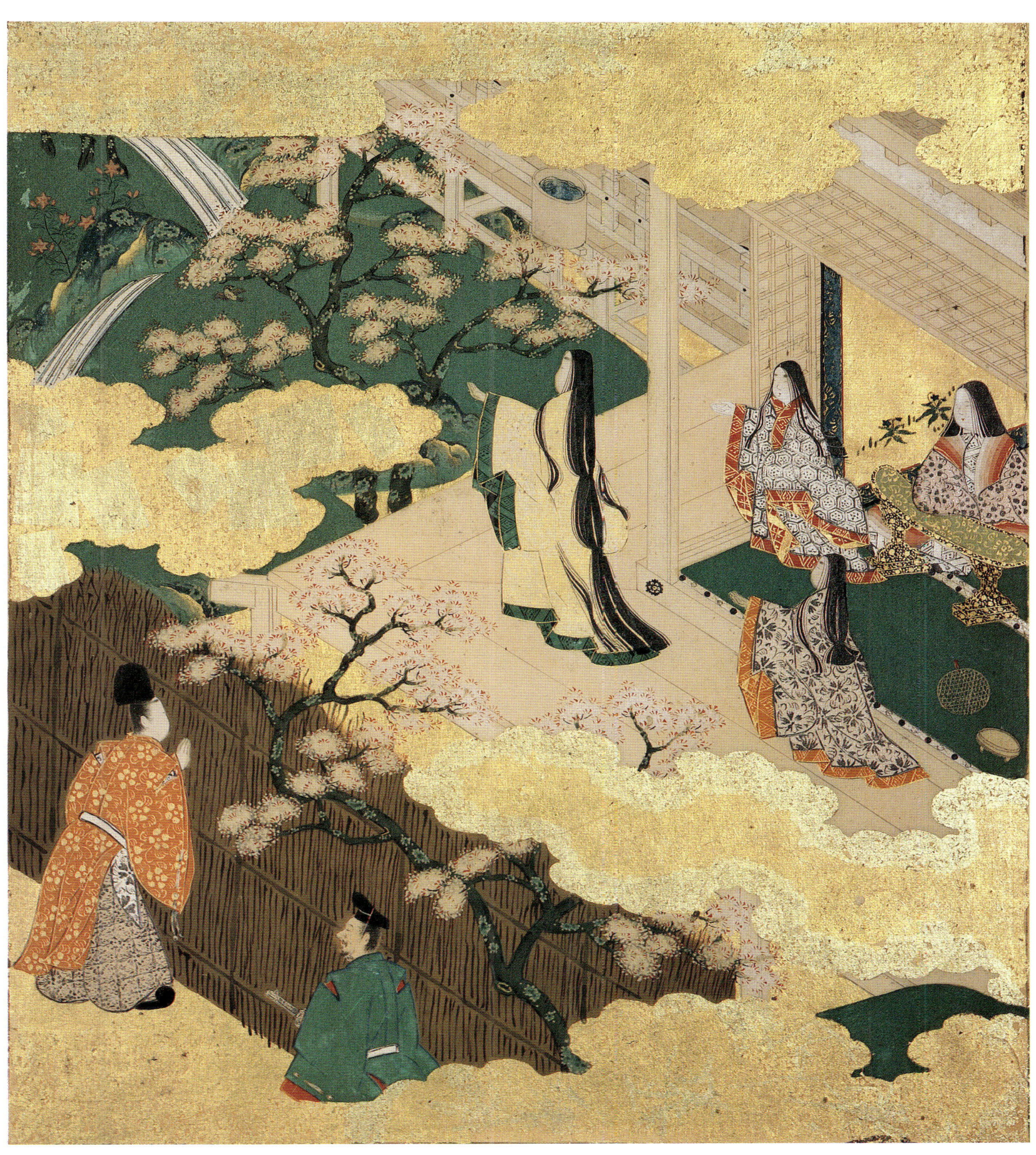

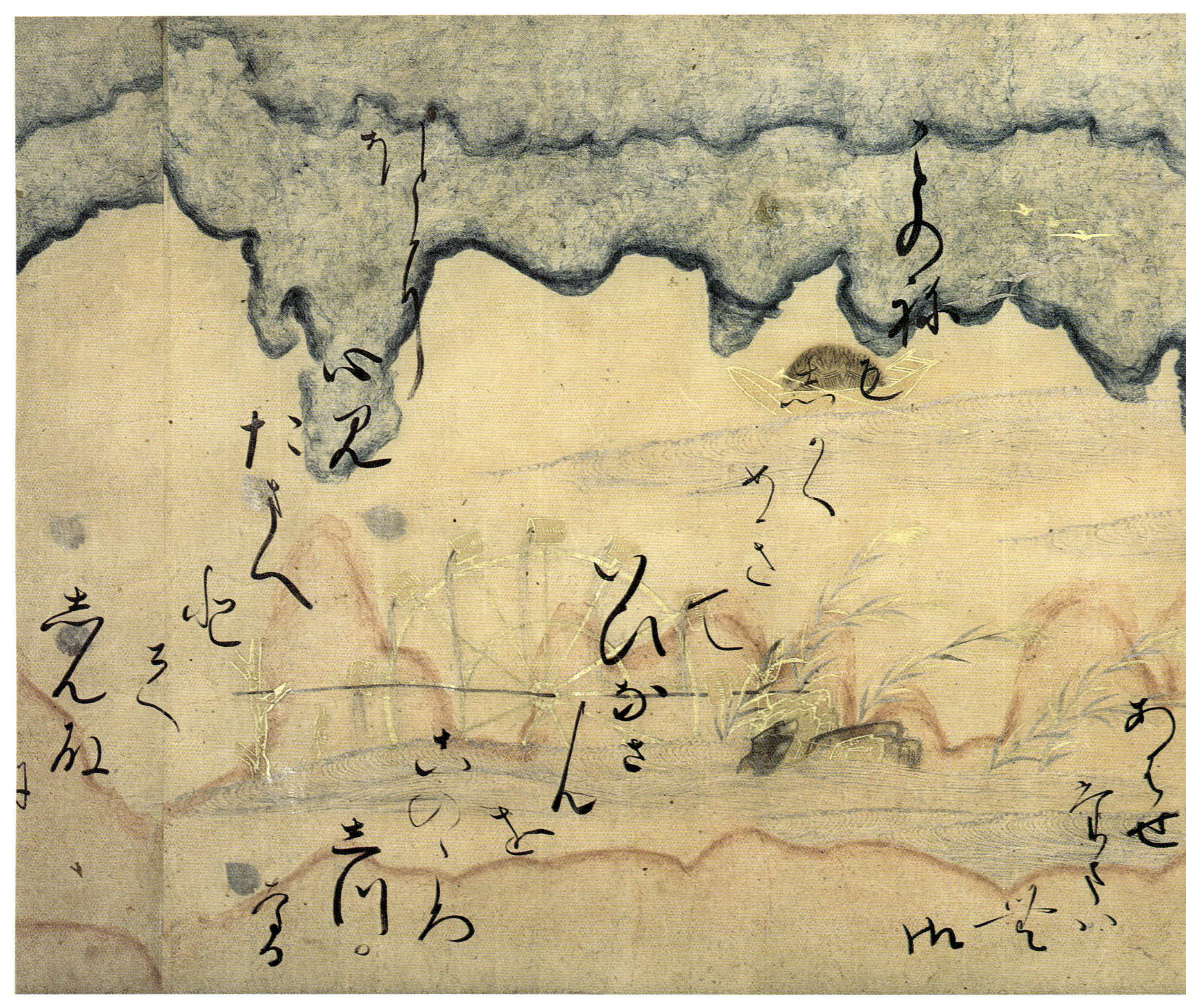

48 ◎

Model Calligraphy Text of Extracts
From THE TALE OF GENJI
Hand attributed to Emperor Fushimi
伏見天皇宸翰源氏物語抜書

Kamakura period, late 13th century
Handscroll; ink on decorated paper
30.8cm × 540cm
National Museum of History and Ethnology,
Chiba

The scroll consists of random extracts from the "New Herbs" (chapters 34, 35), "Lavender" (chapter 5), "A Rack of Clouds" (chapter 19) and "Beneath the Oak" (chapter 46), and includes isolated (*waka*) poems in addition to prose text paragraphs. The work was produced as a model text for calligraphy practice, with the extracts chosen for their edifying value as well. There is no colophon, but the calligraphy is judged to be in Emperor Fushimi (1265–1317)'s distinctive style. The lines of writing are freely placed, often forming sloping diagonals from right to left aross the pages in the "scattered writing" *chirashigaki* beloved of the Japanese-style (*wayō*) calligraphers. Emperor Fushimi is noted for bringing a greater clarity (with fewer vertical connections between characters) and boldness, influenced by Song Chinese calligraphy, to the flowing, run-together script of the late Heian period, in particular of the aristocratic Seison-ji calligraphy school.

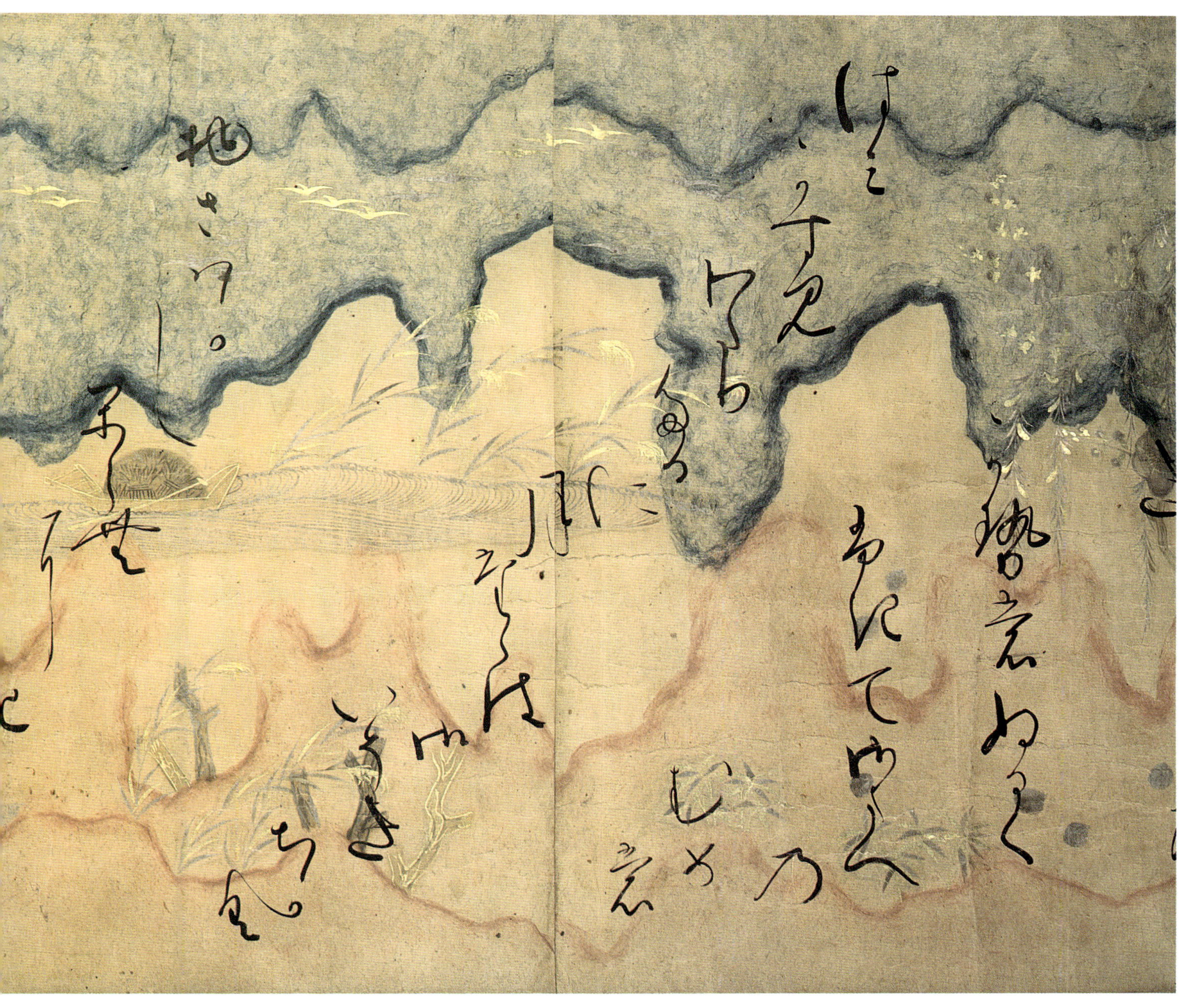

The indigo blue and purple cloud bands of the paper, called "pounded cloudiness" or *uchigumori-shi,* were made by adding dyed paper fibers into the paper pulp. The finished paper was then further embellished with gold and silver painted motifs of the four seasons. The back support of the body of the scroll is also richly decorated in gold and silver birds and butterflies. Around the 15th century, the scroll, while still in the Imperial Collection, was re-covered in an elegant Muromachi design of phoenix and grape-vine scrolls scattered with pieces of gold leaf, and given an inside cover (end paper) also decorated with scattered flakes of gold, on a solid ground.

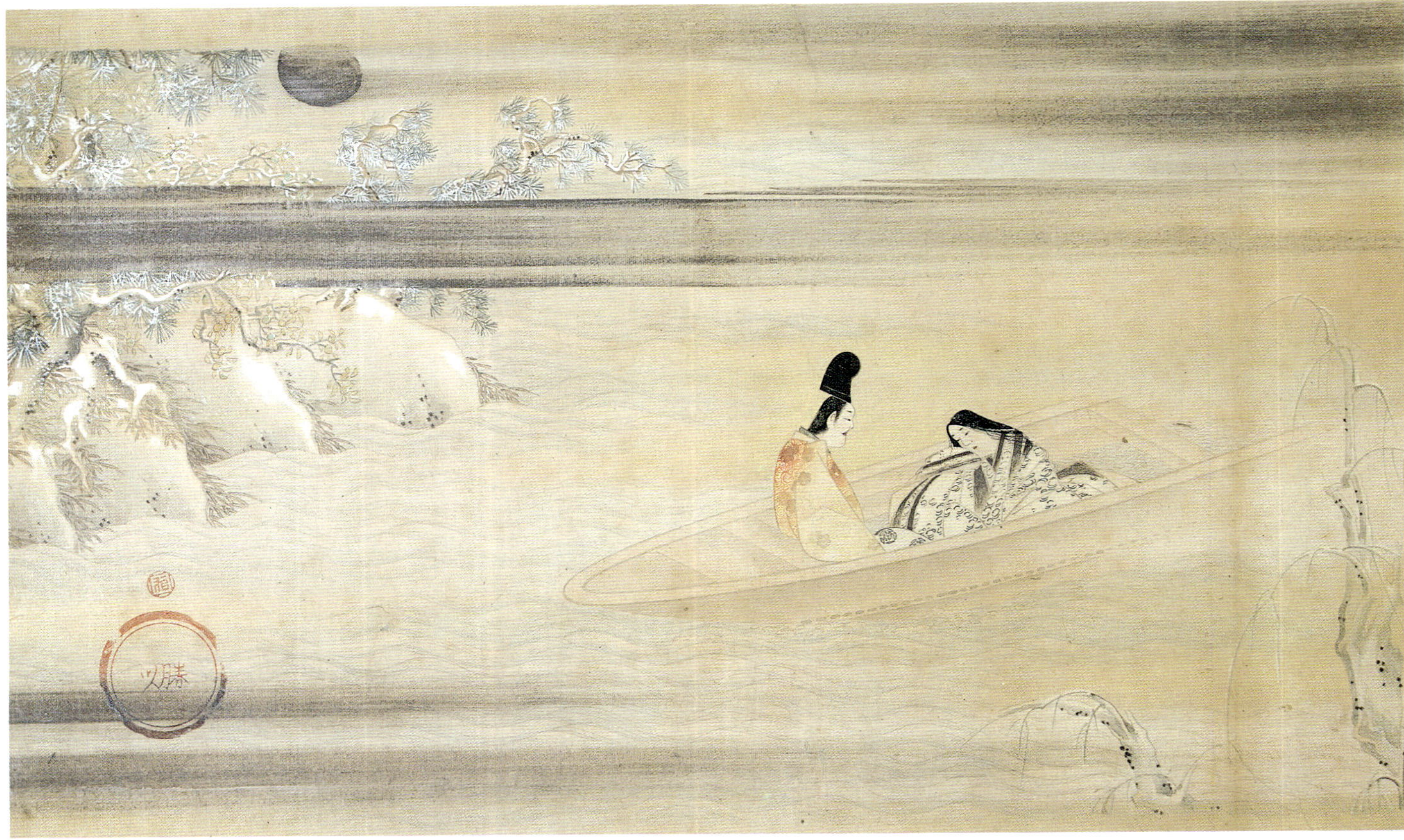

49-3

49

Famous Characters from THE TALE OF GENJI
By Iwasa Matabei (Katsumochi)
故事人物図

Edo period, early 17th century
Three paintings from a set of 12; ink and colors
on paper; each 36.0cm × 59.0cm
Fukui Prefectural Museum

Iwasa Matabei (1578-1650) working in the individualistic style that marks his best work captures in these three paintings the psychology or inner state of various characters in THE TALE OF GENJI. Despite the intervening centuries since its appearance around 1015 THE TALE OF GENJI continued to inspire Japanese artists and craftsmen.

The first painting shows the novel's main hero, the "Shining Prince" Genji, at the nadir of his court career, exiled from the capital to the storm-visited coast of Suma. The scene, although extremely elegant in details, reflects Genji's unsettled state — unjustly exiled, Genji was yet guilty of the far greater sin of having sired the Crown Prince, thought by the world to be Genji's father's legitimate heir. The stereotyped conventions of pine-studded beach, rain, and simple house have been transformed by the raking, oblique viewpoint of the composition and the disquieting, snaking fence.

The second depicts Yūgiri, Genji's recognized son and, in contrast to his father, a modest man of basically upright principles who is mostly in love with one woman, his wife. The autumn scenery with mists and the lowing deer and its mate capture the delicate irony of Yūgiri on a clandestine visit to Princess Ochiba, very much not his wife.

The third painting shows Prince Niou, in a boat on the moonlit river at Uji, seducing Ukifune whom his rival Kaoru, thought by the world to be Genji's son, has kept protected.

The three paintings formed part of a hand-scroll of 12 scenes of famous personages from literature and history (without text) now all mounted as hanging scrolls in the Fukui Prefectural Museum.

Iwasa Matabei, also known as Katsumochi (as reads the large red seal on these paintings), was born the son of Araki Murashige, a warrior retainer of the hegemon Oda Nobunaga. That year Murashige apparently rebelled against Nobunaga and he and more than 30 of the family were executed. Matabei escaped to grow up in Kyoto under his mother's name. He studied with both the Kanō and Tosa schools, but early developed an individualistic style distinct from both traditions and noted for its full-faced elegant human figures. He painted for the Matsudaira lords in Fukui and from 1637 served the Tokugawa shogun, Iemitsu, in Edo. Matabei took many of his painting subjects from THE TALE OF GENJI and other literary classics in the Japanese aristocratic tradition.

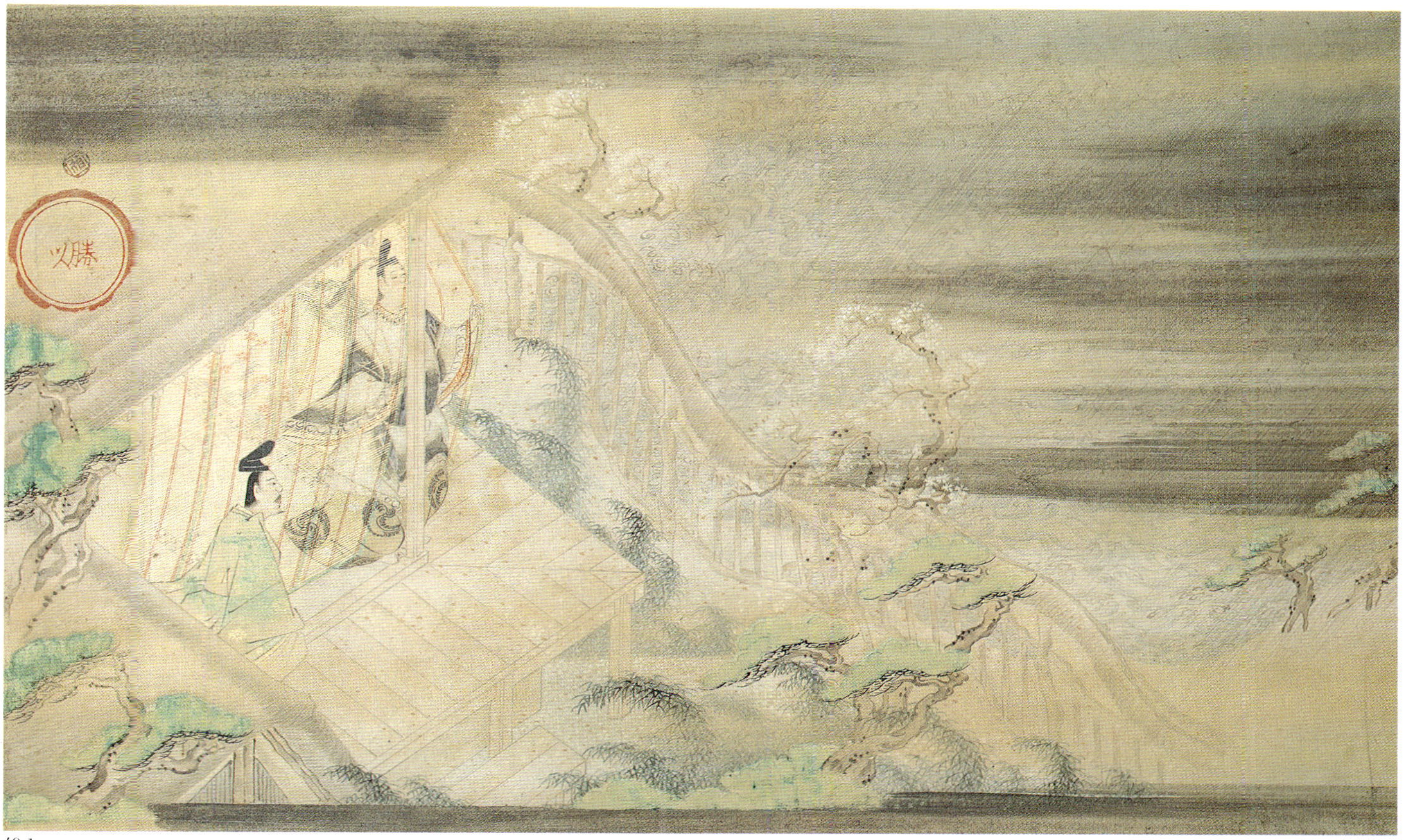

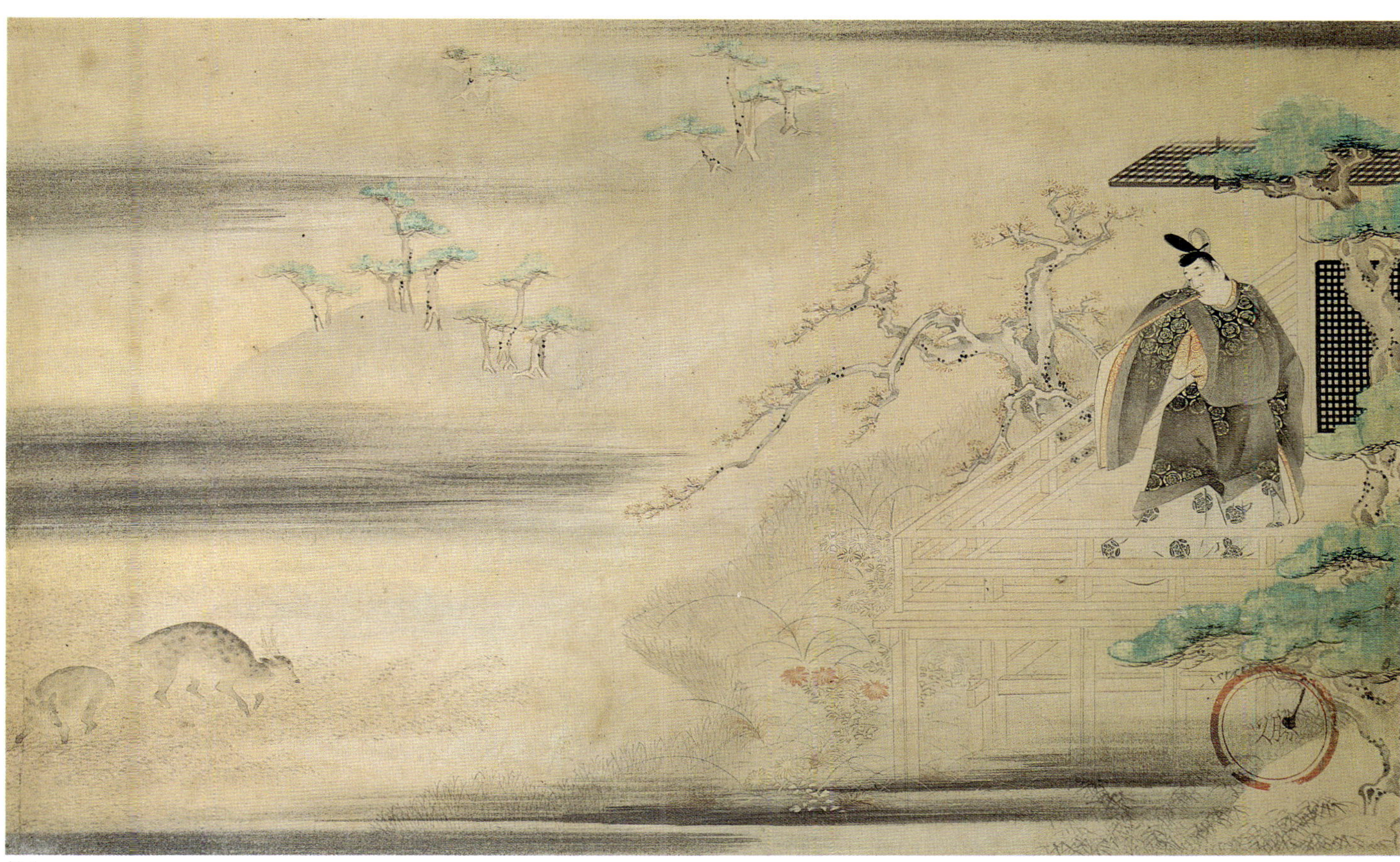

49-1

49-2

50 ○

Genji at the Shrine Gate of Nonomiya
By Iwasa Matabei
野々宮図

Edo period, early 17th century
Ink and light colors on paper; 131.0cm × 55.5cm
Idemitsu Museum of Art, Tokyo

This painting, with no explanatory inscription, was probably immediately identifiable to its audience as the scene from "The Sacred Tree" (chapter 10) in THE TALE OF GENJI where the hero, Genji, considers a visit to his old love, the Lady Rokujō who is staying at the shrine of Nonomiya. The sacred precincts are indicated by the conventional motifs of simple brushwood fence and *torii* gate with white cut-paper pendants. Iwasa Matabei (1578-1650), see Cat. No.49, depicts Genji, who fastidiously shakes his hem wet with autumn dew, at the penultimate moment of hesitation, with a young attendant poised at his side.

Lady Rokujō, meanwhile, is aware that Genji's love for her has faded and while consumed with a jealousy that has caused her spirit to haunt some of her rivals, is yet too proud and cultivated to wish to prolong the relationship. She has resolved to accompany her daughter, the Princess Akikonomu, who on the ascension of the new emperor has been honored to be chosen to serve as the priestess (*saikū*) at Ise Shrine. After a year of purification and training at the temporary shrine of Nonomiya, on the outskirts of the capital, the entourage is preparing to move on to distant Ise. They will not return as long as the emperor reigns. Genji will break numerous taboos should he enter the precincts, yet he cannot bear, now, to let Lady Rokujō go. The lady, her resolve weakening, grants him an audience...

The seal at lower right reads Hekishōkyū, one of the artistic names (*gō*) used by Matabei.

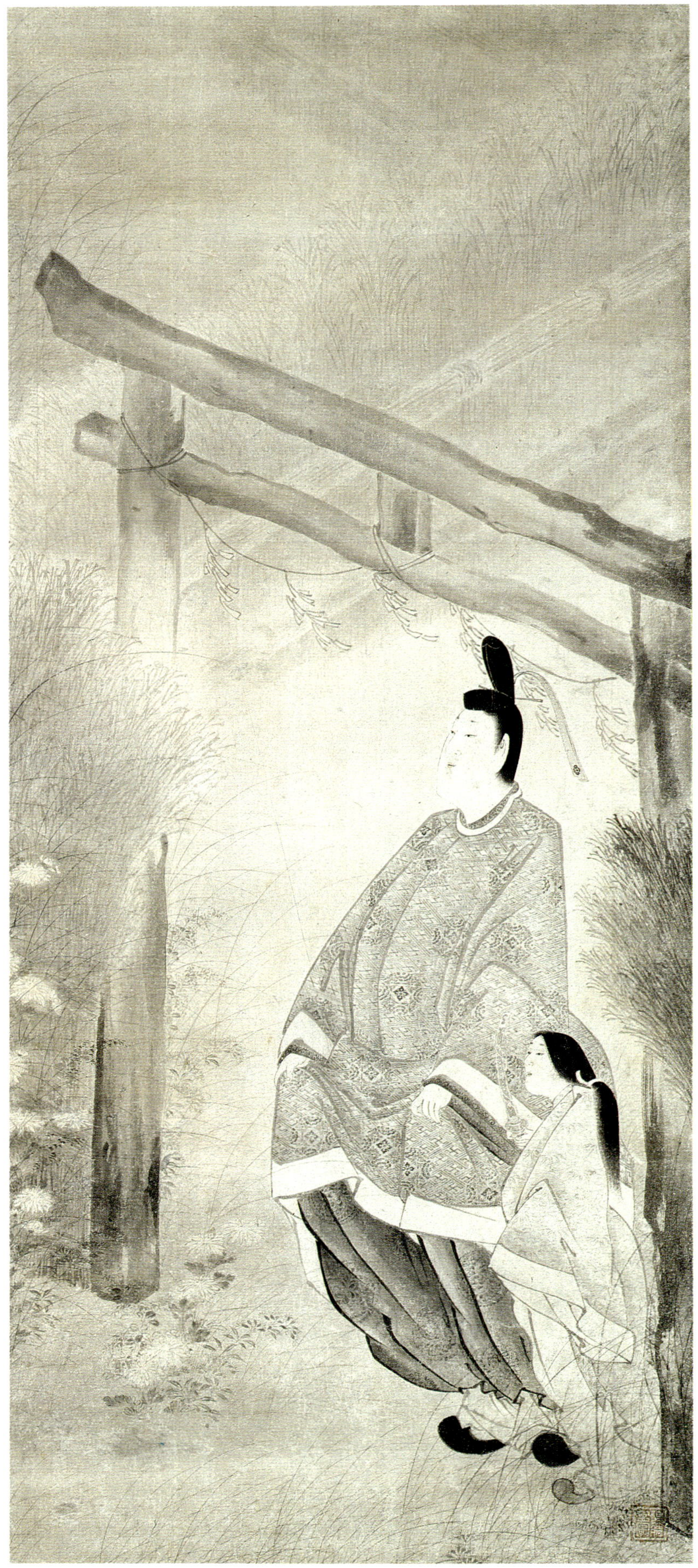

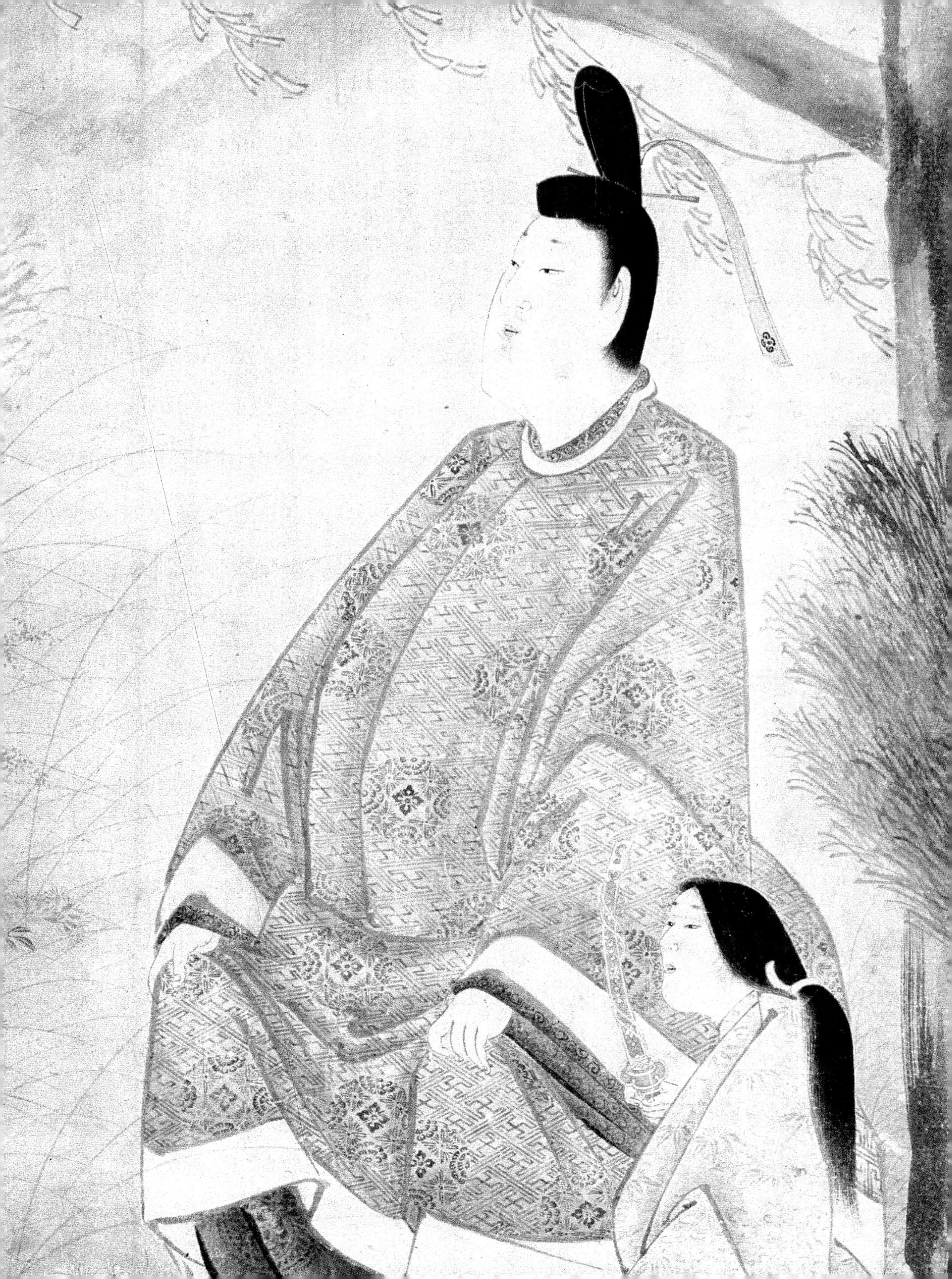

51

Box for Inkstone and Writing Utensils, With Designs of Nonomiya

野々宮蒔絵硯箱

Edo period, 17th century
Lacqured wood with *maki-e* decoration
22.8cm × 4.55cm
Suntory Museum of Art, Tokyo

The design motifs for this box (*tsuzuri-bako*) are all suggestive of Genji's visit to Lady Rokujō at the temporary shrine of Nonomiya (see Cat. No.50) in THE TALE OF GENJI. On the cover, under the misty autumn moon we find an empty aristocrat's carriage. Inside the lid is the simple, unfinished *torii* gate and brushwood fence that represent the shrine. And, accompanying the colored maples and flowering bushclover (*hagi*) depicted inside round the inkstone and bronze water-dropper is one cricket (*suzumushi*) whose plaintive cry is mentioned in the poems exchanged between the two old lovers. To achieve the decoration various lacquer techniques were employed over a wood base. The craftsman used metal inlays, such as a silver piece for the moon, shell inlay (*raden*) for the cricket, and silver and gold powders for the *maki-e* motifs of the carriage. Gold filings were sprinkled in varying densities to induce shading for the grounds.

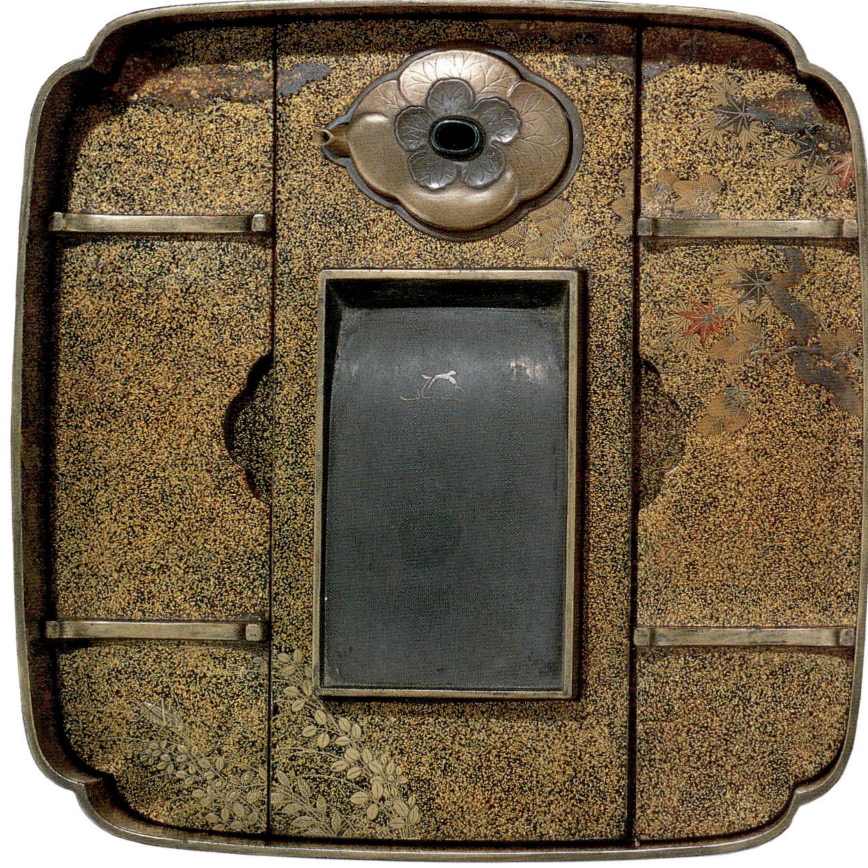

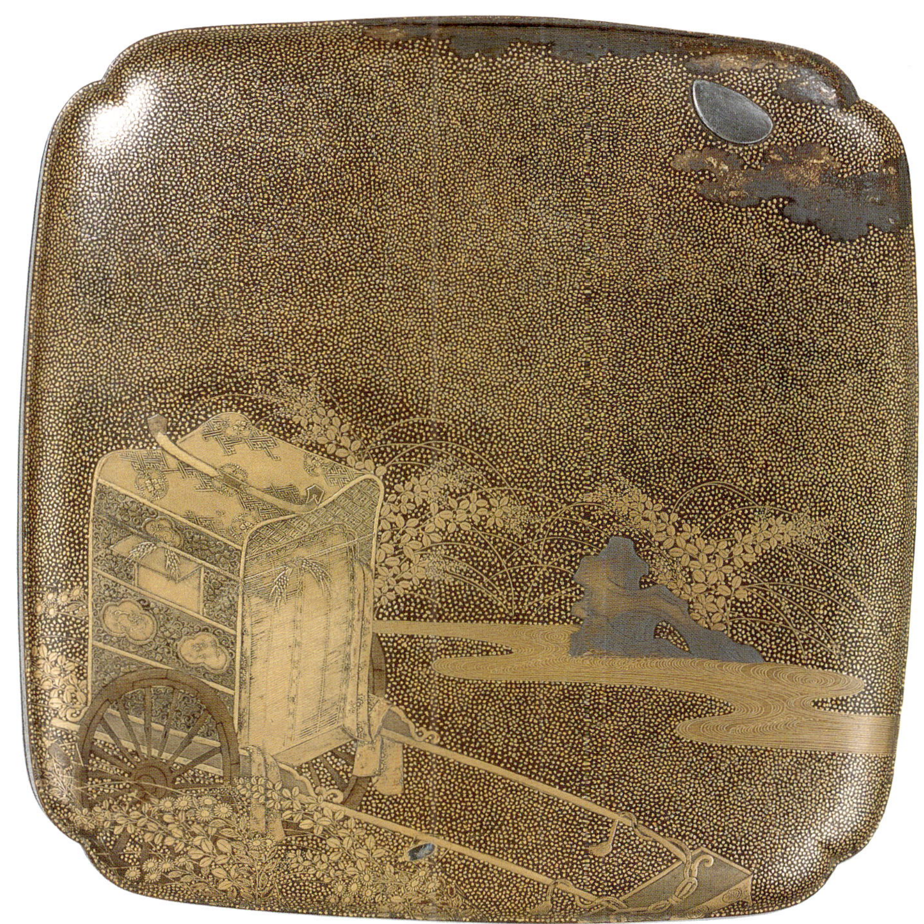

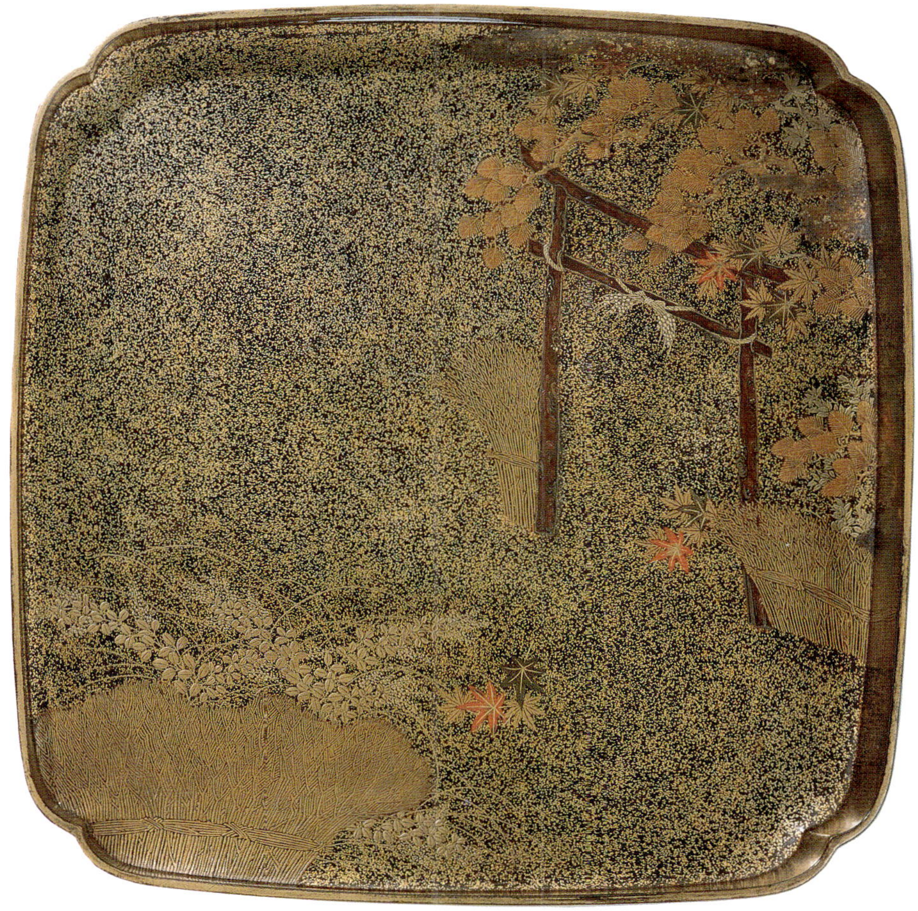

52 ◎

Incense Burner, With Designs from the "First Warbler" Chapter

初音蒔絵火取母

Muromachi period, 15th century
Lacquered wood with metal mesh and lining
Height 5.0cm
Tōkei-ji, Kanagawa

This type of incense burner (known as a *hitorimo*) with metal inner-cup and mesh cover set in a lacquered wood outer-body was used to scent clothes, a custom widely practiced from the Heian period. Because the 6-lobed shape resembles a gourd, this particular piece is also known as an *akoda* (type of gourd)-*kōro*.

The design of bush warbler *(uguisu)* in a flowering prunus tree, along with the cryptic syllables inlaid in the tree trunk, come from "First Warbler" *(Hatsune,* chapter 23) of THE TALE OF GENJI. The motif, which symbolizes conjugal happiness, was one of the most popular derived from the TALE. The gold filings in clear lacquer of the ground set off the *maki-e* (gold-dust sprinkled on a motif painted in wet lacquer) design of the tree trunk and the gold-plate inlay employed for the bird and silver-plate inlays for the plum blossoms and syllables.

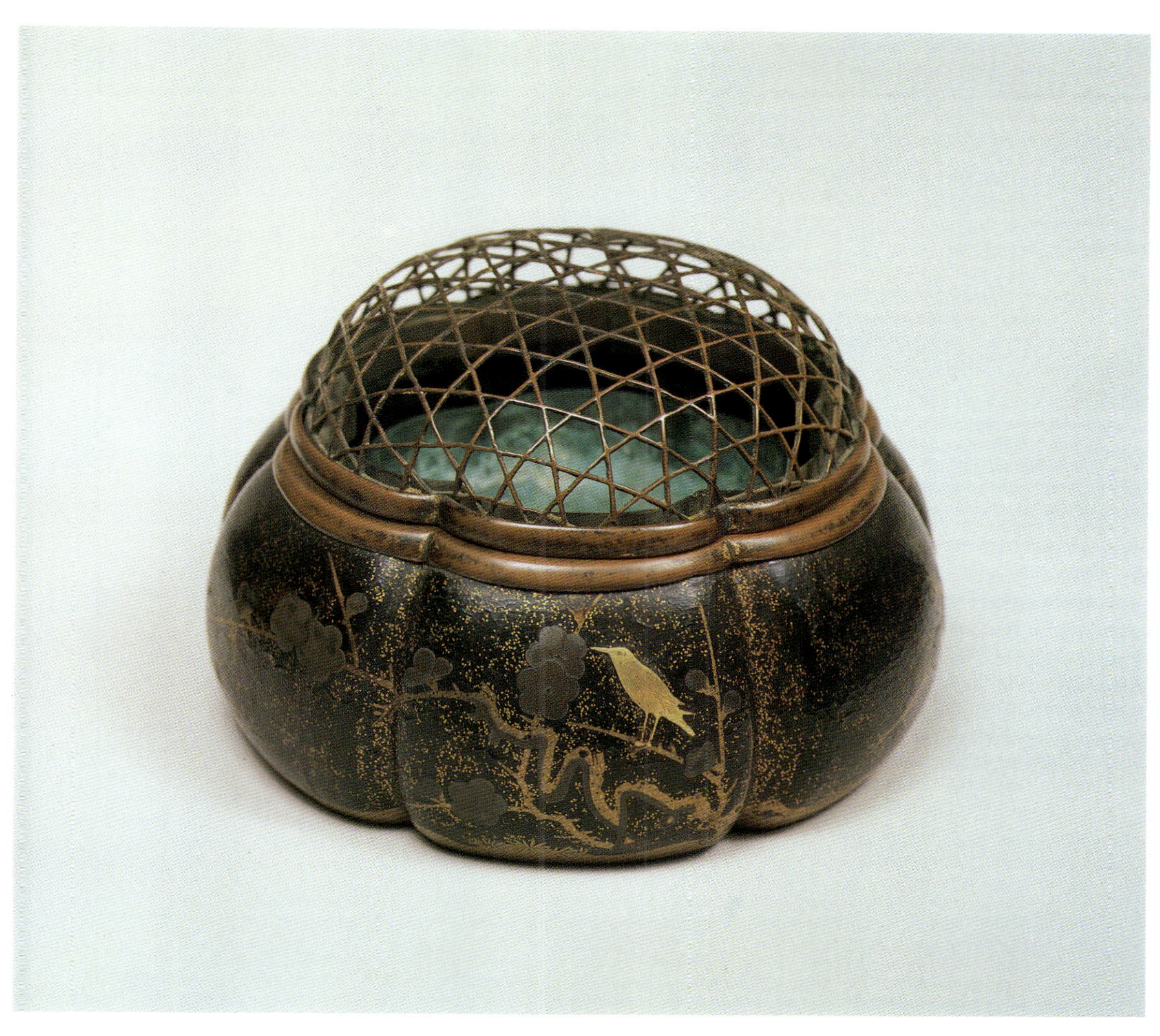

53

Small Cabinet for a Complete Booklet Set of THE TALE OF GENJI

石山寺蒔絵源氏箪笥

Edo period, 17th century
Lacquered wood with silver fittings
21.2cm × 39.5cm × 24.5cm
Suntory Museum of Art, Tokyo

This small chest *(genji-dansu)* was made to hold the 54 booklet chapters of THE TALE OF GENJI. The set now contained in the box was written out by Higashizono Motokata (1626-1704), an aristocrat, who like many from old noble families, was known for his calligraphy. The set bears a colophon with the date of 1660. The chest with its dazzling lacquer techniques on stylistic grounds too is credibly datable to mid-late 17th century. This type of lacquered, boxed set of THE TALE OF GENJI was a standard showpiece item in the trousseau of women from well-born warrior families. The elaborate lacquer decorations include richly modeled relief *takamaki-e*, various inlays and flat *maki-e* designs, with every remaining area covered in a sumptuous *nashiji* (gold-particles set in clear lacquer) ground. The designs covering the box depict landscapes centered around the temple of Ishiyama-dera in Otsu, present-day Shiga prefecture. From a very early period the legend arose that Murasaki Shikibu had written THE TALE OF GENJI while staying at the temple overlooking Lake Biwa. The chest is thus another example of the vast number of designs inspired by the novel.

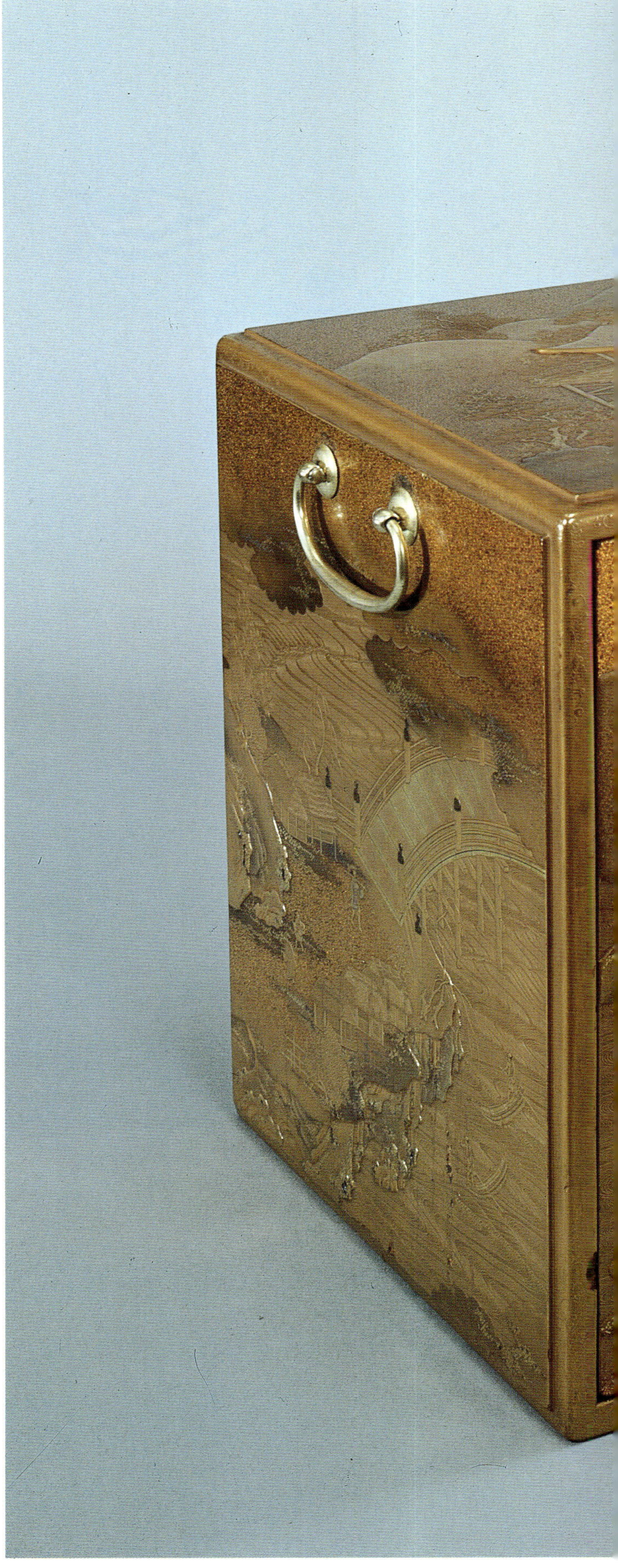

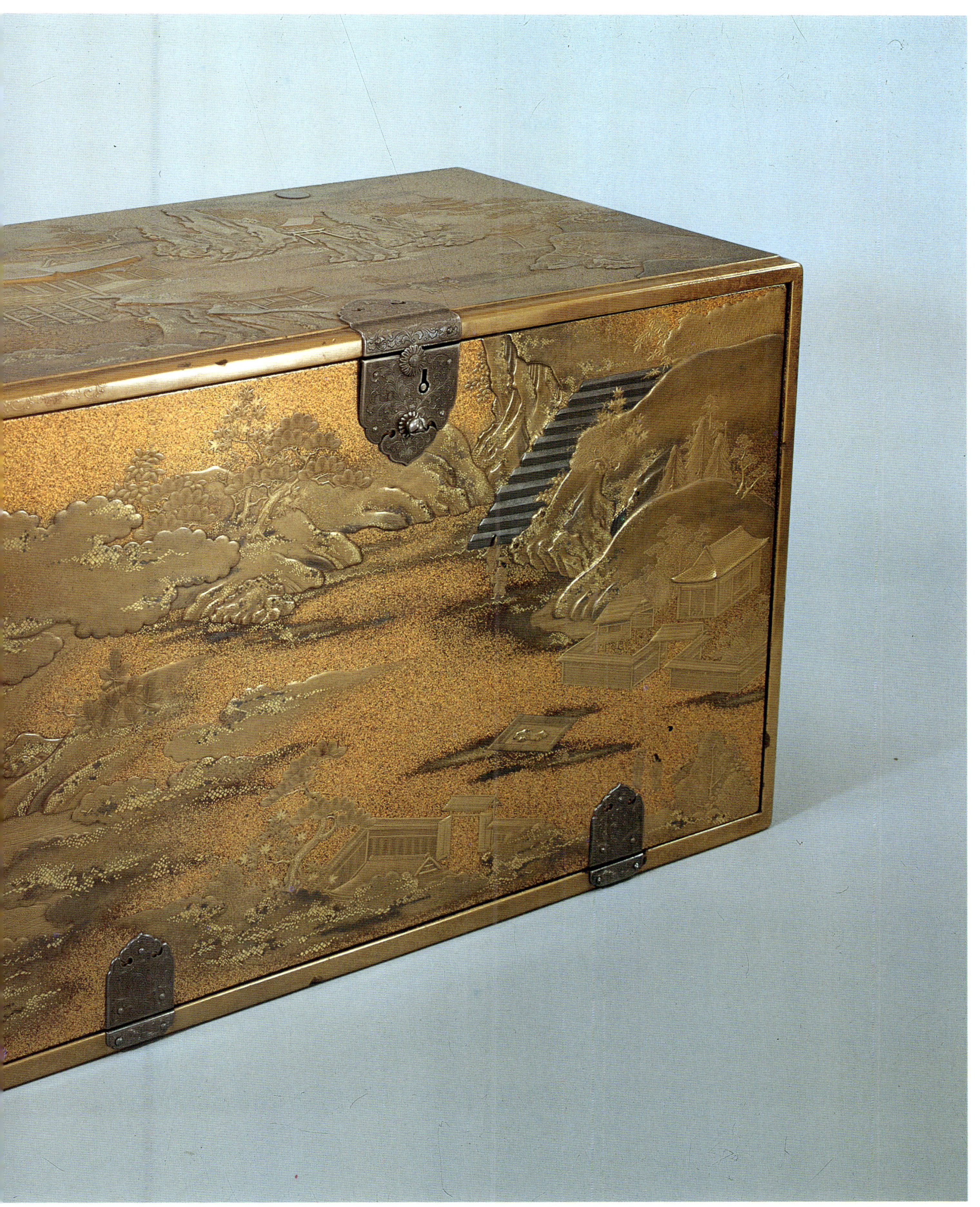

54 ◎

Shelf, With Designs from THE TALE OF GENJI
子日蒔絵棚

Momoyama period, beginning of the 17th century
Lacquered wood, with bronze fittings
32.7cm × 72.8cm × 65.5cm
Agency for Cultural Affairs

This type of shelf, often fitted (as here) with doored-compartments is called a *zushi-dana,* and would have been used in the semi-formal or private chambers of a well-to-do mansion. Cosmetic or writing utensil boxes or other personal furnishings would have been displayed on it and kept within reach. The bold designs often staggered over adjoining surfaces against a dark lacquered ground reflect the vigor and freedom from restrictions of the Momoyama period (16th-early 17th centuries). They were executed mainly in *maki-e* combined with large inlays cut from gold, silver and pewter (or tin) plates, along with mother-of-pearl (*raden*).

The motifs can all be related to THE TALE OF GENJI. The piece is known as the "Day of the Rat Shelf" (*Ne-no-hi-dana*), after the auspicious day of the zodiac rat at New Year's, when Heian nobles went gathering young pine shoots. The young pine branches depicted on the top shelf are derived from the "First Warbler" (chapter 23) which opens with the New Year's "Day of the Rat" in Lady Murasaki's section of Genji's Rokujō mansion. On the second level a fan decorated with evening-blooming gourd flowers (*yūgao*) represents Genji's tragically short-lived love, the Lady of the Evening Faces (or Yūgao), from chapter 4 of the same name. The aristocrat's carriage (*gosho-guruma*) and attendant groom come from chapter 16, "The Gatehouse" (*Sekiya*), where Genji and his retinue, passing the barrier outside the capital, meet the carriages of the Vice-governor and his wife with whom Genji long ago had an affair. The bridge and flowing water are motifs from "Lady at the Bridge" (*Hashihime,* chapter 45).

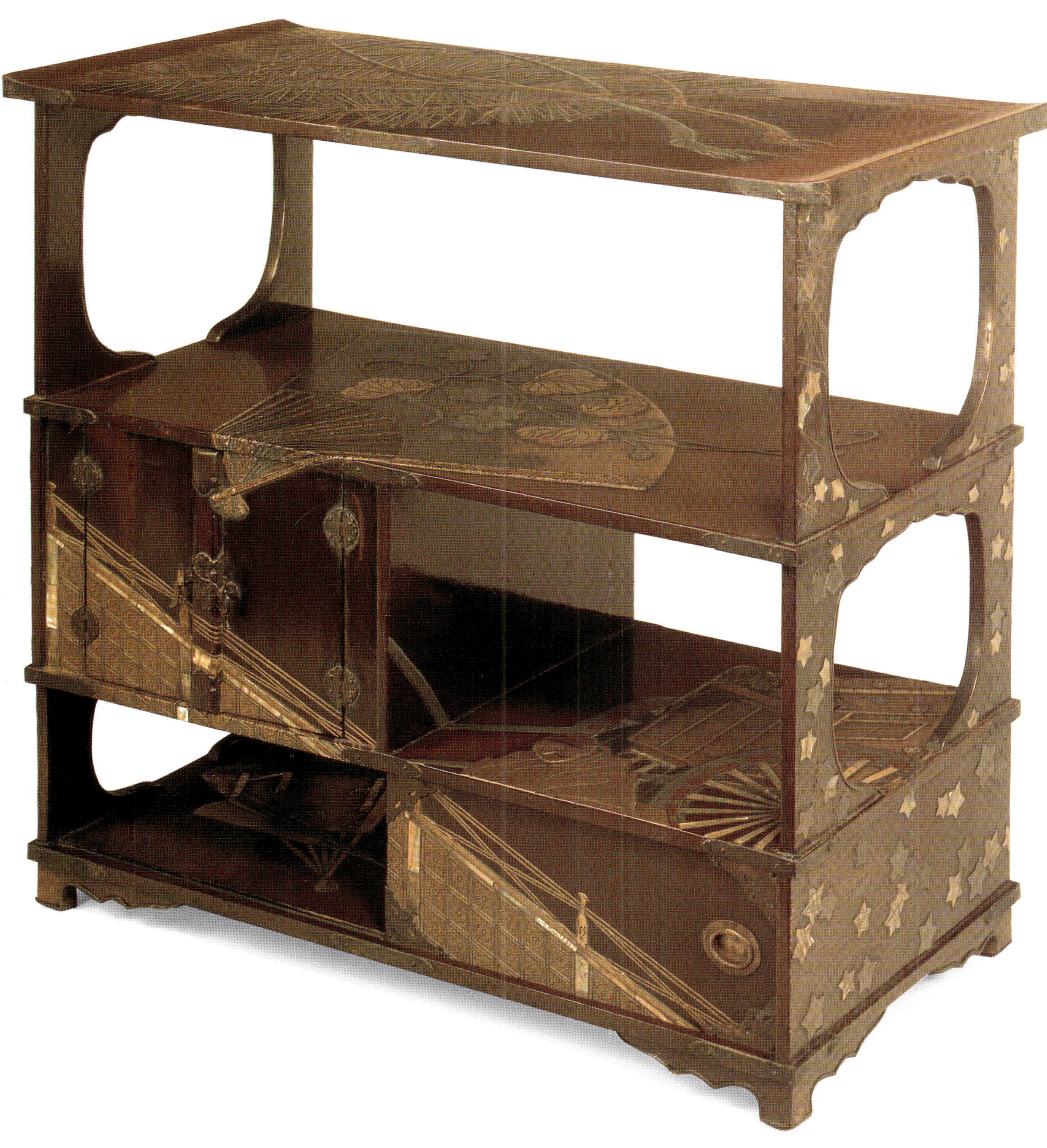

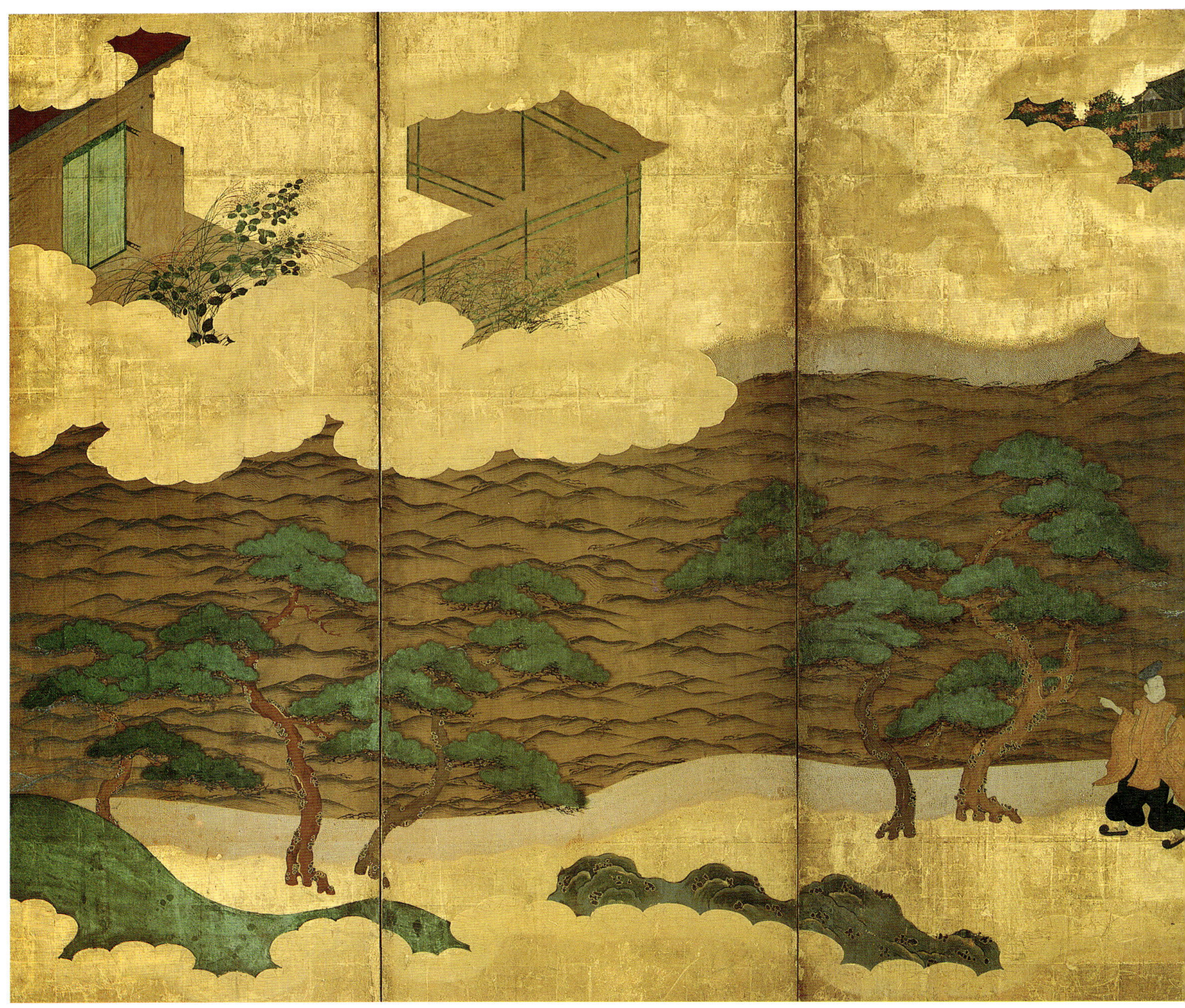

55-1

55

Scenes from the "Akashi" and
"Wormwood Patch" Chapters of
THE TALE OF GENJI
明石・蓬生図屏風

Momoyama period, 16th century
Pair of six-fold screens; ink, colors and gold-leaf
on paper; each 151.5cm × 354.0cm
Tokyo National Museum

The right screen depicts Genji, as the
mounted nobleman with his entourage, going
along the pine-studded beach in autumn from
his house in exile (at Suma) to visit the former
governor of Harima, now living at nearby
Akashi (from chapter 13, "Akashi"). There
Genji falls in love with the old governor's
daughter, the Akashi Lady, who will bear the
daughter who becomes the Akashi Empress.
This child of all Genji's progeny (along with

the provincial wealth brought to Genji's
household by her mother) helps to ensure the
revival of Genji's fortunes at court.

The other screen shows the scene from
"The Wormwood Patch" (*Yomogyu*, chapter
15) where Genji, having been called back from
exile to the capital, is bent on another assigna-
tion one night in the spring drizzle. He hap-
pens upon a dilapidated mansion lost in weeds
and blooming wisteria and recalls his visit

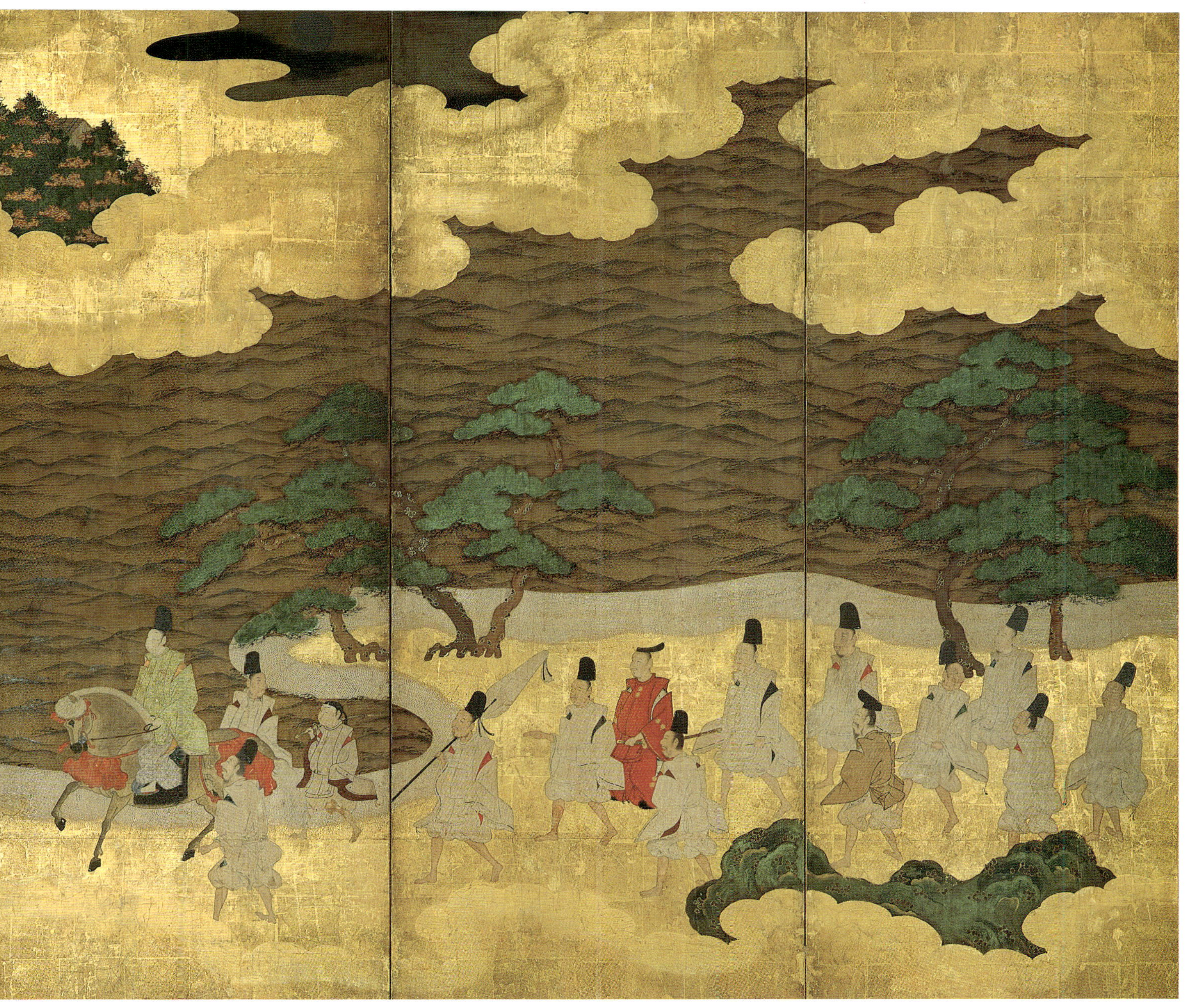

there one night long ago. Genji cannot bear to pass by without at least sending his trusted retainer Koremitsu (seen standing before the veranda) to inquire of the lady, known as the Safflower Princess. Although never a major love in his life, Genji, always honorable in some senses, will accept responsibility for the lady now fallen into such straitened circumstances, and eventually installs the princess at his Nijō mansion.

Both depictions thus signal an auspicious improvement in fortune. The screens were done in the style of the studio of Tosa Mitsuyoshi, see Cat. No.47.

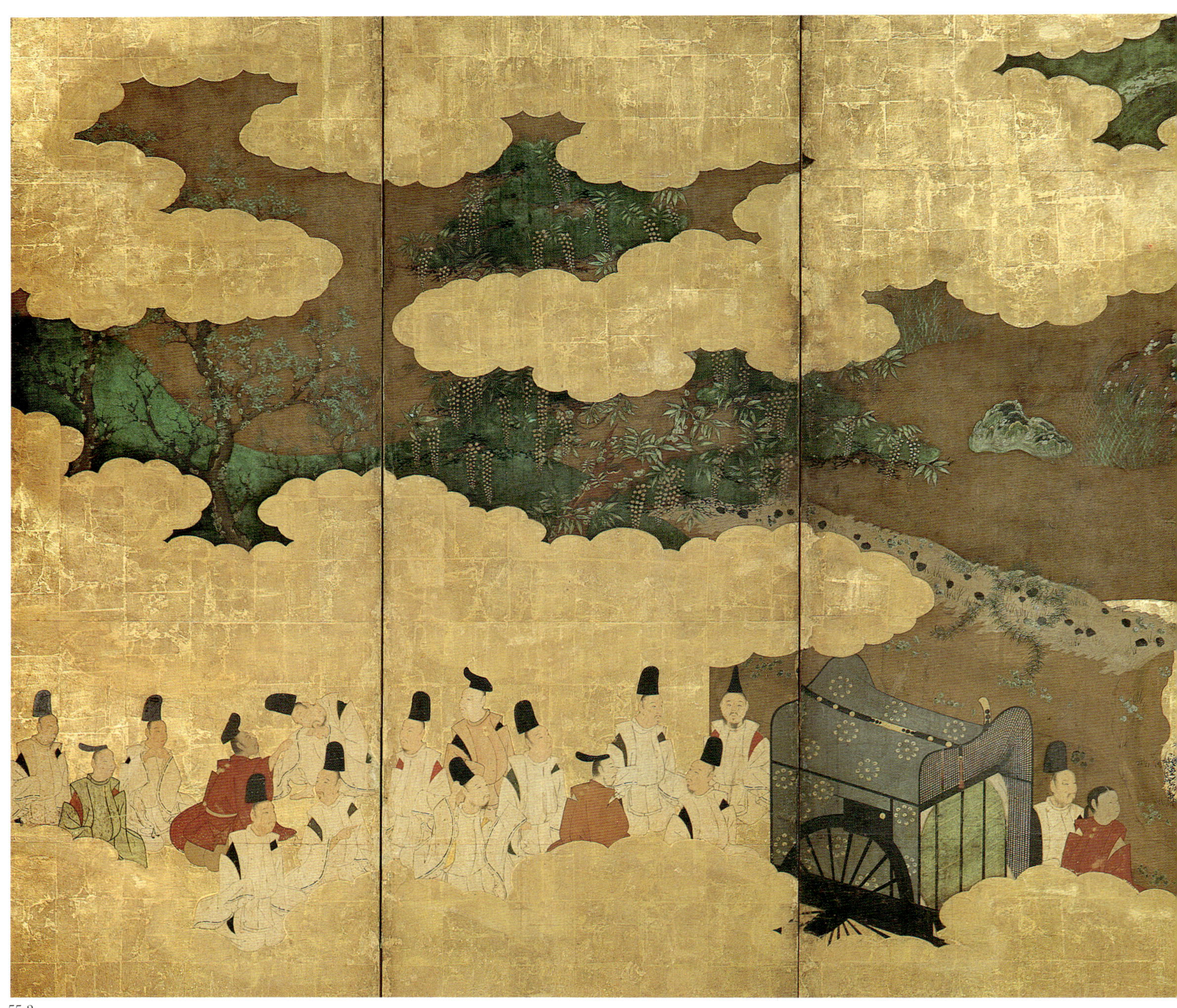

55-2

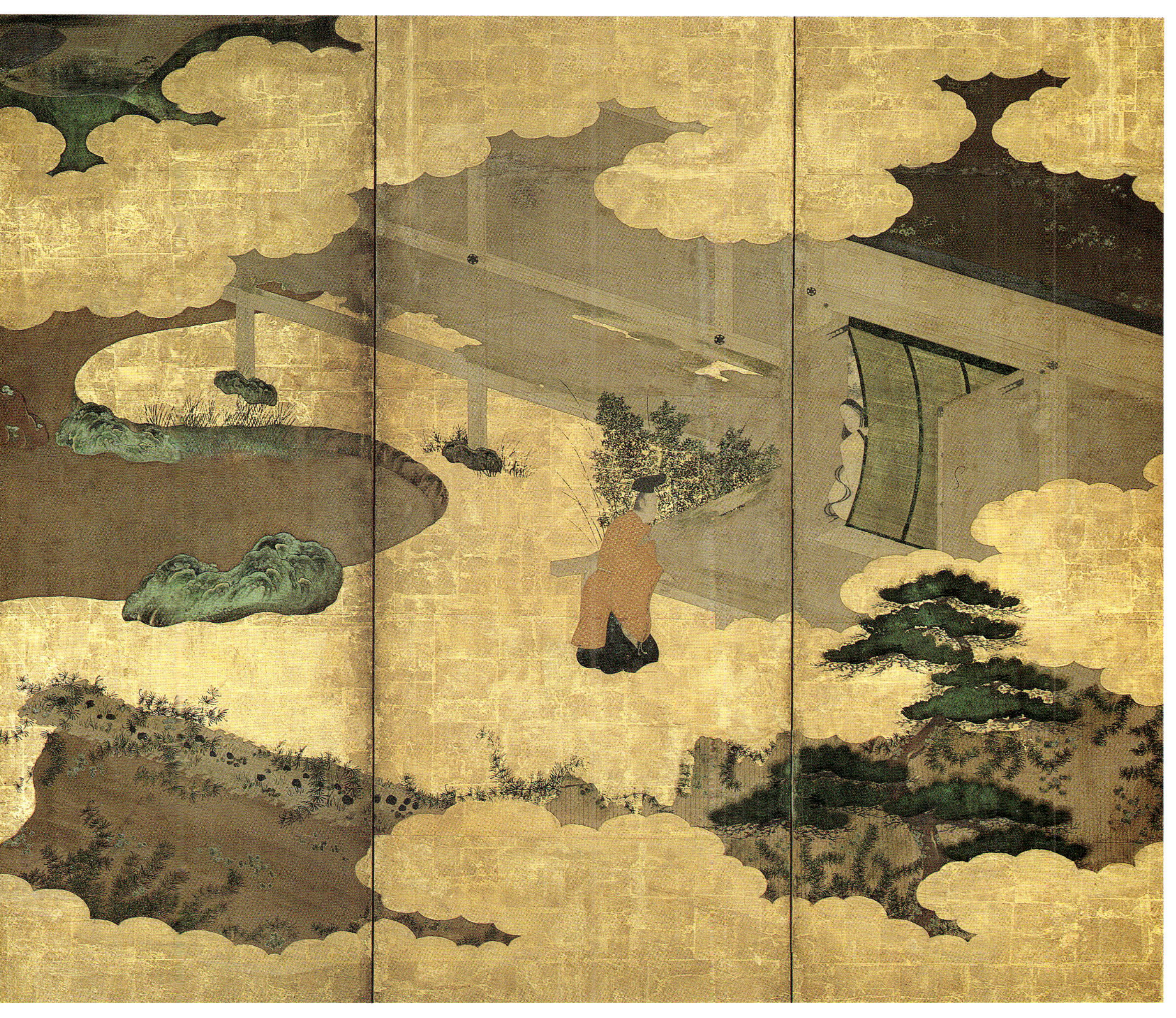

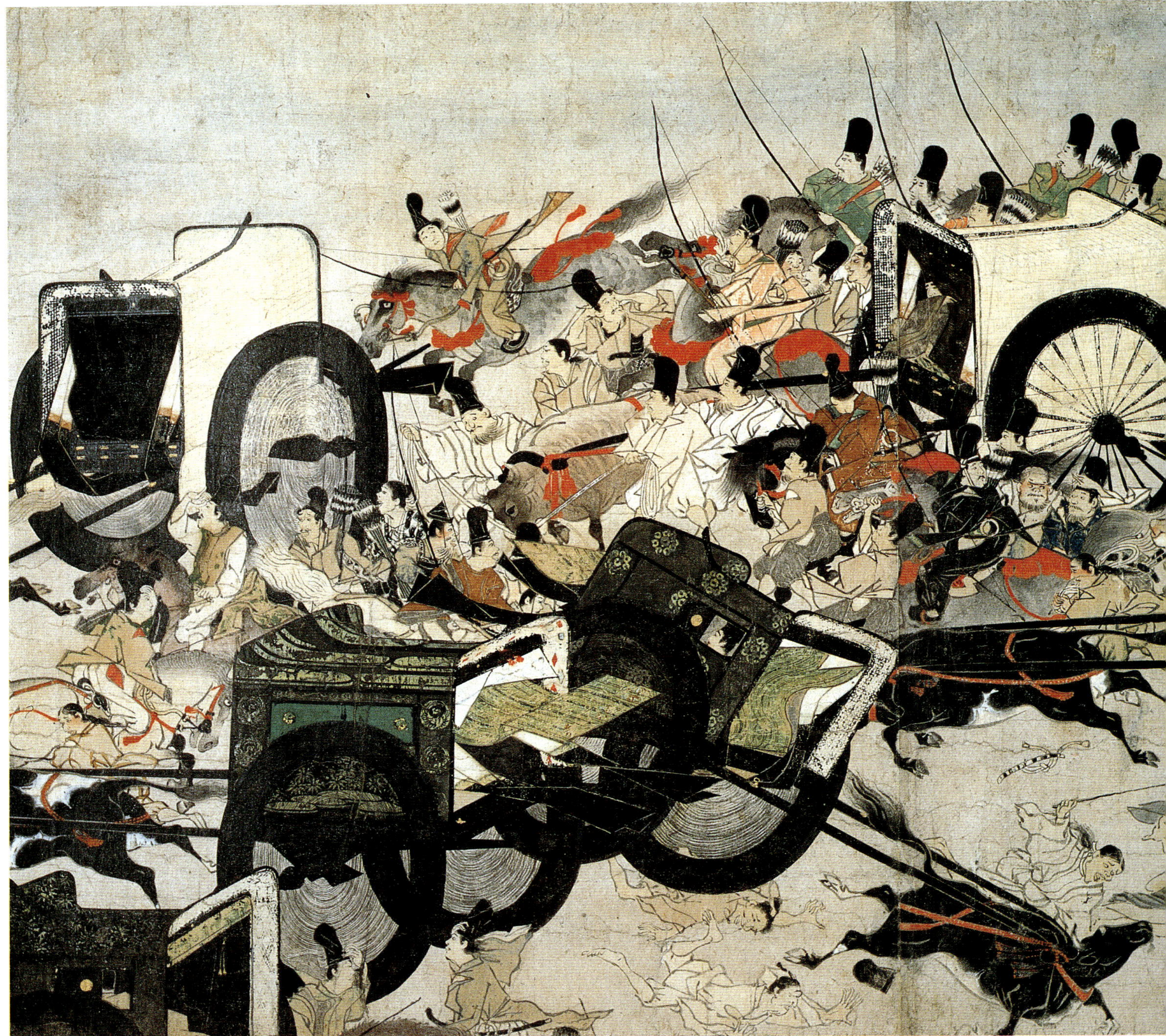

Boston-1

Illustrated Handscrolls of the Heiji Era Rebellion

Special Exhibit
"The Night Attack on the Sanjō Palace"
平治物語絵詞（三条殿夜討の巻）

Kamakura period, late 13th century
Handscroll; ink and colors on paper
(Fenollosa-Weld collection 11.4000)
41.3cm × 699.7cm
Museum of Fine Arts, Boston

56 ◎
"The Death of Shinzei"
平治物語絵詞（信西の巻）

Kamakura period, late 13th century
Handscroll; ink and colors on paper
42.7cm × 1117.0cm
Seikadō Library

57 ⊙
"Flight of the Imperial Family to
Taira Kiyomori's Mansion at Rokuhara"
平治物語絵詞（六波羅行幸の巻）

Kamakura period, late 13th century
Handscroll; ink and colors on paper
42.3cm × 957.0cm
Tokyo National Museum

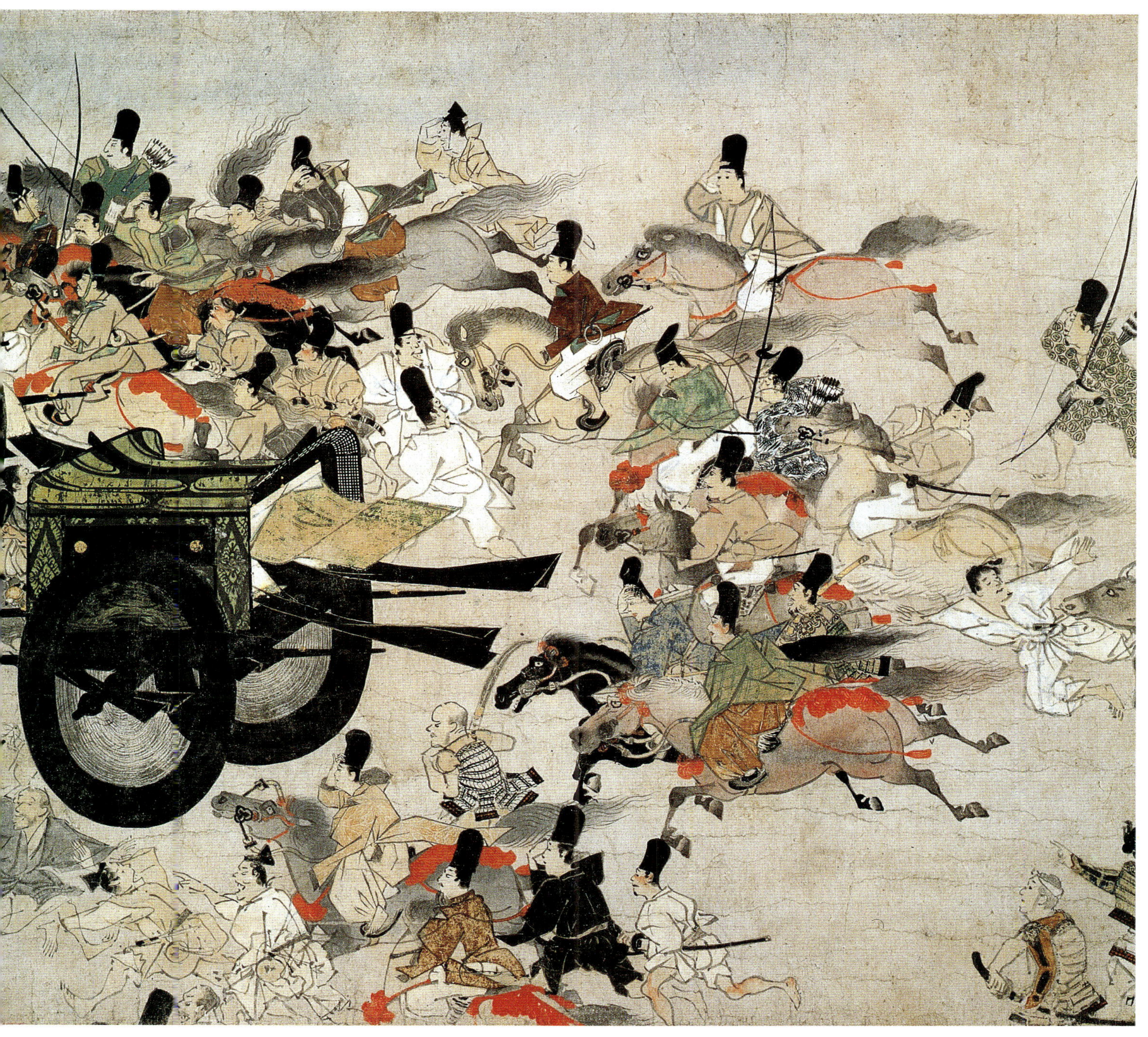

The bloody wars between the Taira and Minamoto clans during the latter half of the twelfth century served as a perennial source of inspiration for narrative reciters and artists in subsequent centuries. The earliest extant examples of pictorial narratives that relate these events are three scrolls and fourteen fragments (now in various collections) from a fourth scroll known together as *The Illustrated Tale of the Heiji Era Rebellion, also known as "The Tale of Events of the Heiji Era", (Heiji monogatari emaki)*. These extant scrolls depict only the opening episodes in the civil war that began in the first year of the Heiji era (1159) and ended thirty years later with the Minamoto (or Genji) clan's destruction of the Taira (or Heike) at Dannoura (see Cat. No.41). Originally they must have been part of an extensive set, perhaps as many as fifteen handscrolls. The surviving narrative text passages appear to be written by a single calligrapher. While the paintings differ slightly in stylistic details and expression, scholars believe them to be the product of one studio, probably the court affiliated atelier.

Although the warriors (*bushi*) were the main sponsors of war tales (*gunki*) and their visual depictions, the scrolls of *The Tale of the Heiji Era Rebellion* may well have been commissioned by an aristocratic patron. The heros are the aristocrats and imperial family members, along with the Taira, who it is always said ultimately went down in defeat because they had too completely adopted the aristocratic ways and "non-warrior" culture of the capital. The scroll set was made in the late 13th (or perhaps early 14th) century when several figures in the imperial family, notably Godaigo (r.1318–39, see Cat. No.22) seemed about to restore the reigns of power to the emperor and court. In the end, it proved an ephemeral reassertion, and in fact rivalries within the

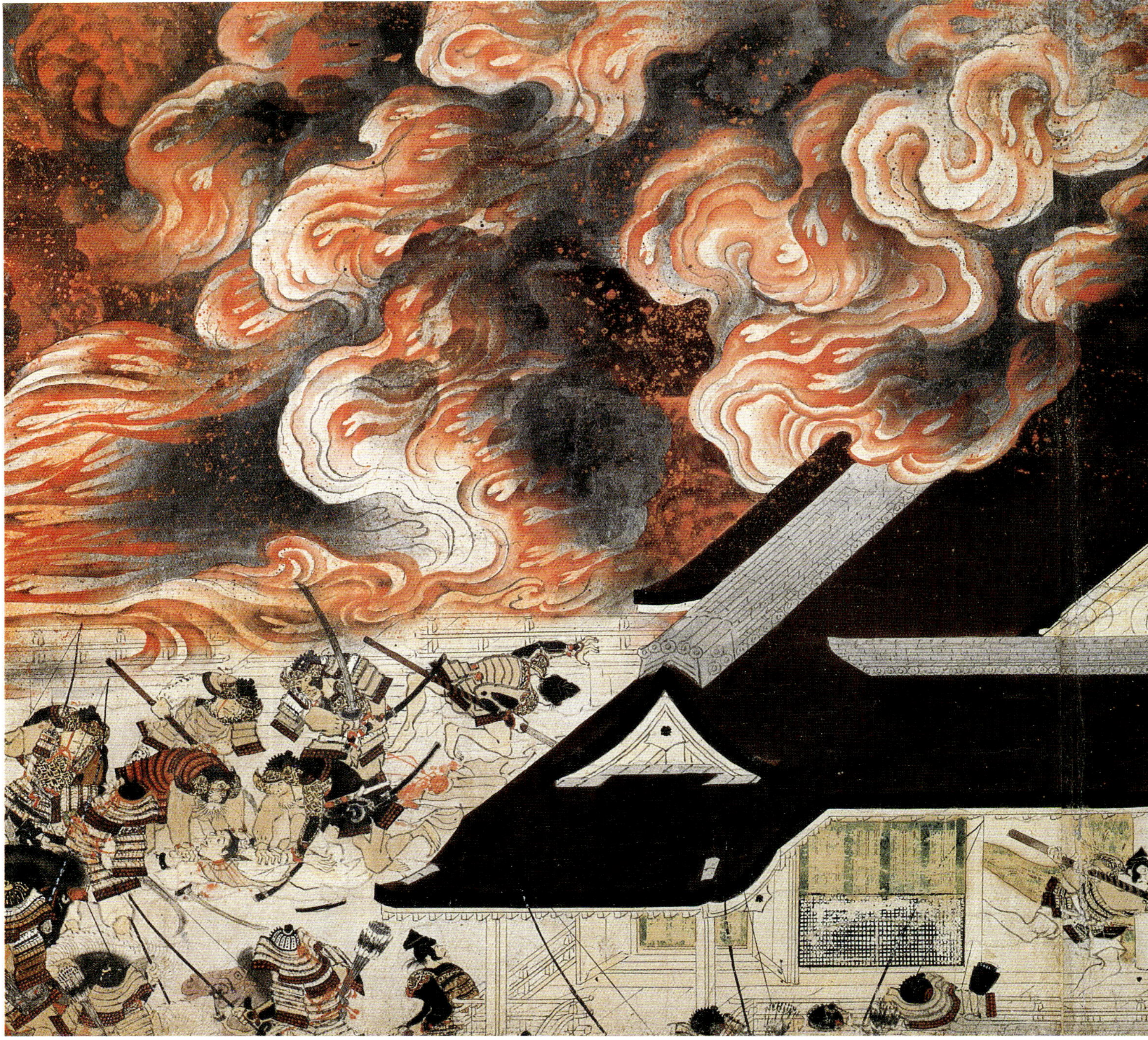

Boston-2

imperial family exploited by warrior factions helped to plunge the nation into a century of civil disturbances marked by the Ōnin War (1467-77) which left most of Kyoto (once the great Heian capital) in ashes.

The Museum of Fine Arts handscroll is the first in order of events, and illustrates "The Night Attack on the Sanjō Palace". Many consider it artistically the finest of the extant paintings. The artist depicts the night attack launched against the Sanjō Palace in 1159 by the combined forces of Fujiwara no Nobuyori and Minamoto no Yoshitomo and their subsequent abduction of the influential retired emperor Goshirakawa.

The painting represents the culmination of a conceptual and artistic specialty for which Japanese narrative scroll painters were justly renowned: the skillful depiction of large crowds of people. The artist conveyed the nervous tension of the bloody encounters by imbuing groups of figures with an organic, vital unity as they move toward the scene of the battles and regroup afterward around the imperial carriage carrying Goshirakawa. Between these two crowds of figures lies the palace in flames, while the scene dissolves into scattered hand-to-hand fighting full of the fierce brutality that characterized these civil wars.

The Seikadō Library's "The Death of Shinzei" handscroll describes events that fall next in sequence. It contains three paintings preceded by three passages of narrative. Starting with the triumphant entry of Minamoto no Yoshihira (Yoshitomo's son) into the capital (Kyoto), the story continues with the forced suicide of Shinzei (or Fujiwara no Michinori), a clever courtier-priest aligned nominally with the Taira, who had ruthlessly suppressed the Minamoto while advancing his own faction against Nobuyori's at court. His head,

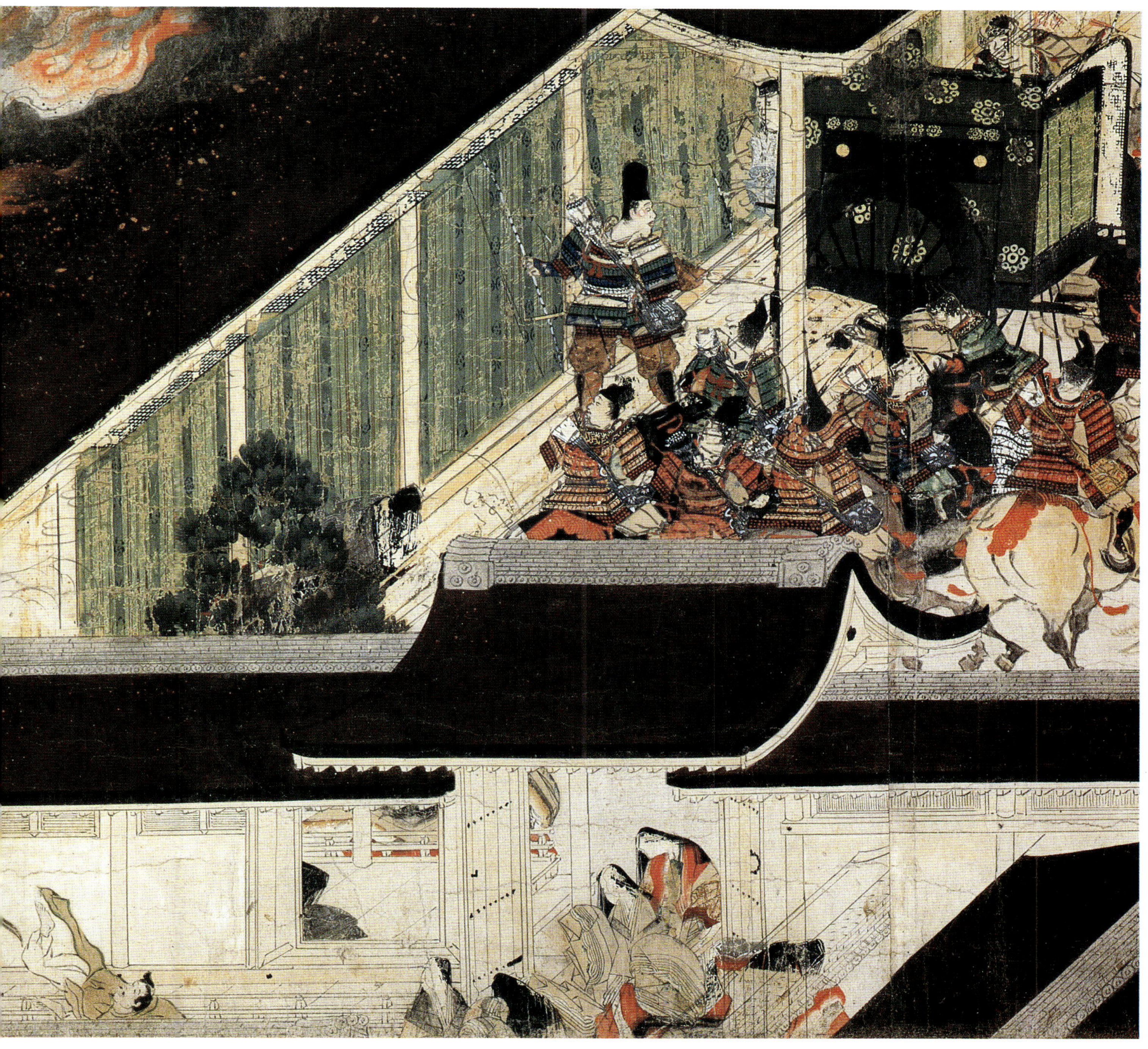

ignominiously discovered in the Iga region, is brought back to the capital, verified by Fujiwara no Nobuyori, and paraded through the streets until finally gibbeted on the west prison gate. The representation of the violent events is controlled and reserved. The overall aesthetic effect of the colors and detailing is one of elegant beauty more than sympathy for the characters involved.

The third scroll, owned by the Tokyo National Museum, illustrates the "Flight of the Imperial Family to Taira no Kiyomori's Mansion at Rokuhara", in four sections of text and paintings. The first scene shows Emperor Nijō, disguised as a court lady, escaping from the Imperial Palace (held by Nobuyori's men) in an ox-drawn carriage. Next, his party is greeted at Rokuhara by the Taira general, Shigemori. The third scene shows Bifukumon-in, consort of the retired emperor Toba, leaving for Rokuhara with various court nobles in a flurry, while in the last scene Fujiwara no Nobuyori and other rebels are angered at the news of the Emperor's escape. As with the Museum of Fine Arts work, the compositions in this scroll show a masterly ability to group figures in a way that draws the eye into the scenes and action.

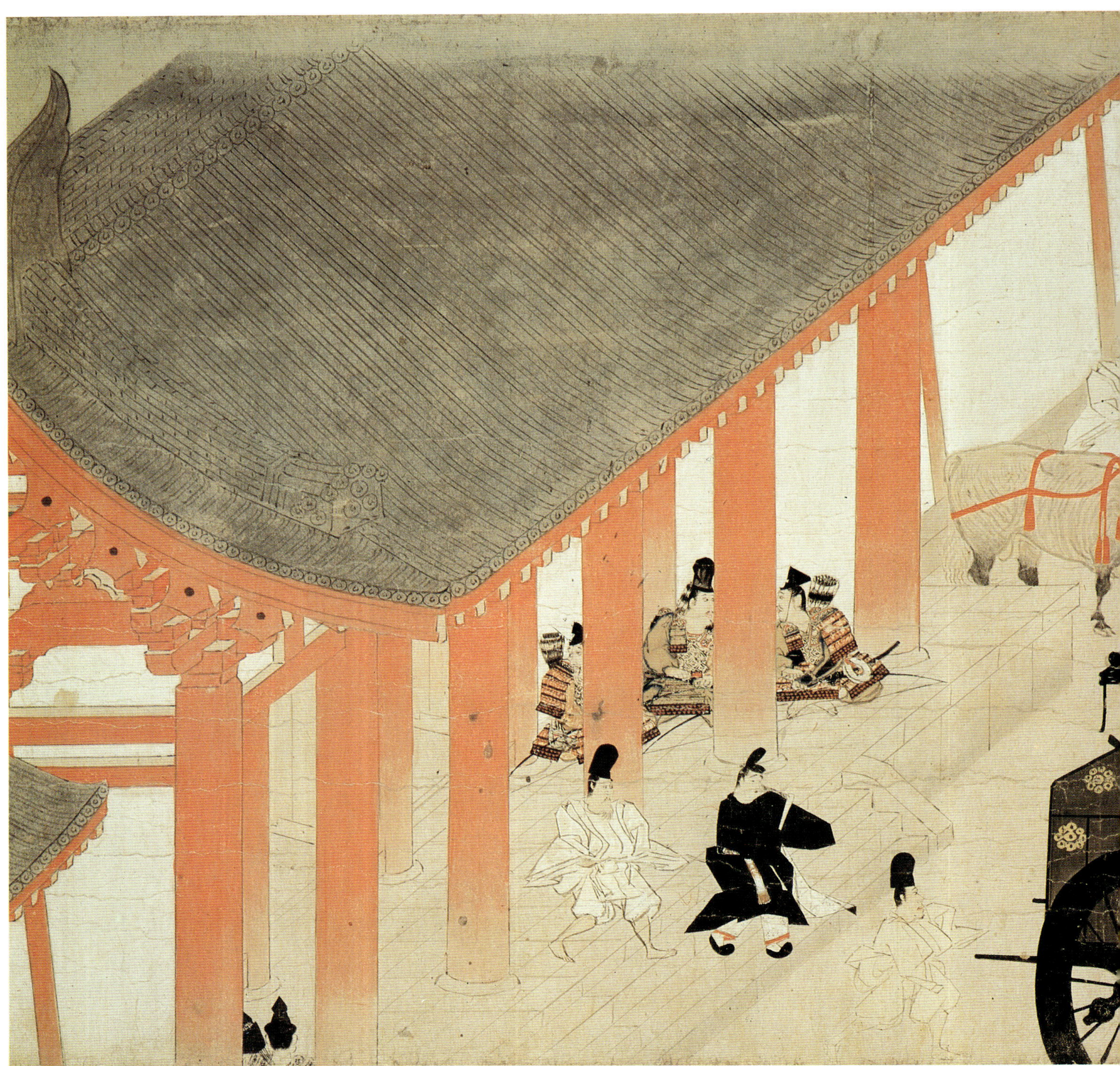

56-1

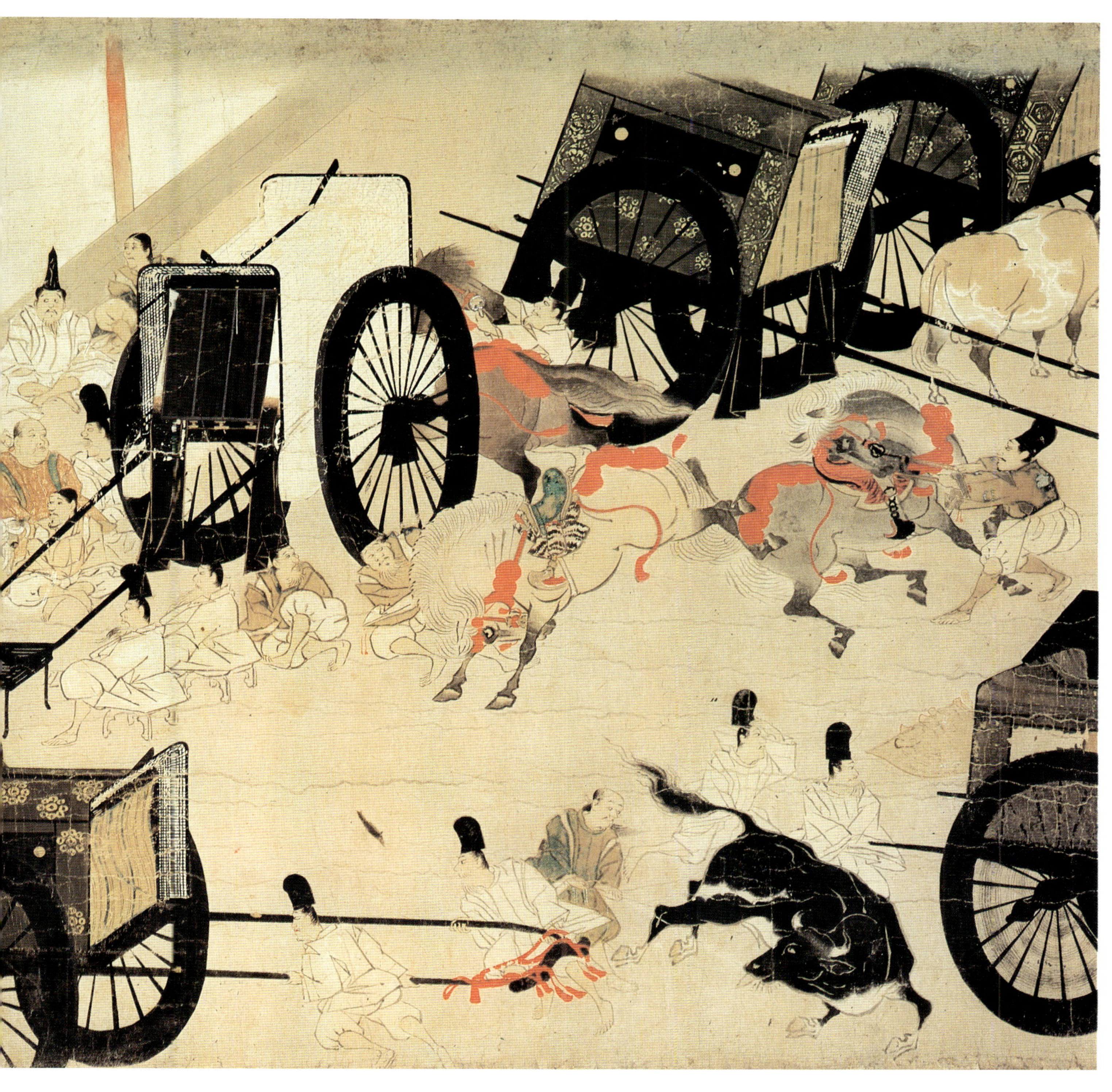

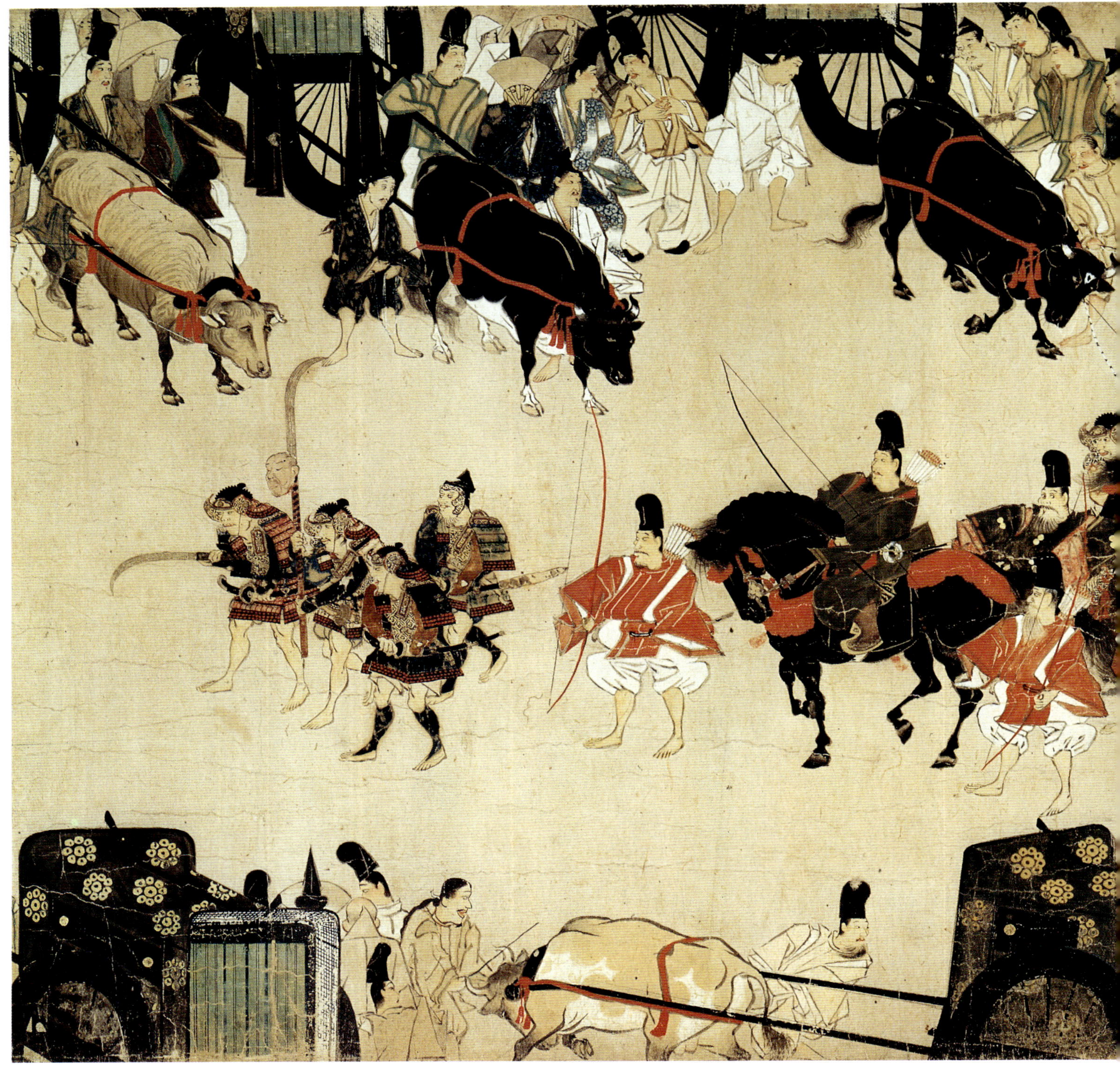

56-2

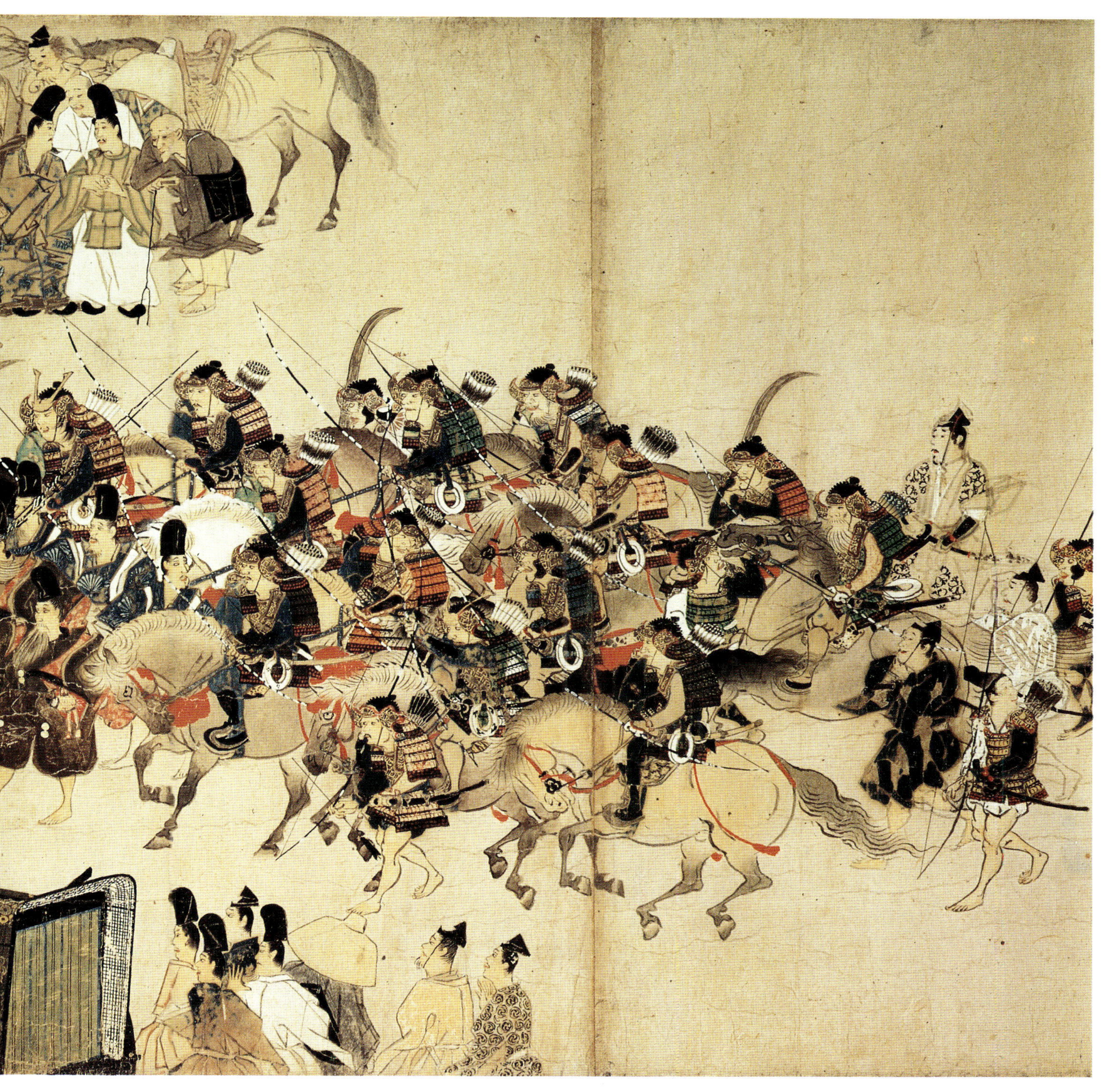

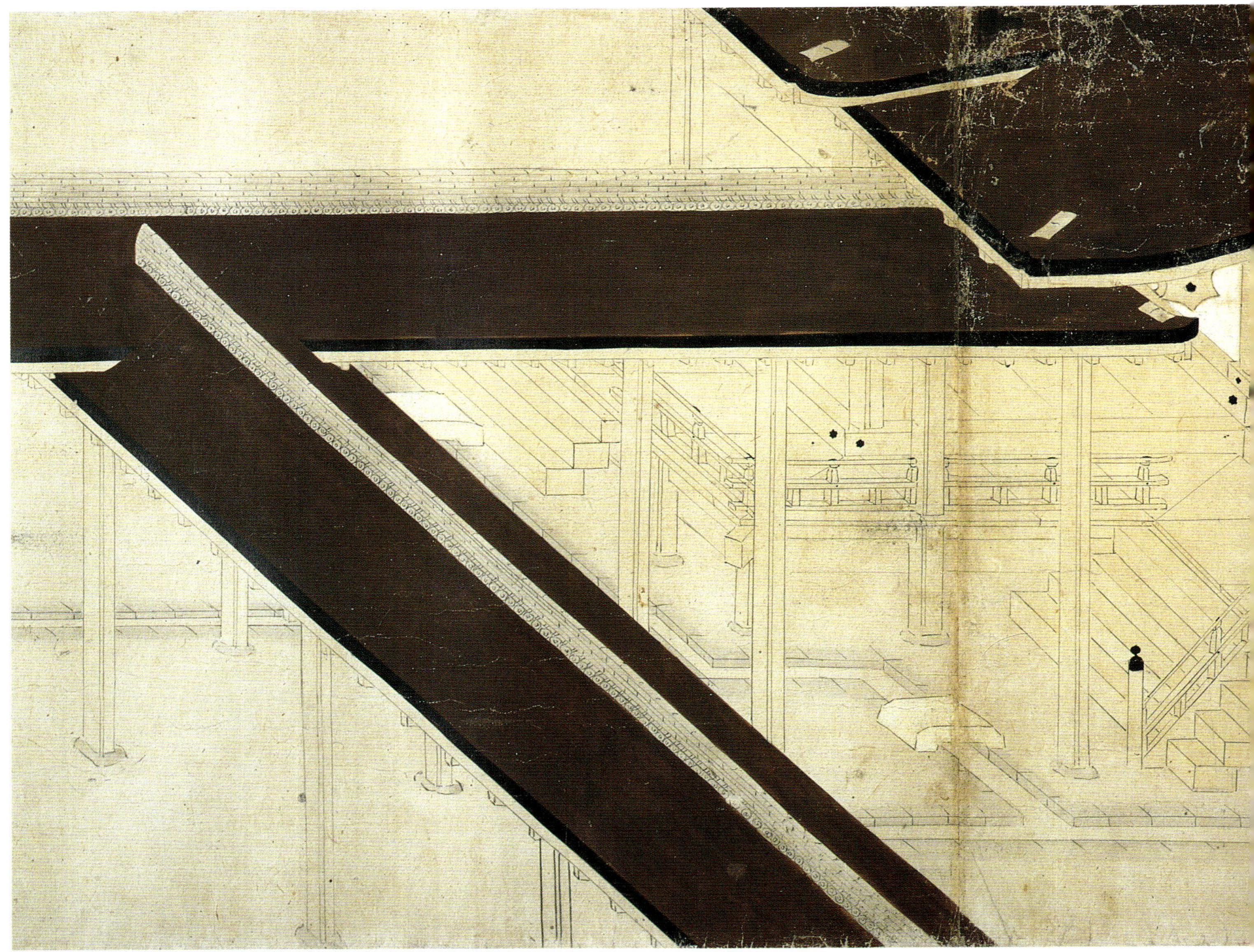

57-1.

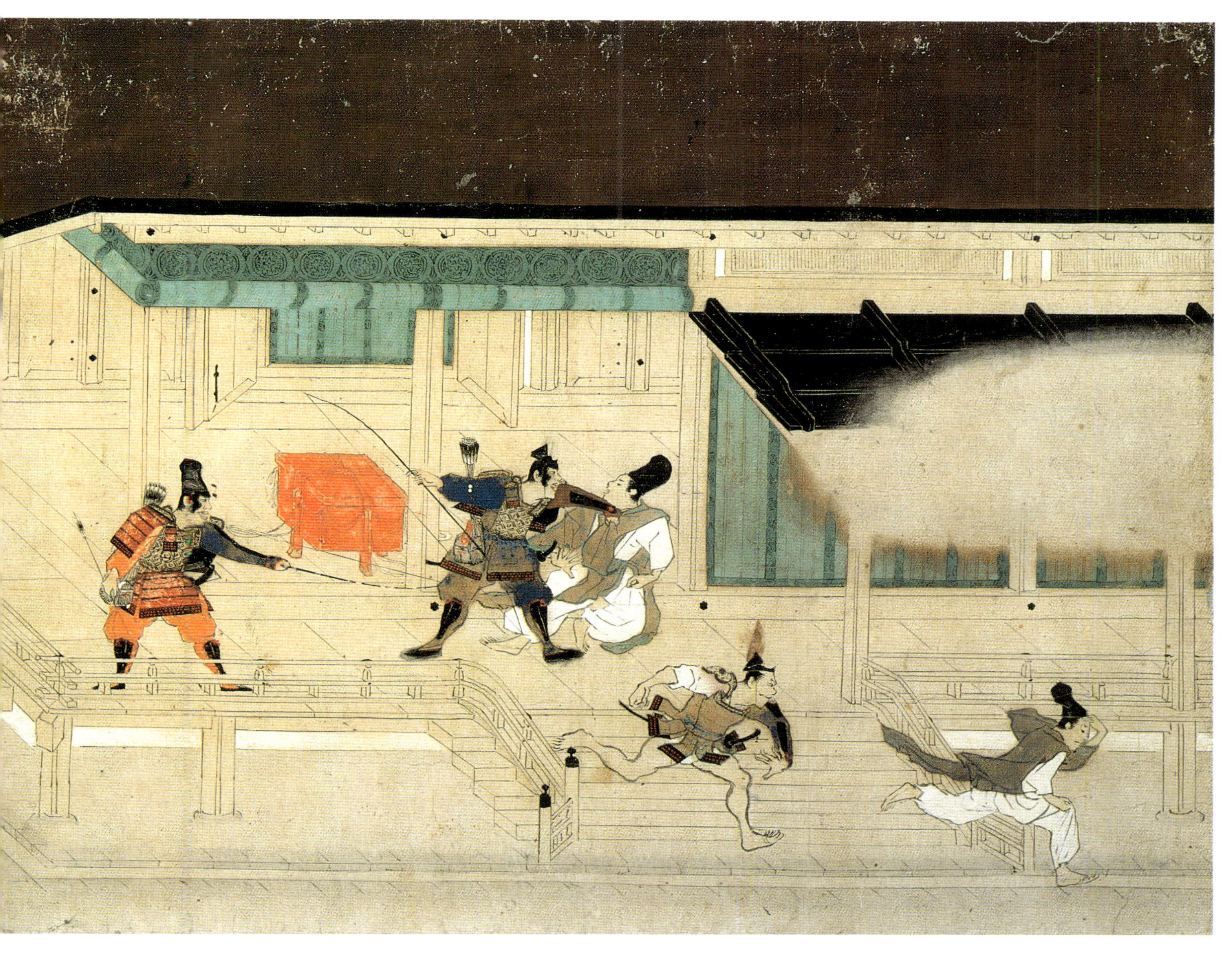

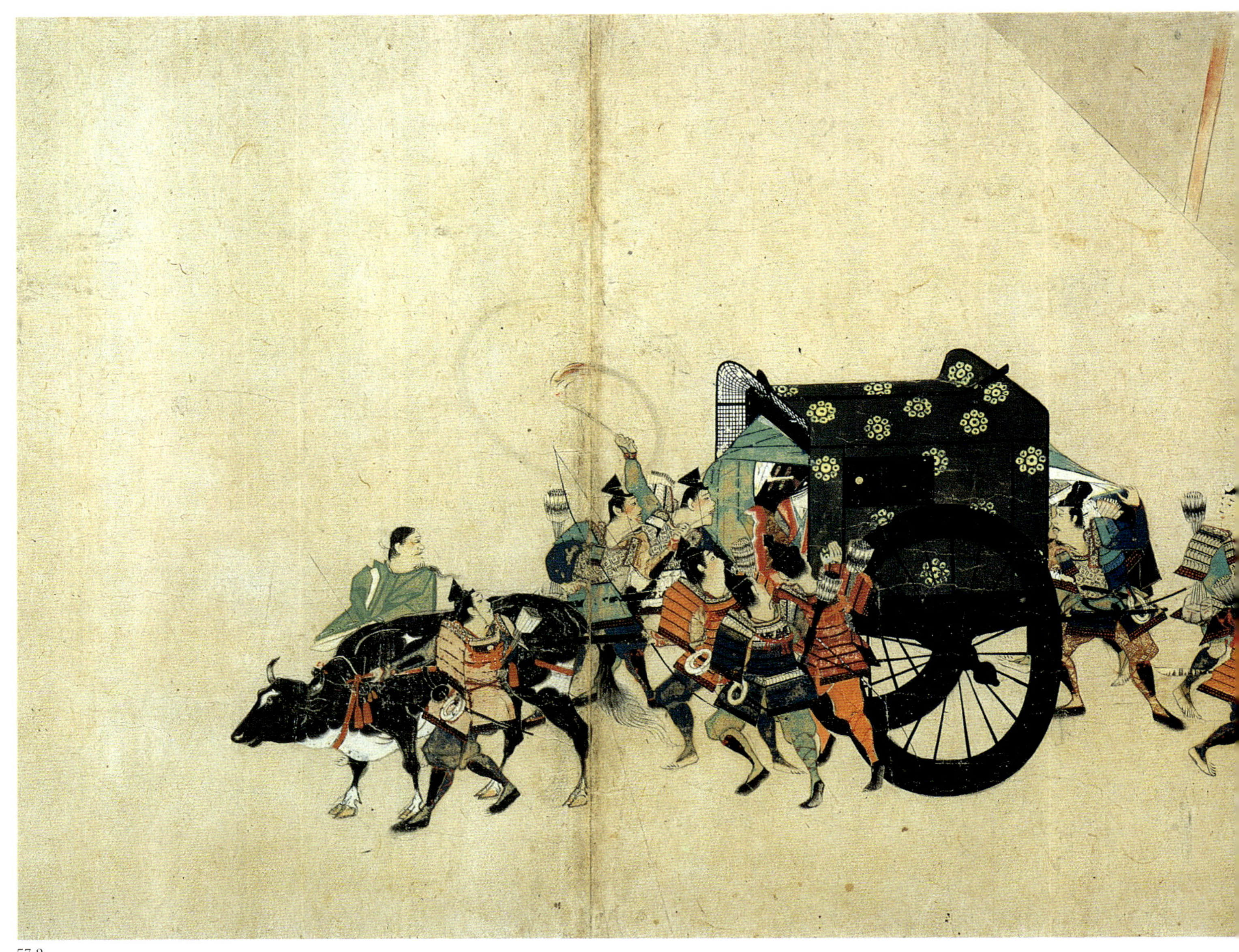

57-2

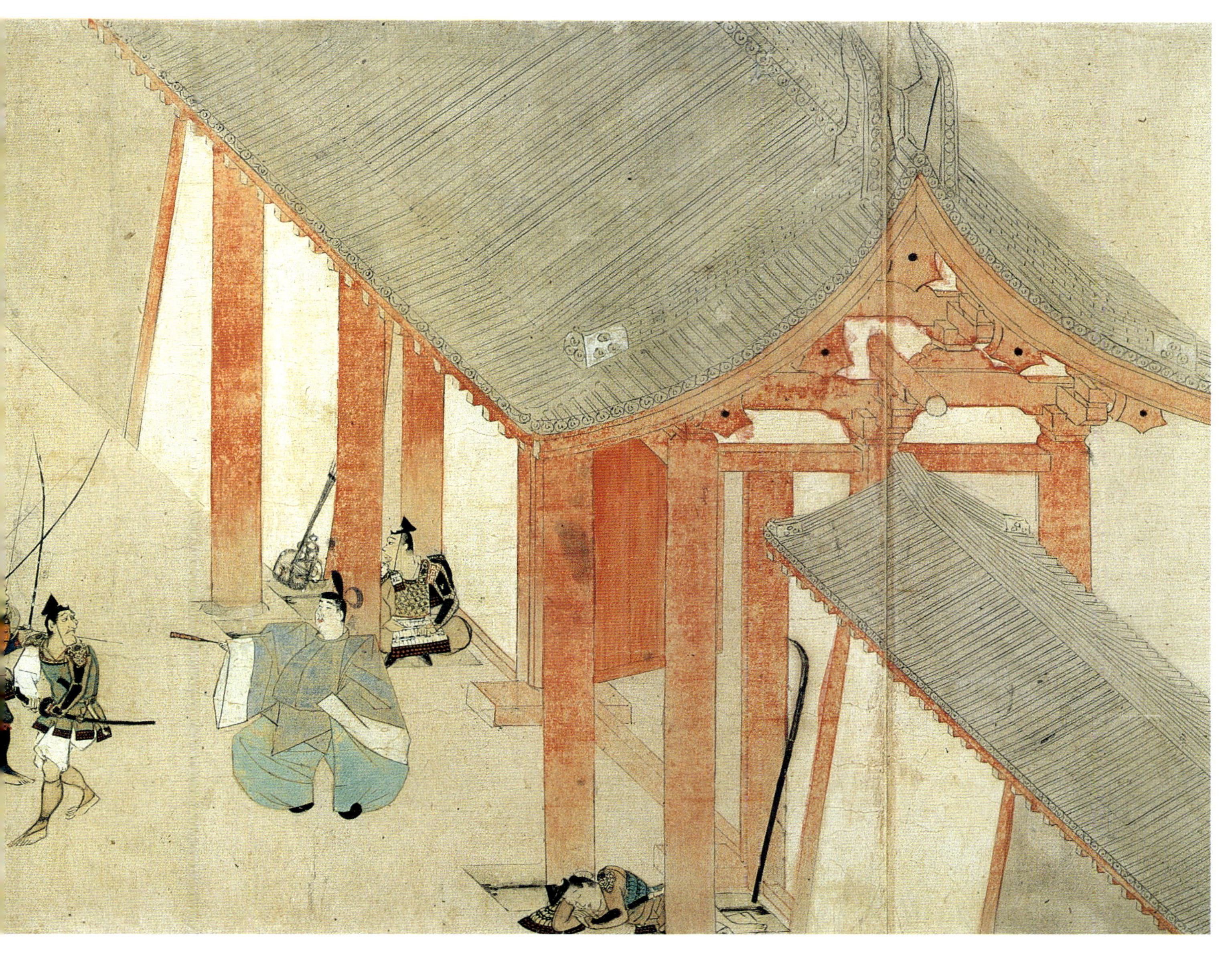

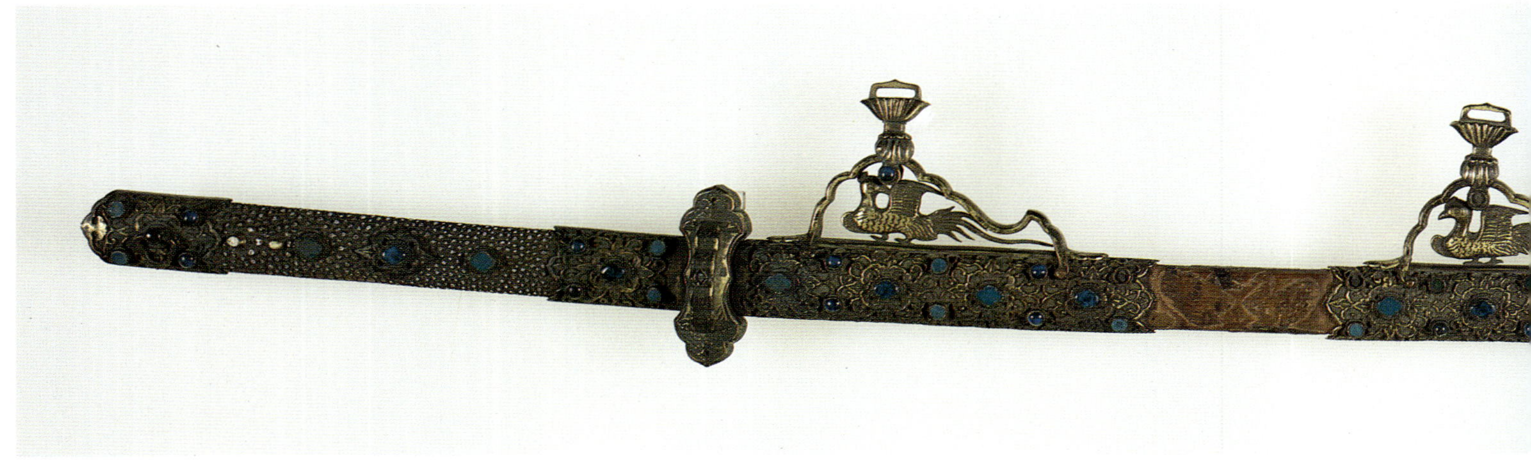

58 ◎

Ceremonial Sword Mounting
沃懸地螺鈿金荘餝剣

Heian period, 12th century
Mainly gilt bronze fittings and lacquer on fabric
base; 110cm
Tokyo National Museum

The elaborate sword hilt, scabbard, and
fittings were designed based on Tang Chinese
sword prototypes for use at Heian court ceremonies. According to the Heian period record
of court protocol, the *Saigū-ki*, only the crown
prince or highest ranking noblemen were
permitted to carry this type of ceremonial
sword (*kazari-tachi*). No functional sword
blade was ever included, only, as with most
Heian ceremonial pieces by the 9th century, an
iron bar in the shape of a long sword, or *tachi,*
is fitted into the scabbard. The *tachi* was worn
suspended from the belt on cords attached to
the two triangular chains (*yamagata-gane*), in
this case graced with sculpted phoenixes, so
that the hilt and blade-point ends curved up.
(From the Kamakura period warriors on the
battle field had replaced the *tachi,* adopting
instead by the 13th century, the *katana* sword,
which was worn, when sheathed, slashed
through the belt, blade-edge up and ends
curving down.) Only about 12 Heian examples
of ceremonial *tachi* mountings have survived
from the 12th century, and this piece, although damaged and missing inlays, is one of
the few that has not been extensively repaired
or remodeled.

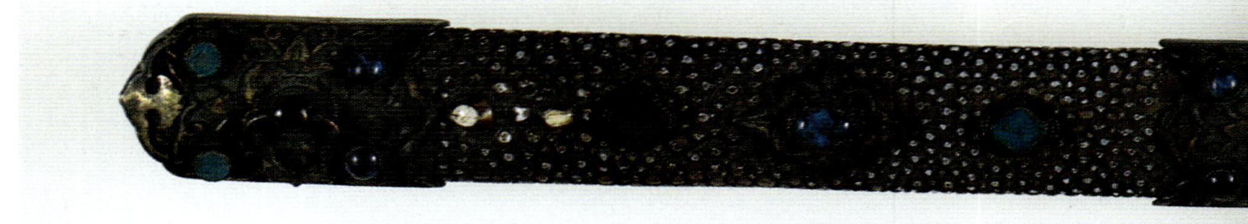

The gilt bronze sword guard (*kara-tsuba*) is
ingraved with *hōsōge* designs. Gilt bands
(*nagakazari*) set round the scabbard in openwork *hōsōge* arabesques and the diamond
shapes on the hilt are selectively inlaid with
blue-green glass and semi-precious stones.
Hardly any of the gold *ikake-ji* lacquered
ground remains on the scabbard which also
has lost the mother-of-pearl mandarin duck
and peacock inlays.

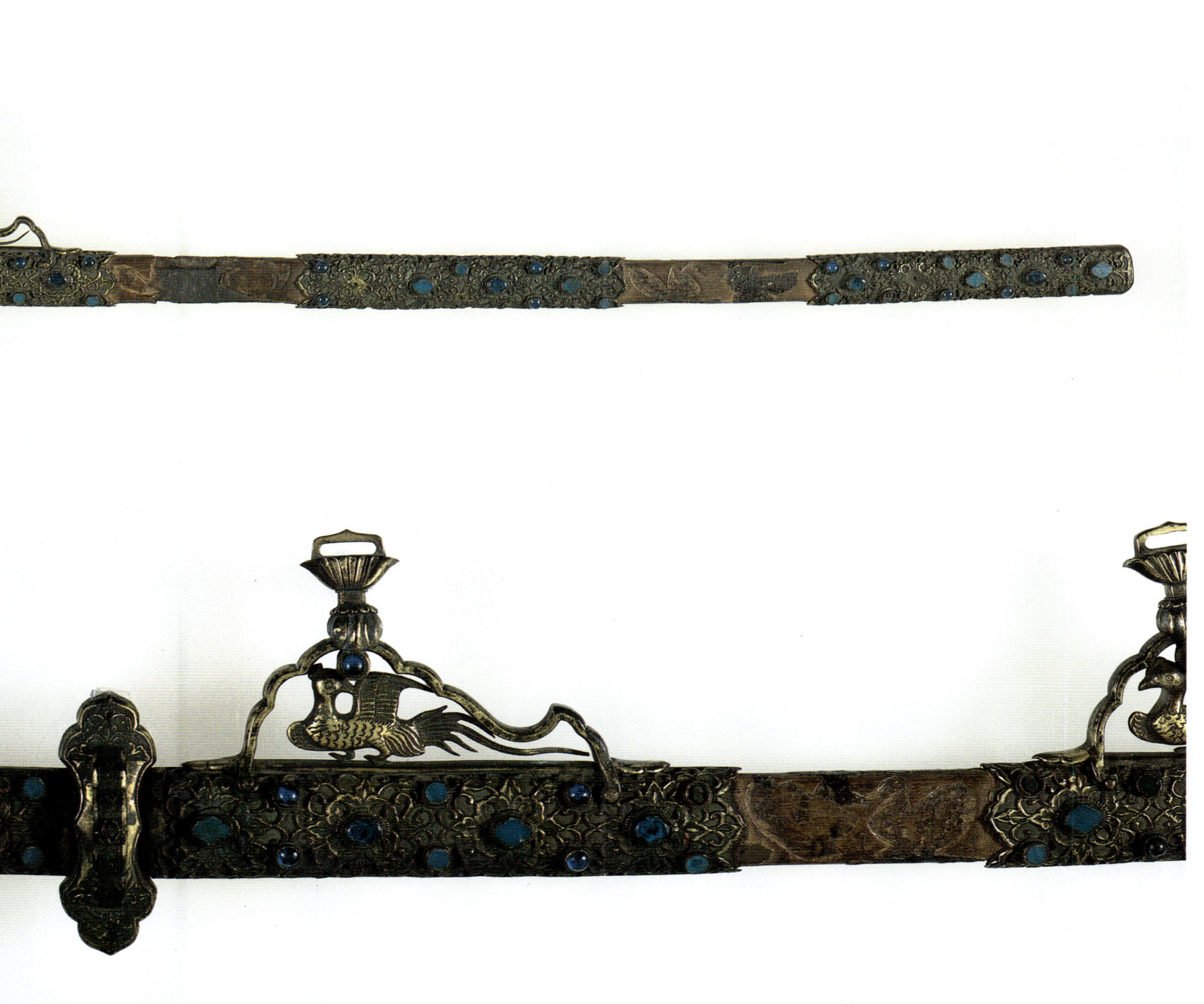

Saddle, With Lion Motifs
沃懸地獅子螺鈿鞍

Heian period, 12th century
Lacquered wood, mother-of-pearl inlay, metal
fittings
28.5cm × 41.4cm × 32.5cm
Tokyo National Museum

The shape of this saddle as well as the mother-of-pearl, or (in other examples) *maki-e,* lacquer decoration on wood is typical of Heian period saddles (extant or mentioned in documents) intended for actual use by a nobleman. Unlike many modern western-style saddles there is no pommel, but a high cantle at front as well as back. Each legged-cantle was carved for extra strength from one continuous piece of a forked tree trunk; the saddle seat was fitted from additional sections of wood.

The three lions are cut pieces of shell or mother-of-pearl (Jp: *raden*) set into a ground finished in a dense scattering of fine gold filings, termed *ikake-ji.*. The use of mother-of-pearl originated in S.E. Asia or China, but as with other lacquer techniques received technical refinement and spectacular variations in the hands of succeeding generations of Japanese lacquer-masters. Heian period records frequently mention the *ikake-ji* technique but this is one of the few extant examples of the ground, and the only Heian saddle known to show it.

Heian courtly taste favored floral and animal motifs taken from nature and the changing seasons. Here, each lion boasts a slightly different posture and expression heralding an interest in realistic detail that marks the art of the following centuries of the Kamakura period. Indeed, although we often think of Heian aestheticism as refined, delicate and "feminine" especially in contrast to the later periods of "masculine" warrior rule these bold and proud lions remind us of the continuity rather than break in the artistic motifs and stylistic approaches of the late Heian with that of following centuries.

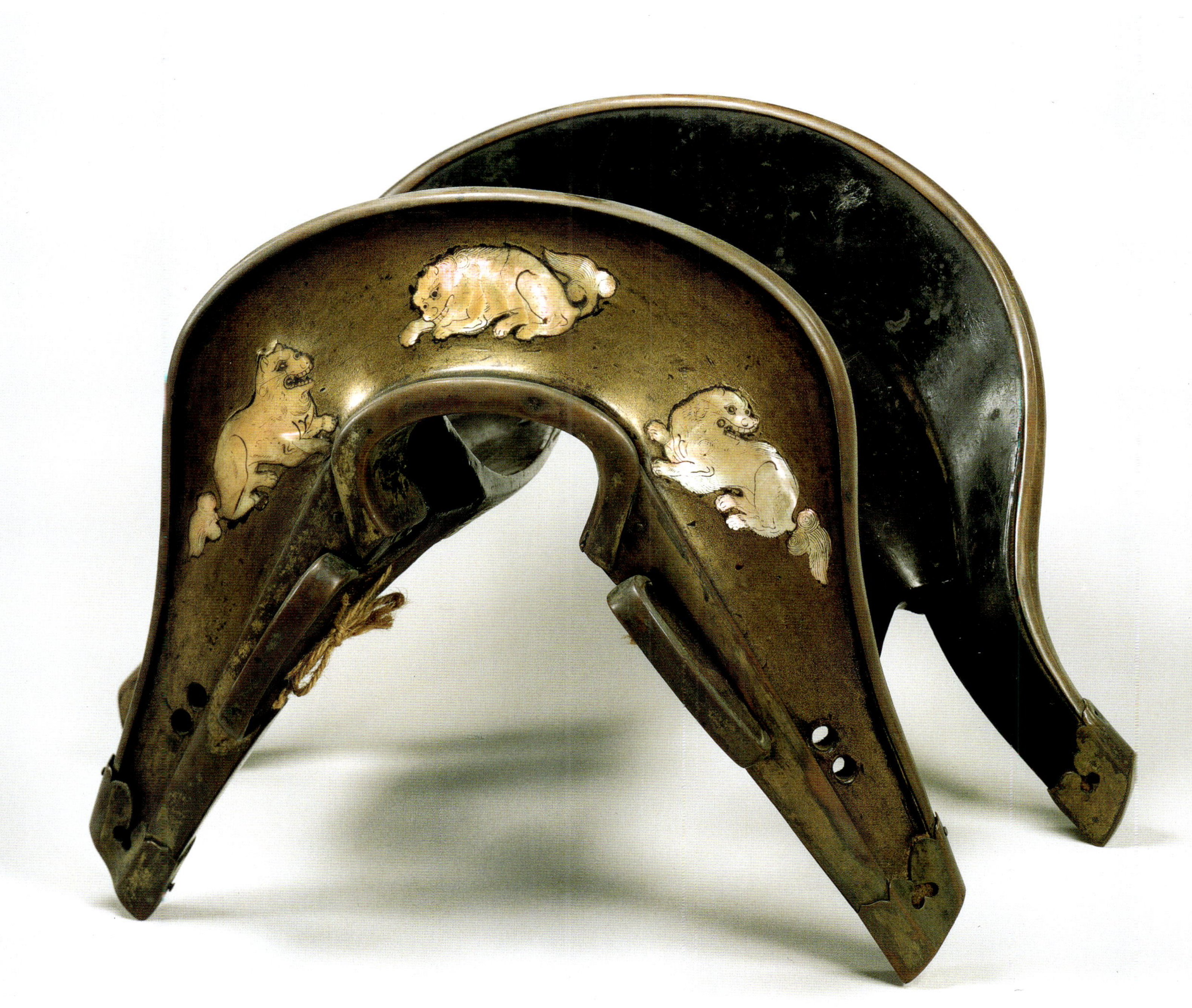

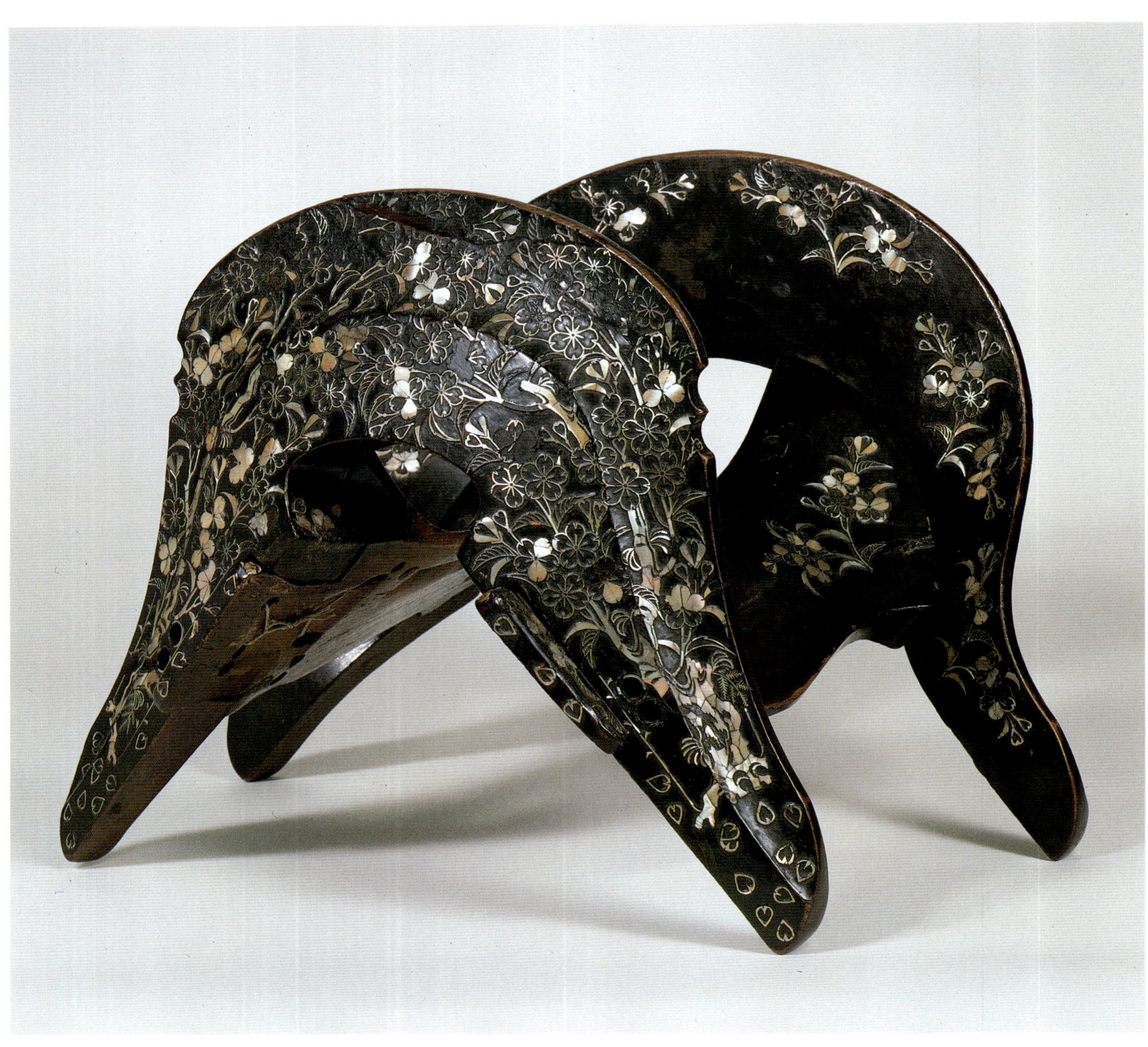

60 ◎

Saddle, With Blossoming Cherry Trees
櫻螺鈿鞍

Kamakura period, 13th century
Lacquered wood with mother-of-pearl inlay
Height 30.0cm, l.41.5cm
Agency for Cultural Affairs

This decorated saddle (see Cat.No.59) is of the type intended for use in the field. Of course its very survival in such fine condition indicates it was probably never actually used in battle, but was perhaps used in ceremonies or treasured as a family heirloom or donation to a religious institution. The late 13th century dating suggests it was made for a high-ranking warrior rather than a member of the old Kyoto aristocracy, by then generally reduced in numbers and circumstances. However, the cherry blossom was a beloved motif of the Heian nobility and their exuberant yet delicate profusion here is completely in the courtly taste.

The decoration was achieved by setting thin pieces of shell (a variety called *yakō* or turbanshell), cut in both solid shapes and fragile openwork, in a ground of black lacquer. The technique of cut open-work or outlining in shell (*raden*) is first seen on late 12th century-early 13th century examples and seems to have been replaced by other lacquer inlay techniques in the 14th century.

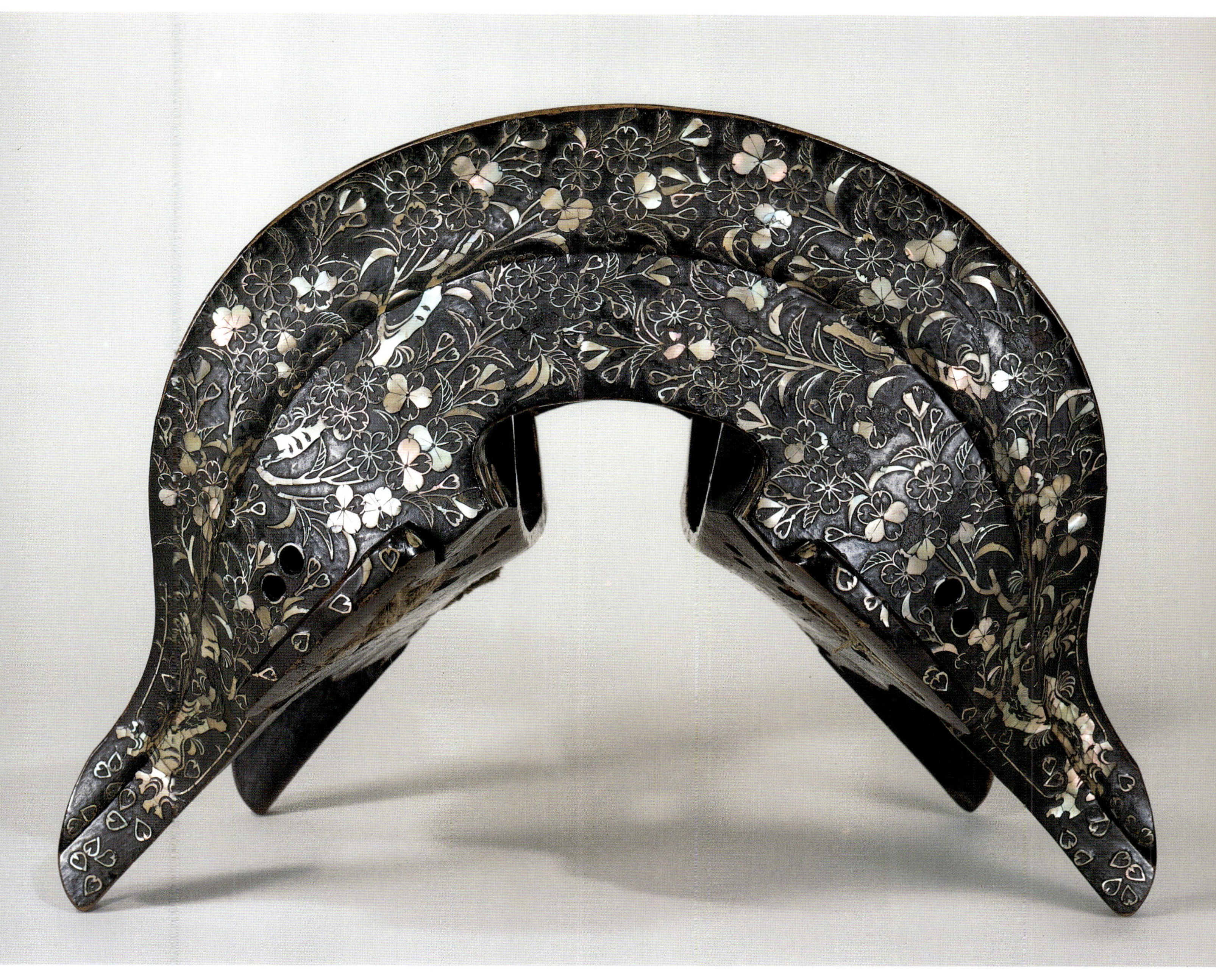

The more accentuated moulding in the cantle is typical of Kamakura saddles, as compared to earlier Heian examples (see No.59); and produced a more difficult curved surface on which to position the shell pieces. The cutout hand grips on the left and right flange of the front cantle also are found more frequently on Kamakura (or later) saddles rather than earlier ones.

Listing of Japanese Terms and Names That Appear in The Text

Numbers refer to catalogue entries (or the introductory historical essay), and where a term appears more than once the first entry number indicates the fullest definition.

CHRONOLOGY OF JAPANESE CULTURAL
HISTORY

Yayoi ca 300BC-AD ca 300
Tumulus period ca 300-538 (552)

(Early Historical Periods)
Asuka 538-645
Nara 645-794
Heian 794-1185

(Medieval Periods)
Kamakura 1185-1333
Nambokuchō 1336-1392
Muromachi 1392-1568

(Early Modern Periods)
Momoyama 1568-1603
Edo 1603-1868

List of Plates